WHAT REMAINS

WHAT REMAINS

Searching for the Memory and Lost Grave of John Paul Jones

ROBERT HORNICK

UNIVERSITY OF MASSACHUSETTS PRESS
Amherst and Boston

Printed in the United States of America

ISBN 978-1-62534-271-3 (paper); 270-6 (hardcover)

Designed by Sally Nichols
Set in Minion Pro
Printed and bound by Maple Press, Inc.

Cover design by Sally Nichols
Cover art: (foreground) Detail from photo of bust of John Paul Jones by Jean-Antoine Houdon, 1780. NH 48628 courtesy of the Naval History & Heritage Command. (background) Detail from engraving of naval battle during Revolutionary War between John Paul Jones of the *Bonhomme Richard* and Capt. Richard Pearson of the British naval vessel *Serapis,* Sept. 22, 1779. Courtesy of the Library of Congress, LC-DIG-ppmsea-19865.

Library of Congress Cataloging-in-Publication Data
A catalog record of this book is available from the Library of Congress.

British Library Cataloguing-in-Publication Data
A catalog record for this book is available from the British Library.

For Gabrielle and Will

CONTENTS

PREFACE

John Paul Jones is justly celebrated today as a Revolutionary War hero and father of the American navy, the intimate of famous men like Ben Franklin, Thomas Jefferson, and Lafayette. His defiant words to an English captain calling for his surrender—"I have not yet begun to fight!"—inspire schoolboys and sailors as the perfect example of courage under fire, of never giving up, of the American way. It was not always so. Jones's brief celebrity vanished quickly when the War of Independence ended. His death a decade after the English surrender at Yorktown went unremarked. He was buried in a foreign grave and forgotten.

This book tells the story of why Jones was forgotten, the subsequent recovery of his memory and remains, and the much-delayed commemoration of his achievement. It is not a biography of Jones; it is, rather, a history of the several men and women who did remember him, promoted his achievement, searched for (and finally found) his lost grave, and returned both his physical remains and his memory to a place of honor. It is, therefore, a story of opportunists as well as evangelists: not only of politicians who needed the memory of Jones to advance agendas of their own but also of fellow warriors committed to recovering one of their own from obscurity and shame. This book is also about, centrally, a singular moment in American history, one that followed Jones's death by 115 years, when President Theodore Roosevelt, after staging a great military and naval pageant to celebrate the return of Jones's remains to the United States, sent an American fleet—the "Great White Fleet," comprising the most advanced battleships ever assembled—on a fourteen-month cruise around the world, signaling by its presence at each port of call the coming of age of U.S. global power, a moment, not coincidentally, that coincided with the restoration of John Paul Jones to the American archive.

ACKNOWLEDGMENTS

I WOULD LIKE TO THANK the following individuals who helped me with this book: Paul Friedland, Will Hornick, and John MacLennan—history enthusiasts and excellent writers all, each of whom read and reread early drafts of my manuscript and gave me many valuable comments; the library staff at the University of Arizona who facilitated my research; Renny and Julie Stackpole who responded courteously to my questions about Alexander Pinkham; the men and women who assisted me with identifying, locating, and obtaining permissions to use photographs for this book, including Jennifer Bryan at the U.S. Naval Academy's Nimitz Library, Cynthia Buffington at Philadelphia Rare Books & Manuscripts, Lisa Cruck and David Colamaria at the Naval History and Heritage Command, Carolyn Cruthirds at Boston Museum of Fine Arts, Jascin Finger and the Coffin School Trustees, Ralph Marie Henke at the Nantucket Historical Association, Thomas Lisanti and David Rosado at the New York Public Library, Dennis Robinson at Seacoast New Hampshire, Lara Szypszak at the Library of Congress, Scott Whitman at the South Coast Chapter of Sons of the American Revolution, Fred Wilshire at NavSource Destroyer Archive, and Inna Young at the City of Annapolis; Matt Becker and the editorial staff at University of Massachusetts Press, who guided me through the editing and production process and helped make this a better book; and my wife, Gabrielle, who made room in our lives for John Paul Jones.

WHAT REMAINS

1

COMMEMORATION CEREMONY APRIL 24, 1906

> We have met to honor the memory of that man who gave our Navy its earliest traditions of heroism and victory.
>
> —Charles Bonaparte, secretary of the navy, April 24, 1906

IT WAS CALLED THE GREATEST military and naval pageant ever witnessed in the United States.[1] Five thousand guests, there by invitation only, crowded the Naval Academy's recently completed armory at Annapolis. Thousands more lined the streets from the railway station to the armory to cheer President Roosevelt and the dignitaries accompanying him as they made their way from their special train to the great hall.

The hall was decorated simply but elegantly in the red, white, and blue colors of the French and American flags, the French tricolors as well as the Stars and Stripes, because it was in France that the lost remains of John Paul Jones had been buried for a hundred years and then recovered. It was the French who had given him his first funeral when the Americans would not, the French who with special foresight had anticipated a future day when the United States might regret its oversight (therefore preserving his mortal remains, unusually, in a lead coffin filled with alcohol and straw), the French who indulged the six-year search for his grave, and the French who, when the grave was finally found, delivered those remains to the custody of an American naval squadron to be returned to American shores.

In addition to the dignitaries, naval officers, and other seated guests (not, however, the diplomatic corps; it was decided to exclude all of them except for the French—how could one invite Great Britain's ambassador to glorify the victories of John Paul Jones over the English fleet?), there stood at attention along both sides of the hall the academy's uniformed midshipmen as well as marines and sailors from three French and eight U.S. war vessels anchored in the nearby bay: *Admiral Aube, Condé,* and *Marseilles* from France and *Alabama, Indiana, Illinois, Iowa, Cleveland, Minneapolis, Des Moines,* and *Denver* from the United States. "The great hall," observed one attendee, "glistened with gold lace and flashing steel." There were also primary colors and quaintness: the brilliant red coats of the Marine Band, the minutemen uniforms of the Maryland militia.

The purpose of this pomp was to commemorate the achievement of Revolutionary War naval hero John Paul Jones and to commit his mortal remains to a final place of honor on American soil. The body of Jones, sealed in the lead coffin in which it had originally been buried, was now further encased in an oak casket with eight silver handles, the lid secured by sixteen silver screws. It had arrived on American soil the previous year after being carried from Paris to Cherbourg to the deck of the U.S. battleship *Brooklyn* and then across the ocean to a pier at Annapolis and a temporary vault at the Naval Academy, where it would await formal commemoration ceremonies and final burial. The details of Jones's long-delayed return from a lost Paris grave are the subject of later chapters. We begin the story near its end, in June 1905, on the northern shores of France, nine months before the April 24 commemoration.

A squadron (officially the "John Paul Jones Squadron") had been dispatched to retrieve Jones's remains and return them to the United States. It consisted of four vessels: the flagship *Brooklyn, Tacoma, Galveston,* and *Chattanooga,* these vessels' names representing the principal sections of the country (East and West Coasts, the Gulf, and the interior).[2] Rear Admiral Charles Sigsbee, former commander of the battleship *Maine,* was flag officer. The squadron set sail on June 18 and arrived at Cherbourg on June 30. Cherbourg was the destination port chosen rather than the larger

Channel port of Le Havre because the shops and houses of Cherbourg were farther from the harbor, and it was thought the requisite cannon salutes to be fired when the remains were brought on board would smash fewer windows there than at Le Havre. (Le Havre's locks would also have posed a challenge.)[3] The American warships were joined the next day by a French squadron of three vessels, the black-painted French hulls and dull-gray upperworks contrasting sharply with the stainless white American hulls and copper-colored funnels.[4]

Admiral Sigsbee and entourage left Cherbourg for Paris by train on July 1, there to receive the formal handover of John Paul Jones's remains and transport them back to Cherbourg for uploading to *Brooklyn* and the return voyage to America. Meanwhile, the many American and French sailors remaining behind temporarily transformed Cherbourg into a festival town, their merrymaking culminating in a grand Fourth of July celebration featuring, according to one observer,

> an immense torchlight procession, an open-air concert, a lunch offered to the American sailors by the French sailors and soldiers, a garden party given by [French] Vice-Admiral Besson at the Préfecture in honor of the American officers, a reception by the Maire on the Exhibition Grounds, boat races between the French and American crews, in which honors were fairly even, and, as a grand climax, a superb Venetian fête in the harbor, in which the American ships were fairly outdone by the brilliancy and originality displayed in the illumination of the French ships, which were most elaborate and unique in design.[5]

The formal ceremonies in Paris on July 6 (the birthday of John Paul Jones), accompanying the transfer of Jones's remains to the Americans, were even more elaborate. They included the arrival of an American escort detail from Cherbourg at the Gare des Invalides—five hundred American sailors and marines met by French officers, French infantrymen, and a military band; a memorial service in Jones's honor at the American Church of the avenue de l'Alma; and a triumphal procession through the streets of Paris from the church to the Champs-Élysées and then down the Champs-Élysées to the Pont Alexandre III, dense multitudes of reverent spectators lining the streets and avenues along the way. The coffin was placed on a bier at the Esplanade des Invalides, salutes were sounded, and anthems were played. In the evening the coffin was transferred to the funeral train, placed in a sealed compartment, and transported to Cherbourg.

At Cherbourg the next morning, the seal on the compartment of the mortuary car was broken, and the remains were removed to a temporary tent chapel set up on the commercial wharf. An enormous crowd surrounded the railway station and witnessed the removal and then slowly and respectfully filed past the coffin.[6] On July 8 there were additional ceremonies to mark the transfer of the coffin from shore to ship. The casket was loaded onto the French torpedo boat *Zouave,* transferred on board the flagship *Brooklyn,* and placed on a catafalque on the quarterdeck, near the entrance to the cabin of Admiral Sigsbee, where a sentry would stand guard for the duration of the voyage. Appropriate naval honorifics were also provided throughout the transfer, including a fifteen-gun salute by the French flagship *Bouvines,* the flying of the colors of both squadrons at half-mast, and a profusion of French and American flags waving in the breeze.

The battleship *Brooklyn* and the rest of the John Paul Jones Squadron steamed out of Cherbourg Harbour at five thirty in the evening, "firing a national salute upon leaving the shores of France." The ships were "enshrouded in smoke from the guns of the fort and the combined [French and American] squadrons." The American sailors gave a parting cheer to their French comrades as they passed the Cherbourg roadstead, and the French sailors returned the favor.[7]

The voyage back to America was "leisurely"—thirteen days at a speed of ten knots. Henry Marion, a professor of modern languages at the Naval Academy who was the official interpreter for the squadron that brought Jones back to the United States and later wrote a detailed chronicle of the retrieval and return, summarized the thirteen days in a sentence: "On the return voyage nothing of special interest occurred."[8]

The pomp and circumstance resumed the morning of July 21, about 150 miles east of New York. There the battleship *Maine,* bearing the flag of Rear Admiral Robley Evans, commander in chief of the North Atlantic Fleet, together with the battleships *Missouri, Kentucky,* and *Kearsarge,* had been on the lookout for the Jones Squadron. Sigsbee sighted *Maine. Maine* fired a fifteen-gun salute; *Brooklyn* returned fire. Then *Maine,* trailed by the three other battleships, formed an escort of honor for the return of John Paul Jones. At four o'clock they were joined by a second squadron of battleships under the command of Rear Admiral Charles Davis—*Alabama,*

Illinois, *Massachusetts*, and *Iowa*. They formed, eyewitness Marion tells us, "a grand procession of twelve war ships, carrying over six thousand men and presenting an imposing sight with the flagship *Brooklyn* in the center of the column."[9]

On Saturday, July 22, the fleet arrived inside the Capes of Virginia. There Admiral Evans's squadron broke formation and took up a position off Cape Henry, making room for *Brooklyn* and the other vessels to pass slowly by. All flew their flags at half-mast, *Brooklyn* played the national anthem, and the Evans squadron fired a fifteen-gun salute. Then Admiral Sigsbee's John Paul Jones Squadron, including *Brooklyn*, escorted by the battleships under Admiral Davis's command, headed for Annapolis, anchoring for the night off Thomas Point and arriving at Annapolis the following morning at nine o'clock. The French man-of-war *Jurien de la Gravière*, which had come to take part in the exercises, was visible in the distance. Meanwhile, Evans's battleships had returned to Hampton Roads the previous evening.[10]

Monday, July 24, the remains of John Paul Jones were brought ashore on the naval tug *Standish* and placed in a temporary vault at the center of the grounds of the Naval Academy, near the unfinished chapel, where, it was expected, Jones would be finally buried when the chapel was done. The day began with heavy rain. However, significantly it was thought, the rain stopped and the sun shone brightly on the unfolding events. Suitable naval ceremonies accompanied each step of this transfer, including booming guns from the anchored men-of-war, honor escorts, funeral dirges, another funeral service (Jones's third since 1792; there was a fourth to come), prayers, a volley of marine fire over the vault, a bugler sounding taps.

The bones of John Paul Jones had at last returned to American soil, welcomed with honors reserved for an admiral. That Jones's highest commission in the U.S. Navy was only that of captain and that his rank of admiral had been conferred by Catherine the Great of Russia for his service in the Imperial Russian Navy was an inconvenient truth not highlighted.[11]

Nine months later, on the early morning of April 24, 1906, Jones's casket was moved from its temporary vault and taken to the armory for the official commemoration. The date chosen for the ceremony, April 24, was not random. It was the anniversary of one of John Paul Jones's most celebrated deeds: the capture of HMS *Drake*. The capture was a significant achievement. Jones's ship *Ranger* and *Drake* were evenly matched in terms of guns and speed. *Drake*, however, was commanded by a seasoned British naval officer and manned by a well-trained crew. Jones was a young, untested captain with a mutinous crew. The odds, therefore, favored *Drake*. The victory, though, was Jones's. It was not, to be sure, his greatest Revolutionary War victory (that would be the later capture of *Serapis* off Flamborough Head) but a memorable deed nonetheless—and a fitting anniversary on which to commemorate the captain.

The casket, when it reached the armory, was set on a bier in front of the speaker's stand, slightly to the right, and draped in a naval Union Jack. Three items were laid on top: at the head, a single laurel wreath, symbol of victory and glory; at the foot, a spray of palm, placed by the academy's cadets; and in the middle, the sword presented to Jones by Louis XVI, king of France, to commemorate Jones's capture of *Serapis* in 1779, its hilt, or handle, wrapped in gold.

Directly in front of the casket, in the first row of the hall now filled to capacity, sat the two admirals George Dewey and Paul Campion—Dewey, victor in 1898 at the battle of Manila Bay and the only officer in American history with the rank of "Admiral of the Navy," and Campion, his French counterpart. Officers of the two navies were seated nearby. Eight sailors, four French and four American, stood behind the casket. President Roosevelt, U.S. navy secretary Charles Bonaparte, French ambassador J. J. Jusserand, the governor of Maryland, the superintendent of the Naval Academy, and former U.S. ambassador to France Horace Porter (the man who found Jones's lost grave) were seated on the speaker's stand, overlooking the casket.

Not everyone, not even all of those in the great hall, believed the body in the casket was really that of John Paul Jones. An editorial in the *Literary Digest*, published in July only days after the casket was delivered to Annapolis, insisted there were "many doubting Thomases."

> The possibility that the American and French governments are going through a series of elaborate ceremonies over the body of some unknown Frenchman which they are mistaking for the body of John Paul Jones creates a situation that may easily turn from the sublime to the reverse. The American press, therefore, are reviewing with considerable concern the

> evidences that the leaden casket found in the almost forgotten cemetery on the Rue Grange-aux-Belles in Paris holds all that was mortal of the famous sea-ranger of the Revolution. The two governments have officially accepted the body as that of the Admiral, but nevertheless there are many doubting Thomases who are not satisfied with the identification.[12]

The doubters were not just the Americans. A *Washington Post* story from about the same time, relying on an anonymous source "just returned from Paris, of high position," reported that the French "looked upon the ceremonies attending the transfer of this body with cynical amusement, the conviction being almost universal, apparently, that the body was not that of John Paul Jones, but of an unknown and unknowable Frenchman." Even the trainload of dignitaries traveling from the capital to the commemoration ceremony on July 24 had its doubters. According to a reporter on the train, there was "much discussion" of the subject during the one-and-a-half-hour passage to Annapolis. All agreed, however, "even if it were the wrong man, he was in the right place."[13]

It is unclear whether the reporter's conclusion about the remains being in the "right place" was meant to refer to the Naval Academy at Annapolis or more lightheartedly to the casket itself. There had certainly been competition and controversy about choosing Annapolis and the Naval Academy as the final resting place for John Paul Jones. Early speculation was that the national cemetery in Washington would be picked.[14] No less a naval hero than Admiral Dewey favored the national cemetery site, arguing for Arlington over Annapolis on the grounds that John Paul Jones was, even above his character as a naval officer, "a great American citizen. He belongs to the navy, but in a greater sense he belongs to the nation."[15]

Other cities came forward and made a case for their selection as well. Fredericksburg, Virginia, for example—arguing that Fredericksburg was the only home Jones had had in the United States and that he had lived there in a house belonging to his brother, William Paul, at the time of his appointment as a lieutenant in the Continental navy—urged that he be buried there and that a monument be erected there in his memory.[16] Philadelphia argued that it should be selected because Jones's naval career was closely associated with that city—for example, his naval commission was issued in Philadelphia, and his first vessel under the American Congress sailed from there.[17]

The most audacious claim—and campaign—was on behalf of New York

City. Three New York congressmen (Representatives Timothy Sullivan of the Eighth District, William Sulzer of the Tenth, and Joseph Goulden of the Eighteenth), no doubt at the express urging of *Evening World* publisher Joseph Pulitzer, stated that Jones should be buried in New York City. Pulitzer then took up the cause. "Paul Jones loved the country for which he fought so bravely, and of all parts of it he loved New York the best. A far-seeing man, he realized all those years ago that the time would come when New York would be the greatest city in the country he did so much to create, and he frequently expressed a desire to spend his last days here." Doubling down on these dubious claims of special New York affection, Pulitzer added that Jones himself wanted to be buried in New York. "Before he left the country Jones declared time and again he was coming back, coming back to live in or near New York, so that when he died his body should be buried here."[18]

Responding to Pulitzer's drumbeat, the New York Board of Aldermen unanimously adopted a resolution that Jones should be buried in the city, purportedly quoting Jones himself in support. "When he sailed from the port of New York, Jones took affectionate leave of his beloved country, saying on that occasion: 'When I return to America I shall build a home in this city, destined to be great, and within her confines shall I spend my remaining years. It is here I desire my grave be established.'" The aldermen were followed in turn by a carefully orchestrated series of endorsements, culminating with the New York State Assembly.[19]

The decision was Theodore Roosevelt's to make, and Roosevelt chose the Naval Academy. For him, unlike Dewey, the naval hero trumped the national one. As he would explain in his commemoration address:

> I feel that the place of all others in which the memory of the dead hero will most surely be a living force is here in Annapolis, where year by year we turn out the midshipmen who are to officer in the future Navy, among whose founders the dead man stands first. Moreover, the future naval officers, who live within these walls, will find in the career of the man whose life we this day celebrate, not merely a subject for admiration and respect, but an object lesson to be taken into their innermost hearts. Every officer in our navy should know by heart the deeds of John Paul Jones. Every officer in our Navy should feel in each fiber of his being an eager desire to emulate the energy, the professional capacity, the indomitable determination and dauntless scorn of death which marked John Paul Jones above all his fellows.[20]

Choosing the naval hero over the national one was consistent with Roosevelt's broader theme for the commemoration, one that he would elaborate more fully elsewhere in his address.

The atmosphere in the great hall, waiting for the ceremony to begin, was festive, notwithstanding the solemnity of the occasion and the playing of Chopin's Funeral March in the background.[21] The French naval officers, when they came forward to take their seats, were generously applauded. There was more applause for Mrs. Donald McLean, president general of the Daughters of the American Revolution, and for "Uncle" Joe Cannon, Speaker of the House, who went at once to where Mrs. Roosevelt and Madame Jusserand, the French ambassador's wife, were seated. Admiral Dewey, the crowd favorite, had to rise and bow repeatedly to acknowledge his welcome. When President Roosevelt finally appeared (thirty minutes late), the five thousand rose and cheered.[22] Then the 350-voice Oratorio Society of Baltimore on a terraced platform at the end of the armory, accompanied by the Marine Band, sang "The Star-Spangled Banner," and the ceremony was launched.

There were four speakers: President Roosevelt, French ambassador Jusserand, former American ambassador Porter, and the governor of Maryland, Edwin Warfield. The speeches of the first three of these are directly relevant to our theme. The president spoke first. He began his address with the exhortation to "know by heart the deeds of John Paul Jones" and then singled out the capture of *Serapis* for special commendation: "In his fight with the *Serapis,* Jones's ship was so badly mauled that his opponent hailed him, saying 'Has your ship struck?' to which Jones answered 'I have not yet begun to fight.' The spirit which inspired that answer upbore the man who gave it and the crew who served under him through the fury of battle, which finally ended in their triumph." "It was," added Roosevelt, "the same spirit which marked the commanders of the *Cumberland* and the *Congress,* when they met equally glorious though less fortunate fate."[23]

This sudden pivot, from Jones's most famous Revolutionary War triumph to the sinking of USS *Cumberland* and the burning of USS *Congress* by a Confederate ironclad in the Civil War, is interesting. It provides insight into Roosevelt's ulterior motive for the address and, more broadly, his promotion of John Paul Jones. Many, probably most, in the audience were perfectly aware of the referenced battle—the first-ever encounter between an ironclad vessel and a squadron of wooden battleships. Both Melville and Longfellow had immortalized in poetry the bravery of the *Cumberland*'s doomed crew (they fought beyond hope yet refused to surrender). However, their gallantry notwithstanding, they lost. New technology easily defeated old. It is futile, Roosevelt seemed to be saying, to expect exemplary behavior alone to protect the nation. The best warships and weapons were also necessary.

This point would be made explicit as the address continued. Though conceding that personal courage was an essential element of any successful naval engagement, it was not, the president insisted, a sufficient condition. "No courage," he said, "can atone for the lack of that efficiency that comes only through careful preparation in advance, through careful training of the men, and careful fitting out of the engines of war." In other words, the prodigious inequality of skill or force can overwhelm even a brave captain who refuses to surrender. In the end, "The courage which never yields can not take the place of possession of good ships and good weapons and the ability skillfully to use these ships and these weapons."[24]

It was a stirring call to armed preparedness, for character, the best training, and the right ships and weapons with which to deploy. The remainder of Roosevelt's address was an elaboration of this theme, laced with sharp reprimands for those public officials not on board with the commander in chief's desire for a larger, more modern navy. Because the president spoke first, the theme got submerged in the glorification of John Paul Jones that would follow—notably, the oration of Horace Porter much praised in the newspapers the following day. The power of the presidency, though, even in 1906, was substantial, and Roosevelt was nothing if not persistent. His message would eventually command the nation's attention.

The next to speak was France's ambassador to the United States, J. J. Jusserand. His theme was France's contribution to the American Revolution and what he called "Jones's connection with things and men of France." France had been America's chief ally in the War of Independence. Although it was motivated more by antipathy to Britain than the justness of the American cause, its support was vital to America's success. Throughout, it provided money and supplies to the Americans. Young French officers—among them the marquis de Lafayette—trained American soldiers and led them in combat. In 1781 French infantry and artillery commanded by the comte de Rochambeau, French naval forces commanded by Admiral François de Grasse, Continental troops commanded by Lafayette, and the Continental army commanded by General Washington trapped General Cornwallis and his British troops on the Yorktown peninsula and forced their surrender, thus ending hostilities and resulting in the Treaty of Paris in 1783 that ended the war and recognized the independence of the colonies.

As for John Paul Jones, the French provided money, supplies, and crew members for his most successful missions against the British, a base of operations in France from which to launch attacks, and a safe haven to which he could return. Jones while in command of *Ranger* also received the first salute given by a foreign navy—the French navy—to the American flag. Ambassador Jusserand, in his address, reprised these French connections. He also highlighted the mutual affection that developed between Jones and the people of France ("After each of his campaigns he returned to Paris more and more popular at court, in society, and among officers, the good will toward him almost equaling that which everyone there bore to [Benjamin] Franklin [the American representative in France during the war]"). Finally, he told the story of how, when the news reached Annapolis that the war was over and independence was won, thirteen toasts were drunk to the accompaniment of thirteen cannons, the first three of which were to "the third of February, 1783 . . . on which day a virtuous war was concluded by an honorable peace," "the United States," and "friendship with France."[25]

The person chosen to deliver the principal celebratory oration honoring John Paul Jones was Horace Porter, the man who led the search for and finally found Jones's lost grave. Porter was a most interesting man in his own right: Civil War hero and Medal of Honor recipient, aide-de-camp to General Ulysses S. Grant, secretary (what we would now call chief of staff) to President Ulysses Grant during the first half of Grant's presidency, vice president of the Pullman Car Company and manager of their New York office, and U.S. ambassador to France from 1897 to 1905. Porter was also an acclaimed public speaker. His oratorical style and skills were formidable, well suited to the occasion.

Porter portrayed Jones as a "many-sided man" (fair enough; he was), not only a "wizard of the sea" but also "an adept in the realms of diplomacy," recounting political as well as military achievements of the man. Porter also wove into his narrative personality traits of Jones that were not strictly military—for example, Jones's "easy manner and marked elegance in the brilliant salons of the most polite courts of Europe" and his "graceful" replies in fluent English, French, and Spanish to "the compliments of kings and queens"—thus showing he could "tread the polished floor of a royal palace as becomingly as the blood-stained deck of a man-of-war."

But it was the bloodstained deck of the man-of-war on which Porter trained his rhetorical skills, recounting in one long sentence and a short one the singular triumph of Flamborough Head.

> We find him aboard the *Bonhomme Richard,* the frail merchantman he had hurriedly converted into a man-of-war, equipped with condemned guns, whose explosion early decimated his crew, attacking the *Serapis,* a superior British ship, just off her own shores, his vessel soon a wreck and sinking, most of his guns disabled, half of his motley crew of Americans and French lying about him dead or dying, the scuppers running with human blood, his ship a charnel house, over 200 prisoners confined in the hold rushing up from their prison and attacking the remnant of his exhausted crew . . . the mad carnage raging till it seemed that hell itself had usurped the place of earth . . . and when asked by his antagonist, who saw his desperate condition, whether he had struck his flag, replying, "I've just begun to fight!" Then, by the inspiration of his example, forging weaklings into giants, capturing his opponent, snatching victory from defeat.[26]

Thus went Porter's address, building slowly to a climax that (so the newspapers of the day uniformly reported) brought the entire armory to tears (Roosevelt included). "Leaning far over the [speaker's] stand," an observer wrote, Porter "looked solemnly at the flag-draped bier" and then, "in choking accents," said these final words:

> Farewell, noblest of all spirits, bravest of all hearts. The simplicity of the rugged sailor was mingled with the heroic grandeur of your nature. Wherever blows fell thickest, your crest was in their midst. The story of your life rises to the sublimity of an epic. Untitled knight of the blue waters, "Wrathful Achilles of the Ocean," conqueror of the conquerors of the sea, the recollection of your deeds will never cease to thrill men with the splendor of events and inspire

> them with the majesty of achievement. You honored the generation in which you lived, and future ages will be illumined by the brightness of your glory.[27]

Such rhetoric, well received at the time, is now sometimes dismissed as the overwrought romanticizing of war. It is worth remembering that Porter himself was a decorated battlefield hero who hated war. He had earned the right to speak this way about John Paul Jones.

When the speeches ended and the prayer was given, the audience rose. Eight petty officers, four American and four French, lifted the casket, carried it out of the armory, and placed it on a wagon. The wagon, drawn by a long line of sailors, proceeded slowly to Bancroft Hall. The chaplain of the U.S. Navy led the way, followed by President Roosevelt, the other speakers, marines, midshipmen, officers, and the Naval Academy band playing the Dead March from *Saul*. The route was lined with cavalrymen, marines, sailors, and midshipmen, presenting arms as the casket passed by. At Bancroft Hall the casket was placed inside, beneath the stairway, pending completion of the new Naval Academy Chapel, where, it was thought, Jones's remains would soon be finally laid to rest. Then the crowd dispersed. The president was taken by automobile back to the railroad station for his return to Washington. Apparently, he seldom rode in automobiles. "He appeared delighted with the experience," wrote the *Washington Post*'s reporter. "When the station was reached he jumped to the ground and greeted the chauffeur cordially." He also presented Mrs. Roosevelt to the driver.[28]

Bancroft Hall, where Jones's remains now temporarily reposed, was the midshipmen's dormitory. Weeks of repose there became months. The middies, not inclined to reverence, composed a song:

> Everybody works but John Paul Jones!
> He lies around all day,
> Body pickled in alcohol
> On a permanent jag, they say.
> Middies stand around him
> Doing honor to his bones;
> Everybody works in "Crabtown"
> But John Paul Jones![29]

What the future naval officers did not know—what most of America did not know—was that the appropriation for Jones's tomb at the soon-to-be-completed Naval Academy Chapel had never been secured. Jones was destined for a very long layover under the stairs of Bancroft Hall—guarded at all times, to be sure, by an armed sentry, but an undignified purgatory nonetheless for the Achilles of the Ocean.

2

THE DEEDS OF JOHN PAUL JONES

Every officer in our Navy should know by heart the deeds of John Paul Jones.
—Address of President Roosevelt, April 24, 1906

President Roosevelt, in his commemoration address, insisted that every naval officer should "know by heart" the deeds of John Paul Jones. However, except for the capture of the English man-of-war *Serapis,* he did not identify specific deeds. What were the deeds of John Paul Jones that President Roosevelt thought should be known by heart? Were they even historical events? The John Paul Jones who was commemorated at Annapolis on April 24, 1906, was both a historical figure and a legend. His memory, lost for decades, had been fitfully retrieved and reconstructed over many years. We now know that several acts attributed to him at the time of the commemoration were fabrications, the work of writers whose intent, evidently, was to sell books and copy, not to enhance the historical record. (The fabrications included the most popular contemporary "biography" of Jones then in circulation.)[1]

There are clues as to what deeds, or at least what kinds of deeds, Roosevelt thought should be remembered. It is noteworthy, in particular, that he addressed his exhortation to officers of the navy, not the broader American public ("Every officer in our Navy should know . . ."). He saw in Jones the qualities of officership that naval officers must have for America to prevail in case of war. He chose Annapolis where future naval officers are trained, not the national cemetery at Arlington, as Jones's final resting place because he hoped to inspire the academy's midshipmen—the navy's future officers—to emulate Jones's qualities of command, foremost among them preparedness and courage.

Roosevelt had elaborated on the qualities of preparedness and courage before, at the academy's 1902 commencement, for example, when he implored the graduates before him to train themselves, and those under them, in the actual work of seamanship and gunnery. Of course, he said, officers and men must have the ability in battle to "stand up to the hammering" as well as "the courage, the daring, the resolution to endure." But such bravery alone was not enough. The navy's officers and men must also realize that, in battle, "the only shots that count are the shots that hit, and that normally the victory will lie with the side whose shots hit oftenest."[2] The president was nothing if not practical. He ended his Jones commemoration address on a similar note, addressing the midshipmen. "You will be worthless in war," he told them, "if you have not prepared yourselves for it in peace."

> You will be utterly unable to rise to the needs of the crisis if you have not by long years of steady and patient work fitted yourselves to get the last ounce of work out of every man, every gun, and every ship in the fleet; if you have not practiced steadily on the high seas until each ship can do its best, can show at its best, alone or in conjunction with others in fleet formation. Remember that no courage can ever atone for lack of that preparedness which makes the courage valuable; and yet if the courage is there, if the dauntless heart is there, its presence will sometimes make up for other shortcomings; while if with it are combined the other military qualities the fortunate owner becomes literally invincible.[3]

The intent of this chapter is to try to identify those of John Paul Jones's "deeds" that manifest the qualities of preparedness and courage Roosevelt had in mind when he admonished the midshipmen at the Annapolis commemoration, deeds it would be well worth it for a naval officer to "know by heart," deeds that justify the inscription on Jones's Annapolis tomb, "He gave our navy its earliest traditions of heroism and victory." For context, we begin with a brief account of his origins (he was born a Scotsman), his early years at sea, and his emigration to America.[4]

The Early Years

He was christened John Paul (Paul was the surname; there was no Jones). His father, also John, was head gardener for the Arbigland estate in the Scottish parish of Kirkbean, near the sea. His mother, Jeannie, was the daughter of a landed family. The Pauls resided at an attractive cottage on the estate, where the younger John was born July 6, 1747, the fourth of seven children. He grew up exploring the nearby sand flats and coves of Solway Firth, watching the great sailing ships make their way out of the firth and into the Irish Sea.[5] At the age of thirteen he was apprenticed for seven years to the shipowner John Younger. His first voyage, as a ship's boy, was out of nearby Whitehaven on the brig *Friendship,* bound for Barbados and Virginia. It was on *Friendship* that John Paul began to learn the trade of seaman.

Friendship, eighty-five feet long and 179 tons, was a two-masted merchant ship typical of the era. It had a crew of twenty-eight; it was also well armed, England being at the time at war with France. In a normal year, it would make one round-trip from Whitehaven to the West Indies to the American colonies and then back to Whitehaven. John Paul's older brother, William, a tailor, had previously emigrated to Fredericksburg, Virginia. John Paul visited William during these trips. The visits provided him his first introduction to America. Evidently, he liked it, writing some years later that it was "my favorite Country from the age of thirteen, when I first saw it."[6]

In 1764 John Younger sold *Friendship* and released John Paul from the rest of his apprenticeship. John Paul then signed on as third mate on the slaver *King George* and first mate on the slaver *Two Friends,* both out of Whitehaven. He obtained his discharge in or about 1768, at Kingston. He would say afterward the business disgusted him.

John Paul got free passage back to Scotland on the brig *John.* This proved a turning point in his young career. Both the captain and the ship's only other officer died during the voyage. Paul assumed command and sailed the vessel safely to its home port of Kirkcudbright. The owners, grateful for the safe return of their cargo and ship, made John Paul its captain. As captain he made two round-trips between Kirkcudbright and Jamaica. It was his first test of leadership. As Samuel Eliot Morison writes, "To be a master of a merchant ship in overseas trade was a great responsibility for a man of twenty-one; and on a vessel as small as *John* [60 tons] the burden was greater. Captain Paul had complete charge of the rigging, the navigation (celestial and otherwise) and the internal discipline of his ship." He was also responsible for selling or bartering the ship's cargo at its port of destination and procuring cargo for the return trip, thus testing his commercial skills as well as seamanship. *John*'s owners sold the ship in 1771. Their letter honorably discharging John Paul states that, on the two voyages he captained, "he approved himself every way qualified as a navigator and supercargo."[7]

John Paul's reputation as a skilled seaman and merchant captain was advancing. In 1772, after a brief time as captain of a packet that plied between Galloway and the Isle of Man, he obtained command (and part ownership) of his first three-masted vessel, *Betsy,* out of London. It traded among the ports of England, Ireland, the Madeira Islands, and Tobago. It was in Tobago, in late 1773, that there occurred what John Paul would later call "the greatest misfortune of my life," a misfortune that ended his promising merchant career, forced his exile to America, and prompted his adoption of the alias Jones.

Before recounting this misfortune, it should be noted that John Paul's favorable reputation among shipowners and traders was not fully shared by the sailors he commanded. He was, evidently, a hard-nosed and bad-tempered captain. His crews respected his seamanship but not always his discipline. A flogging of the ship's carpenter he had ordered while commanding *John* was notorious; the carpenter's subsequent death (albeit unrelated to the flogging) resulted in charges being brought and a brief stint in jail. Although Captain Paul was cleared, the incident is illustrative of tensions with his crews that would dog him throughout his career.

The misfortune in Tobago began when Paul refused to advance wages to the *Betsy* crew; he was, it seems, hoarding cash to invest in the return cargo. A crewman with whom he had had run-ins on the voyage out pressed for payment.[8] An altercation ensued: the crewman rushed the captain and swung a bludgeon at him; Paul drew his sword, ran the sword through his attacker, and killed the man. The captain immediately gave himself up to a local justice of the peace. He always insisted, then and later, that the killing was justified self-defense. Nevertheless, he fled Tobago (the crewman was a Tobago native; perhaps local sentiment was too aroused against Paul), adopted the alias Jones to conceal his identity (for a time he was John Jones, then John Paul Jones), and made for Virginia.

How, exactly, he got to Virginia (or even when) is not known. Presumably, the route was circuitous. We do know he was there in 1774, possibly living in the house of his brother, William, who had died that year. We also know he became good friends there with a Dr. John K. Read, who apparently introduced him to influential men of the time, including Philadelphians (Jones's Masonic connections were probably also an important source of introductions—he had become a Mason around 1770 while in Scotland), and that Jones visited Philadelphia in 1775, on the eve of the American Revolution. The battles at Lexington and Concord had already occurred. The Second Continental Congress had just created an army and a navy. Was Jones looking for a job? Probably. In any event, on December 7, 1775, "John Paul Jones [Esq.]" was appointed first lieutenant in the Continental navy. Congress formalized his commission on December 22.

Our future naval hero had progressed from a thirteen-year-old ship's boy to a captain at twenty-one. By his midtwenties, he had commanded merchant brigs and a three-masted square-rigger. He had learned, in the words of Morison, "about all there was to learn about rigging, loading and handling a full-rigged ship. He could navigate across the ocean by dead reckoning and noon latitudes of the sun. He had gotten the hang of a lucrative branch of commerce."[9] He was meticulous about most things he did, whether fitting out a ship or dressing. He was also a fluent writer, well read (apparently, he used the downtime of his long voyages for self-study), and socially poised; he also had a fiery temper.

Hoisting the Flag; First Cruise of *Alfred*

John Paul Jones's first military assignment was to oversee the naval outfitting of the sloop *Alfred*, one of four merchant ships that the Naval Committee (appointed by Congress, also known as the Marine Committee) had bought to convert to fighters. Jones began the assignment several days before his commissioning. It provided the occasion for his first memorable deed for his adopted country: the first-ever hoisting of an American flag on a naval ship. The event happened at Philadelphia on December 3, 1775. The newly appointed Commodore Esek Hopkins, commander in chief of the grab-bag squadron of which *Alfred* was a part, was rowed from shore to *Alfred* and piped on board. Next the commodore's battle flag—a version of the Gadsden flag with the motto "Don't Tread on Me" on it—was raised. Then Jones, as the ship's second in command, personally hoisted the Grand Union flag of the colonies onto the jack staff of *Alfred:* thirteen alternating red and white stripes with a miniature British flag in the upper left corner.

The orders to the squadron of which *Alfred* was a part were to sail for Chesapeake Bay, there to "attack, take and destroy" all enemy ships. Instead, the four newly outfitted vessels—revolutionary America's first battleships—sat in the Delaware River for six weeks, until mid-February, icebound and unable to move. When the ice broke, Commodore Hopkins made for warmer climes, specifically New Providence (now Nassau) in the Bahamas, not Chesapeake Bay. (A loophole in his orders allowed for alternatives if "bad Winds or Stormy Weather" or other unforeseen events should intervene; evidently, Hopkins determined that his circumstances fitted the loophole.) New Providence was undefended. The squadron (technically now a fleet, two smaller schooners having joined them as they left the Delaware) captured two local sloops, sundry weapons and ammunition, and the lieutenant governor and then headed with their booty to Rhode Island, Hopkins's home state. On April 6, twenty miles southeast of Block Island, they encountered HMS *Glasgow,* engaged and badly damaged it but did not defeat or capture it, and proceeded to Providence. *Alfred* (among others) was badly damaged as well. Still, John Paul Jones had completed his first naval mission and survived his first sea battle. He had also impressed his commodore. On May 10, 1776, Hopkins made him captain of the twelve-gun *Providence.* (Hopkins himself did not fare so well. Although Congress—and the American press—initially hailed him for his "great victory" over *Glasgow,* subsequent inquiry determined that, given his numerical superiority in the battle, he had made a botch of it. He was censured and dismissed from service in 1778.)

The Enemy; Cruise of *Providence*

The British navy at the start of the American Revolution was the most powerful navy in the world. Larger by a third than either of its nearest rivals, France and Spain, it comprised some 270 ships, including more than 100 so-called ships of the line (very large ships, usually having fifty to one hundred guns each, intended for direct close-range combat and powerful enough to participate in a line of battle, that is, a single line of ships that would face a single line of enemy ships and engage in close-range combat) and more than 80 cruisers (smaller, usually faster ships with fewer guns, including frigates, brigs, sloops, and schooners but intended for combat).[10] Moreover, British naval superiority was not a matter of numbers only: the officers, sailors, and marines who manned the ships (some sixteen thousand in all) were the best-trained, most professional navy on earth. Of course, not all of these ships and men were deployed to the American colonies; the British had other interests to defend as well. But the American deployment was substantial: in 1775 some 90 ships, including 10 or 12 ships of the line and numerous frigates (twenty to forty guns). The numbers, while not overwhelming, were sufficient to disrupt the American economy and war effort. Moreover, these numbers were increased in 1776 when a large British fleet under command of Admiral Richard Howe arrived in New York's East River.

The Americans could not hope to challenge British command of the sea. Initially, therefore, American naval strategy was mostly focused on trying to divert or capture merchant ships that were supplying British land forces in the colonies and, where possible, seize supplies from them for the colonial army. The orders to John Paul Jones, captain of the seventy-foot, single-masted *Providence* with a crew of seventy-three officers, sailors, and marines, were consistent with this early strategy of trying to capture supply ships and their cargoes: "Cruise against our enemies." From August 21, 1776, when he set sail from Philadelphia for the coast of Canada, until October 8, when bad weather (and a depleted crew) forced him back to safe harbor in Narragansett Bay, Jones captured 16 British ships, 7 of which he successfully brought or sent back, 1 of which was retaken by the British, and the rest of which he burned. (So many of his original crew were needed to sail the captured prizes that Jones did not have enough crew left on *Providence* to keep sailing, even if the weather had been good.)

On October 10, Congress permanently conferred on Jones the rank of captain of the Navy of the United States of North-America. It was not exactly what Jones craved; he wanted a ship, not just a rank. But it was public recognition of his talents, and it provided job security. Three weeks later, he was placed in command of *Alfred* and given his next mission: to interdict coal supplies headed for the British army in New York City and rescue captured American seamen being forced to work in the coal pits of Cape Breton Island, Nova Scotia.

Second Cruise of *Alfred*

Alfred, as we learned earlier, was a larger ship than *Providence*—140 feet long, 350 tons, and thirty guns—and therefore a step up in command prestige. It carried a crew of 220. However, at the time Jones took command, there were only 30 men on board. Naval recruiting throughout the War of Independence (but especially at the beginning) was hampered by several factors, the most important of which was the contingent of "privateers" that competed with the navy for manpower. Privateers were privately owned vessels outfitted for fighting that attacked and seized enemy ships and cargo—in effect pirate ships, except that they were authorized by Congress to do what they did, and they were rewarded for their successes by being allowed to sell the "prizes" that they captured (ships and supplies), keeping most of the proceeds of sale for themselves. The proceeds were then shared among the owners, officers, and crew (a token payment also went to Congress for the war effort), thus making the privateers a far more lucrative source of employment than the navy. There was a long tradition of privateers in war. All seafaring nations (including Britain) used them, and their activities were even regulated by international law. The British established a prize system for the navy as well: British crews were allowed to keep two-thirds of their prizes, a percentage that was competitive with what could be earned by the officers and crew of a privateer. By contrast, Continental navy crews could keep only a third of the profits from their captured prizes.

A week after he was commissioned captain of *Alfred,* in the midst of his efforts to sign up a crew, Jones wrote a letter about the prize system to Robert Morris, a member of the Marine Committee of the Continental Congress, recommending that Congress increase the share of prize money for Continental navy crews so that the navy could compete for talent with the privateers. The letter is justly famous for its foresight; it would also become one of Jones's most celebrated writings. Jones begins the letter by lamenting that he has been able to hire only about 30 men for his crew. The average recruit, he says, is motivated by self-interest, not patriotism; as long as the owners of the privateers pay their crews a much larger share of prize money from captured prizes than does the navy, potential recruits will prefer joining the privateers to joining the navy. The only solution, he suggests, is for the navy to offer more prize money to its crews (or, as Jones more colorfully puts it, "enlist the seamen during pleasure, and give them all the prizes"). "What," Jones asks in concluding the letter, "is the paltry emolument of two thirds of prizes to the finances of this vast continent."

> If so poor a resource is essential to its independency, in sober sadness we are involved in a woeful predicament, and our ruin is fast approaching. The situation of America is new in the annals of mankind, her affairs cry haste, and her speed must answer them. Trifles, therefore, ought to be wholly disregarded, as being in the old vulgar proverb "penny wise and pound foolish." If our enemies with the best-established and most formidable navy in the universe, have found it expedient to assign all prizes to the captors, how much more is such policy essential to our infant fleet.[11]

Congress responded, increasing the crew's share of prizes from a third to half, an improvement, but still not fully competitive with the privateers.

Jones was, nevertheless, able to enlist a crew. *Alfred* sailed for Nova Scotia on October 27, 1776. Two additional vessels had been ordered to join *Alfred* on its mission: *Providence* and a fourteen-gun brigantine named *Hampden*. Technically, therefore, Jones would command his first squadron. In the event, *Hampden* ran aground in Providence Harbor shortly after setting sail, and the squadron was quickly reduced to two. By mid-November, though, the tiny squadron had successfully captured several prizes, including *Active, Mellish,* and *Kitty. Mellish* in particular was a major prize: it was a 340-ton transport carrying winter uniforms and supplies for the British army in Quebec, clothing and materials that could now be diverted to General Washington and his troops. Meanwhile, though, the weather was deteriorating, it was cold, winter was setting in, and the crews were homesick. The officers of *Providence* complained that their ship was leaking badly and insisted it would be dangerous to sail any farther north. Under cover of a snow squall, they "gave Jones the slip" and sailed back to Rhode Island.[12] Jones, in *Alfred,* pressed on alone, still hoping to free the American prisoners from the coal mines at Cape Breton. A few days later, during a raid near Canso in which he burned a British supply ship and oil warehouse, Jones learned that the American prisoners had freed themselves—by agreeing to join the British navy. So *Alfred* ended its mission and headed back south, capturing an additional prize, *John,* on the homeward journey as well as a number of colliers, then itself escaping capture by the larger and stronger HMS *Milford* (603 tons and twenty-eight guns) east of Cape Cod. Jones lost *John* to *Milford,* but saved his other prizes as well as *Alfred*—a not inconsiderable feat. *Alfred* arrived in Boston Harbor on December 15. It had only two days of freshwater left on board and no provisions.

Appointment as Captain of *Ranger*

The cruises of John Paul Jones in the late summer and fall of 1776 as captain of *Providence* and then *Alfred* were notable successes. The same cannot be said of the navy's other efforts at the time: most of its few ships had been captured, sunk, or lost to bad weather, and major colonial seaports were blockaded or occupied. It might have been expected, therefore, that Jones would be rewarded for his singular achievements with command of a larger ship and squadron—even a fleet. Instead, he was relieved of command of *Alfred* and spent the first six months of 1777 idle as precious ships and commands were, for the most part, assigned to less deserving captains based on seniority or politics. (Assignments to newly built ships generally went to a captain who was native to the region where the ship was being built. There was logic in this, if not justice: competing with privateers for recruits was difficult; a captain from the local area had the best chance of hiring locals to man a new ship.) Jones was fit to be tied. He made a nuisance of himself to the Marine Committee and Commodore Hopkins, nearly resulting in his court-martial. Finally, in June 1777, he was assigned command of *Ranger*, out of Portsmouth, New Hampshire—a square-rigged, three-masted sloop of war approximately 110 feet long and 320 tons, with twenty nine-pound guns and a crew of 140. Jones reduced the number of guns to eighteen, judging that the ship was too light to carry more. He was always seeking the perfect balance between firepower and speed. As he would later famously write, "I wish to have no connection with any ship that does not sail fast; for I intend to go in harm's way."

Jones's appointment was announced in the *Journals* of Congress on June 14, 1777, immediately beneath the announcement of the resolution establishing the design of the new American flag: "That the Flag of the thirteen United States be thirteen stripes, alternate red and white; that the union be thirteen stars, white in a blue field, representing a new constellation."[13] Many have since remarked on the appropriateness of this coincidental juxtaposition—the appointment that led to Jones's glory and the birth of the American flag.

Crossing the Atlantic; New Orders; the Nine-Gun Salute

Besides being too light to carry twenty guns, *Ranger* was top heavy. Jones knew what to do to fix it but could not get materials, despite Portsmouth being a shipbuilding center. He also struggled to assemble a crew. In both cases, his being an outsider and a Scotsman worked against him. *Ranger* finally sailed on November 1, 1777, more than four months after Jones took command. It was not yet in top fighting shape, but at least it had a crew and was sufficiently refitted to cross the Atlantic.

Jones's orders were to carry duplicate dispatches to the American commissioners in France, including Ben Franklin. The voyage across the ocean was uneventful, although *Ranger* did capture two prizes on the way, arriving in Nantes on December 2. There Jones set about to complete the refitting begun at Portsmouth. He also traveled to Paris to meet the great Benjamin Franklin. It had been anticipated that, once in France, he would be given command of a larger ship to be bought or built in Europe, so the meeting with Franklin was in part to deliver a letter from the Marine Committee to the American commissioners explaining that this was the purpose of Jones coming to France. Jones and Franklin got on well, forging a friendship that would greatly influence Jones. But the larger ship was not forthcoming; the commissioners did not have sufficient funds to procure it, and the French, though sympathetic, were not willing to give it. Jones, bitterly disappointed, was stuck with *Ranger.* What he did get, in lieu of a new ship, was new orders that lifted his spirits considerably—in effect, a blank check to do with *Ranger* whatever he wished: "As it is not in our power to procure you such a Ship as you expected, we advise you after equipping the *Ranger* in the best manner, for the Cruise you propose, that you proceed with her in the manner you shall judge best, for distressing the Enemies of the United States, by Sea, or otherwise, consistent with the Laws of War, and the Terms of your Commission."[14]

John Paul Jones had been convinced for some time that interdicting British merchant vessels off the coast of North America was not the highest and best use of his talents—or the best strategy for the Continental navy. The privateers could do that job well enough. What Jones craved, and believed would best serve the interests of the United States, was to take the fight to the British homeland, that is, raid British commerce off the coasts of England, Scotland, and Ireland and attack poorly defended British ports. He had said as much a year earlier in his letter to Robert Morris, where, in addition to advocating that Congress should increase the share of prize money for Continental navy crews, Jones had proposed a striking extension of Continental naval strategy: taking the fight to the enemy across the Atlantic and in particular interdicting Britain's African trade by attacking English ships along the coast of Africa. "I am persuaded," Jones wrote, this would "give a blow to the English African trade, which would not soon be recovered, by not leaving them a mast standing on that coast." Morris was in perfect agreement with Jones's proposed strategy, writing to Jones in February 1777 that it "has long been clear to me that our Infant fleet cannot protect our own Coasts; and the only effectual relief it can afford us is to attack the enemy's defenseless places and thereby oblige them to station more of their Ships in their own Countries, or to keep them employed in following ours, and either way we are relieved so far as they do it." Now Jones had orders broad enough to let him do precisely that ("Proceed . . . in the manner you shall judge best, for distressing the Enemies of the United States, by Sea, *or otherwise*" [emphasis added]).[15]

Cruise of *Ranger:* The Raids at Whitehaven and St. Mary's Isle

Jones set sail in *Ranger* on February 13, 1778. His crew was mutinous; they wanted home, not glory. Moreover, they had not yet been fully paid for the prizes they captured on the voyage over; they wanted their money.

On his first day out, he sailed northwest along the French coast, anchoring for the night at Quiberon Bay, one of the principal anchorages of the French navy. There a squadron of French line-of-battle ships and three frigates, under command of Chef d'Escadre Le Motte Piquet, was waiting to escort a convoy of American merchant ships out of the harbor. Jones was a man for whom symbols and grand gestures mattered greatly. He sent Piquet a note, presenting his compliments and stating his intent "to salute [the admiral] with thirteen guns under American Colours—provided he will Accept the Compliment and Return Gun for Gun." What Jones was seeking was a thirteen-gun salute from the French to the Americans in exchange for his to them; it would be, if it happened, the first-ever salute by a foreign navy to an American naval vessel flying the Stars and Stripes. Negotiations ensued. The French, it seemed, were willing to exchange salutes—but not an equal number of guns. The admiral offered nine for thirteen. Jones, incensed, asked for at least eleven. In the end he settled for nine. And so it happened in the late afternoon of February 14, 1778, that *Ranger* lifted anchor, sailed by the stern of the French flagship, fired a thirteen-gun salute, and received a nine-gun salute in return. The secret alliance between the French and the Americans, signed two weeks earlier, was now publicly acknowledged.

Jones lingered for two months in and about Quiberon Bay, then Cameret (near Brest), tinkering with rigging, masts, and sails to make *Ranger* faster and more seaworthy. Finally, on April 10, he sailed for the Irish Sea. He had three goals: attack an English coastal city in order to cause panic in the countryside, capture a significant hostage to trade for American prisoners in England, and capture or sink British merchant vessels in British waters. The raids on Whitehaven and St. Mary's Isle were meant to accomplish the first two of these three goals.

Jones knew Whitehaven well: it was the port from which he had first sailed for America at age thirteen as a ship's boy. His knowledge of the port made it an ideal target. The raid itself, though, was something of a farce. First, the crew rebelled; they saw no point to it. Their bread and butter was capturing prizes, not risking their lives landing at an obscure Scottish port. A near mutiny was barely contained when a Swedish volunteer warned Jones just in the nick of time, and Jones was able to stop it with a pistol to the head of the chief provocateur. Then lack of wind forced *Ranger,* at midnight on April 22, to anchor several miles offshore. Jones assembled a reluctant raiding party of forty officers and men in two small boats; they rowed three hours against the tide, arriving in the harbor only after daybreak, thus losing the advantage of darkness.

What Jones had hoped to do was incapacitate the two batteries guarding the north and south sides of the harbor by surprising the sleeping sentinels and spiking the cannons and then set fire to the hundreds of small coasters, fishing vessels, and colliers that Jones knew would be aground in the mud at low tide. The raiding party landed at the town's stone pier. The one boatload (Jones's) made it to the nearest fort, overwhelmed the guards (all of whom were huddled inside the guardhouse for warmth instead of standing guard outside), and spiked the cannons. The other boatload (not Jones's), instead of starting fires, broke into a local pub and got drunk. Jones tried to rally his remaining troops to start the fires. They did manage to set a coal collier ablaze, but hundreds of townspeople were by this time making for the docks. An Irishman in Jones's crew by the name of

David Freedman (he had signed on under the pseudonym David Smith) had betrayed the raiding party and was now running about town sounding the alarm. Jones drew his pistol, waved it at the crowd, and urged his men back to their boats. Jones would later describe his departure this way: "The inhabitants began to appear in thousands; and individuals ran hastily towards us. I stood between them and the ship on fire, with a pistol in my hand, and ordered them to retire, which they did with precipitation. The flames had already caught on the rigging, and began to ascend the main mast:—the sun was a full hour's march above the horizon; and as sleep no longer ruled the world, it was time to retire."[16] The raiding party reboarded their boats and rowed as hard as they could back to *Ranger*, cannon balls from cannons hastily mounted on the beach falling harmlessly about them in the harbor.

Some spiked cannons at the fort, one coal collier in flames, a dozen or so inebriated crewmen, and a deserter who ratted out the mission: the raid on Whitehaven was not a tactical triumph. Strategically, though, it succeeded beyond anything one could have imagined. Anyone, that is, but John Paul Jones—who had, indeed, imagined it. All across the British Isles, word of the raid spread like wildfire: for the first time in five hundred years, a foreign military had landed on Britain's shores, caused harm, and escaped.[17]

> Late last night, or early this morning, a number of armed men, (to the amount of thirty) landed at this place, by two boats from an American privateer, as appears from one of the people now in custody. Whether he was left through accident, or escaped by design, is yet uncertain. . . . This much has however been proved, that a little after three o'clock this morning he rapped at several doors in Marlborough Street, (adjoining one of the piers) and informed them, that fire had been set to one of the ships in the harbour, matches were laid in several others; the whole world would be soon in a blaze, and the town also destroyed. . . . The alarm was immediately spread, and his account proved too true. . . . It appears that this infernal plan (unprecedented except in the annals of John the Painter) was laid at Brest, where, for a considerable sum of money, Paul or Jones, (the latter is only an addition to his name) engaged to burn the shipping and town of Whitehaven. . . . A number of expresses have been dispatched to all the capital sea ports in the kingdom, where any [further] depredations are likely to be made; all strangers in this town, are, by an order of the magistrate, to be secured and examined: similar notices have been forwarded through the country.[18]

Jones, of course, was as yet unaware of the spreading panic onshore. He was focused on the second part of his raiding strategy: the capture of an eminent personage to trade for imprisoned American sailors. His object this time was the Earl of Selkirk, a British lord who lived in a large manor house on St. Mary's Isle in Kirkcudbright Bay. The place was close by Whitehaven; Jones knew of the manor and the earl from his childhood days in Kirkbean. What he did not know was that the earl was in London at the time. He learned this only after he and his raiding party of a dozen or so crewmen landed on the isle around eleven on the morning of the twenty-third. Jones then decided everyone should go back to the ship, but the two officers in the group insisted that the manor must be looted, to avenge lootings that the British had carried out at homes on the American coast but also to compensate the raiders for their risk; after all, they had left Whitehaven a few hours before empty-handed.

Jones hesitated and then proposed a compromise. He would return to the ship himself but allow others to complete the raid and seize the Selkirk family silver, provided they behaved courteously to the occupants, did not search the house, and did not otherwise pillage or molest anyone. A bargain to that effect was struck, the raid was done quickly in accordance with the bargain, and the crew returned to *Ranger* shortly thereafter with the Selkirk silver in hand.

Three observations of relevance to our theme may be made in connection with the raid on St. Mary's Isle. First, the raid was a small illustration of Jones's talent, exercised often throughout his career, for utilizing stealth and camouflage to achieve military objectives. The reason *Ranger*'s tiny raiding party could land in broad daylight on the isle, obtain intelligence about Lord Selkirk's whereabouts, seize the Selkirk silver, and return safely to their ship without local opposition being mustered was due to a ruse that Jones contrived. He informed the Selkirk gardener, who was the first to confront him after landing, that he and his crew were members of a British press gang searching for strong, healthy young men to press into his royal majesty's military service. (Jones's Scottish accent must have been especially convincing in this regard.) The gardener warned what would otherwise have been the manor's likely defenders to get out of town and hide, they did so, and the manor was thus left undefended.

Second, Jones was obsessed by personal honor—quick, therefore, to perceive a slight however small, elaborate in defending behavior that might raise the slightest doubt of his good intentions. In this case, it got the best of him. As soon as *Ranger* returned to Brest two weeks later, Jones wrote a letter to Lady Selkirk, defending the raid (its worthy purpose being to trade her husband for American sailors held captive in English prisons in unspeakable conditions!), seeking her reassurance that his men had acted courteously, and informing her that he would purchase the Selkirk silver from his men with his own funds and return it to the family. The earl responded for his lady a month later, politely but somewhat condescendingly (Jones never saw the letter), saying that Jones's men had "behaved with civility" and that the Earl of and Lady Selkirk could not accept the return of their silver, "as you must purchase it you say for that purpose."

Third, as knowledge of the raid spread, it reinforced the nationwide panic that the Whitehaven raid of a few hours before had aroused. Typical was the following letter from one of the magistrates of Kirkcudbright to the provost of Dumfries:

> This morning [April 23], about 12 o'clock an American privateer, thought to be about 20 guns, appeared in this bay, and has plundered the house of St. Mary Isle, the seat of the Earl of Selkirk, within a mile of Kirkcudbright, of all the silver plate, etc. We expect a visit from them on the return of the tide, as they still hover in our bay. We are not in a state of defense, nor do we believe any thing can be done, unless some of the King's ships had notice of them. If you had any troops, we should be much the better of them; but I suppose all our injury will be over before you can assist us.[19]

Cruise of *Ranger: Drake* Captured

The goal of *Ranger*'s cruise (in addition to attacking an English coastal city to cause panic in the countryside and capturing a significant hostage to trade for American prisoners in England) was to capture or sink British merchant vessels in British waters. An opportunity greater even than this presented itself the following day, April 24, 1778. HMS *Drake,* a British sloop of war, was heading out of Belfast Harbour into the North Channel, a stretch of water between the Atlantic Ocean and the Irish Sea. *Drake*'s Captain Burden had been warned that Jones was in the area, and he could see *Ranger* inside the harbor's entrance. But Jones was careful to disguise its identity: the crew was hidden below deck, and the ship was angled to block any view of its gun ports. Burden sent an officer in a small boat to reconnoiter. Jones invited the British officer on board *Ranger* and then declared him a prisoner of the United States Navy. When the officer did not return, Burden realized that a fight was imminent.

On paper *Drake* and *Ranger* were evenly matched. *Drake* carried twenty six-pound guns and measured 275 tons. *Ranger* carried eighteen nine-pound guns and measured 316 tons. *Drake,* though, had the larger and better-trained crew. The ships engaged an hour before sunset. The fighting lasted an hour. *Drake*'s sails and rigging were shredded, its hull pounded and pocked. Both Burden and his number two in command were killed. *Drake* surrendered. The British suffered 4 dead and 19 wounded; 133 officers and men were taken prisoner. The Americans counted 4 dead and 5 wounded.[20] *Ranger* itself was largely intact.

In the greater scheme of naval history, *Ranger*'s capture of *Drake* was not noteworthy. These were small vessels, not even large enough to be rated frigate class. Even in the context of the American Revolution, this was not the first time the Americans had captured a British warship.[21] But the event was monumental nonetheless. It occurred in British home waters. The combatant ships being an even match in terms of guns and weight, the superior training and size of the British crew should have carried the day. Coming hard on the heels of Jones's raids on Whitehaven and St. Mary's Isle, it now seemed the Americans could threaten and plunder the British homeland and home waters at will. Insurance rates to Ireland jumped fourfold.[22]

The British understood the implications. Attempts were made to explain the loss: the American ship was vastly superior in terms of weight and guns; the British gunpowder was compromised; the British captain was near retirement and not at the top of his game; a proper order of command had not been established, so that when the captain and his second in command were both mortally wounded, *Drake* was effectively leaderless; a part of the crew composed of impressed sailors refused to fight. In the end, though, the difference was Jones. The British conceded as much: "The Drake had 18 six-pounders, and the privateer is said to have 20 guns, which probably were nine pounders; the superiority in point of number was only one gun on each side, and the difference of diameter between a six and nine pound shot, is too small to make the latter so very alarming. In our engagements with the French and Spaniards such a superiority would have been laughed at; but the case is widely different when we engage with our own countrymen; men who have the same spirit and bravery with ourselves."[23]

The British dispatched a number of warships, large and small, to capture Jones: HMS *Stag* and *Doctor, Thetis, Heart of Oak, Boston,* and others. Jones easily evaded his pursuers, sailing north and west around Ireland, instead of south toward France (as the British wrongly anticipated he would do). He arrived in Brest on May 8, 1778, with *Drake,* two other prizes, and two hundred prisoners.

The legend of John Paul Jones was starting to spread—if not in the colonies (where, curiously, Jones's exploits went largely uncelebrated), then at least in the British Isles. Indeed, there—the British Isles—Jones was becoming something of a rogue hero with the locals, the subject of numerous chapbooks and ballads. No better measure of his impact can be had than this.

Prisoner Exchange; Seeking New Commands

Following his return to France, Jones spent nine months trying to get his crew paid, his prisoners exchanged for captured Americans in England, and a new command. One might have thought he would have an easy time of it—and garner accolades as well. He had just won an impressive naval battle for the Americans. His capture of *Drake,* combined with his raids at Whitehaven and St. Mary's Isle, was the talk of England. There had not been many American naval victories; this was surely the finest to date, deserving applause. But it was not Jones's fate.

A draft to pay his men, drawn on the American commissioners in Paris, was dishonored. *Patience* and *Lord Chatham,* his two prizes beside *Drake,* were sold for a fraction of their worth. *Drake,* more valuable, fetched only a fire-sale price. Eventually, Jones took out personal loans to pay the crew, but they blamed him, and him alone, for their late pay and meager shares of prize money.

Jones also borrowed personally to feed, house, and guard his 200 prisoners while efforts to exchange them for their American counterparts in England stalled. The British were reluctant to trade. To them, captured Americans were rebels or pirates, not prisoners of war—therefore criminals to be tried and jailed, not exchanged. Finally, in February 1779, a deal was struck: Jones's prisoners, together with certain others seized by the French, were traded for 228 Americans.

Jones's efforts to secure a new command produced more frustration and humiliation. For a time, it seemed he would get *L'Indien,* a long, sleek forty-gun ship built recently in Amsterdam that he had coveted since before the cruise of *Ranger.* Ben Franklin assured him in June it was his, but it was not. The French offered him a sixteen-gun corvette, a vessel vastly inferior to his talents. He politely refused. There was talk of other possible commands: *Renomée,* the captured HMS *Fox, L'Union.* But it was only talk.

As for accolades, there were none; instead, opprobrium.[24] On May 23, Arthur Lee, one of the three American commissioners in Paris, wrote Jones a letter, the first official communication to Jones since his arrival at Brest two weeks earlier. It contained not a word of acknowledgment or praise for Jones's achievements as captain of *Ranger.* Rather, it excoriated Jones for having arrested a certain Lieutenant Simpson for disobeying orders on the voyage home. Simpson was a popular officer who disliked Jones. Jones believed, probably rightly, that he was responsible for inciting an already disgruntled crew to near mutiny in the early days of the cruise, planning to throw Jones overboard or leave him at Whitehaven. Still, Jones appointed Simpson to command the captured *Drake* on the return to Brest. Simpson was supposed to stay close to *Ranger,* pay strict attention to Jones's signals, and support *Ranger* in the event of enemy contact. Off the coast of France, Jones spotted a possible prize and shouted orders to Simpson to join the chase. In all likelihood, Simpson did not hear the orders clearly and thought he was being told to make for Brest alone. In any event, as Jones turned *Ranger* to pursue the possible prize, Simpson made for Brest. The possible prize turned out to be a neutral Swedish ship, not British, and Jones abandoned the pursuit. Later, when he caught up with *Drake,* he raged at Lieutenant Simpson for defying his order and placed him under arrest.

Once in France, the officers and crew rallied to Simpson. Lee wrote Jones the May 23 reprimand, ordered Simpson released, put Simpson in command of *Ranger,* and sent it back to America—whereupon the charges against Simpson were dropped and Congress promoted the lieutenant to captain! It was a total humiliation for Jones. He could not have been faulted had he quit the service and taken command of a swift and profitable privateer. But Jones persevered—working for nine months to get his crew paid, his prisoners exchanged for captive American sailors in England, and a new naval command for himself. In November, in the midst of it all, when a friend and fellow captain wrote him despairingly about politics in Philadelphia and the mounting failures of the Continental navy, Jones could not suppress enthusiasm for his adopted country and its cause. He replied, "Your account of the Situation in Philadelphia and our poor Marine distresses much—but let us not altogether despond. Tho' I am no prophet, the one will yet become the *first* City and the other the *first* Navy within a much shorter space of time than is generally imagined. When the Enemies land force is once conquered and expelled the Continent, our Marine will rise as if by Enchantment and become within memory of Persons now living the wonder and Envy of the World."[25]

Cruise of the *Bonhomme Richard* Squadron (Ireland, Scotland, England)

In February 1779, Jones finally caught a break. The king of France offered him command of *Le Duc de Duras,* an aging but still serviceable East Indiaman weighing nine hundred tons. It was the smallest of that class of three-masted warships known as frigates, but it was suitable for an aggressive sea captain like Jones. Jones hesitated only briefly, then accepted. He renamed the ship *Bonhomme Richard,* a loose translation into French of Ben Franklin's nom de plume (Poor Richard, as in *Poor Richard's Almanack*), to honor Franklin, the one American commissioner in Paris who had befriended Jones and offered support.

Jones, a meticulous outfitter of ships, spent months tweaking masts, spars, sails, and rigging. (He "enjoyed fitting out," writes Morison, "more than anything except fighting and making love.")[26] He installed forty guns—nine-, twelve-, and eighteen-pounders—and painted the entire vessel black to hide the gun ports. He purchased small swivel-mounted cannons and blunderbusses (massive shotguns) "to line the rails and fortify the tops."[27] And he assembled a crew—no easy task for a Scotsman in a French port who would sail under the American flag. It was a tough, ragtag lot numbering 380, composed of ten or more nationalities, and included drunkards, the homeless, British sailors imprisoned in France, and American sailors freed from English prisons in the exchange Jones had engineered with his captives from *Drake.* "They were generally so mean," Jones said, "that the only expedient I could find that allowed me to command was to divide them into two parties and let one group of rogues guard the other."[28] Jones made liberal use of the cat-o'-nine-tails as well. In one incident, he had twelve men flogged. They had rowed him to shore and then gone off and gotten drunk, leaving him stranded on the beach when it was time to return to the ship. In another, he sentenced the leader of a failed mutiny to 250 lashes. But Jones's skill at commanding men had improved with time, and many of the *Bonhomme Richard* crew came to appreciate not only his seamanship and courage but also his humanity. As a French officer, Captain Antoine Felix Wybert, would later state, "Far from commanding with haughtiness and brutality, as certain persons have endeavored to circulate," Commander Jones "was always (though very strict and sharp in the service) affable, genteel, and very indulgent, not only towards his officers, but also toward the sentries and soldiers, whom he ever treated with humanity."[29]

Gradually, it all came together: ship, armaments, crew. Jones's command was expanded to include four more vessels—*Alliance, Pallas, Vengeance,* and *Le Cerf.* The mission of this *Bonhomme Richard* squadron, as originally conceived, was a peripheral one. Jones would attack Scotland or northern England to distract enemy forces there, while a massive French armada, now assembling in Brest, would rendezvous with the Spanish fleet, take control of the Channel, and invade southern England with an army of forty thousand. (In the event, the combined fleet never engaged the British fleet, and the invasion had to be scrapped; there was a massive outbreak of typhus and smallpox on the ships as they sailed toward England, thousands died, and the fleet returned to port.)

Fortunately, from the American perspective, there was more purpose to the forthcoming *Bonhomme Richard* cruise than to distract enemy forces from defending against a French-Spanish invasion of England. Broadly, the Americans still wanted to disrupt British supplies to North America. More precisely, as Jones had proved in connection with the cruise of *Ranger,* there was much to be gained if one could attack successfully in British waters and show the British people again that they were vulnerable at home, notwithstanding the overwhelming size and superiority of their fleet. "It appears to me to be the province of our infant navy," Jones had said, "to surprise, and spread alarms with fast sailing ships.—When we grow stronger, we can meet their fleets, and dispute with them the sovereignty of the ocean."[30]

On August 14, 1779, Jones set sail, joined by two French privateers, *Monsieur* and *Granville,* therefore seven ships in all. At the last minute, he had been forced by his French patrons to sign a compact regarding the four other naval captains in his fleet: although all of their ships would be deemed part of the American Continental navy, fly American colors, and operate under Continental navy regulations (including with respect to division of prize money), each captain would retain control over the composition of his armaments and crew and, most important, could not be forced by Jones to do anything that made such captain uncomfortable: "You shall not require from the said vessels any services but such as will be comfortable with the orders which those officers shall have."[31] In effect, the other captains were free to disregard orders they did not like. It was an outrage that any commodore should have to share command in this way, and it would prove problematic. But Jones was not given a choice, and so he signed; better a weakened command than none.

The course set was for the west coasts of Ireland and the Hebrides and then around the Orkneys and down the east coasts of Scotland and England to Newcastle. From the start, everything went wrong. On August 18, *Monsieur* captured a prize, refused to share it, and deserted the squadron. On August 19–20, a much larger prize that Jones was chasing got away. On August 23, off the coast of Ireland near Dingle Bay, the wind fell to a flat calm, and *Richard* began drifting dangerously close to the Skelligs. Jones ordered Master Lunt to lower a barge and crew to tow *Richard* out of danger. Unfortunately, Lunt picked six Irishmen for the task and put in charge of them one of the miscreants Jones had had flogged earlier that summer for leaving him stranded on the beach. After dark the barge crew cut the towline and headed for Ireland. When he saw what was happening, Master Lunt took off after them in a second boat with a second crew—and got lost in heavy fog. As soon as the fog lifted, Jones sent *Cerf* in search of Lunt. *Cerf* eventually sighted Lunt but fired a gun that Lunt mistook for the enemy, so Lunt tried to escape, got lost (again), and ended up landing at Ballinskelligs Bay, where he was captured and imprisoned by the locals. *Cerf,* for its part, decided it had had enough and sailed back to France.

There was more. On August 24, Captain Landais of *Alliance* came on board *Richard.* He was angry because the previous day Jones, anticipating a calm, had forbidden him from chasing a prize. Now he berated Jones in front of Jones's officers and crew and announced that from then on, he would chase "when and where he thought proper, and in every other matter" do as he pleased. He then did just that, separating himself from the squadron and not rejoining it again for two weeks. Further compounding the disintegration of the squadron, the privateer *Granville,* like *Monsieur* before it, seized a prize and left. And *Pallas* broke its tiller, putting it out of commission for two weeks.

To make matters worse, the British knew he was coming. A spy (probably Franklin's secretary in Paris, Edward Bancroft) had forewarned them of Jones's plans. Initially, two frigates were sent to track him down, HMS *Ulysses* and HMS *Boston.* Fortunately for Jones, they looked in the wrong place—the east coast of Ireland instead of west. But additional ships were deployed as well along both English coasts. It was only a matter of time.

August gave way to September. *Pallas* and (briefly) *Alliance* rejoined Jones near the northern tip of Scotland. *Vengeance* was also still with them. The squadron captured several prizes, skirted the Shetlands, and turned southward toward the east coast of Britain, where Jones had conceived a rather daring plan to enter the Firth of Forth and threaten Leith (Edinburgh's seaport) with fire unless a large ransom was paid. The captains of *Pallas* and *Vengeance* hesitated and then dickered with Jones for some hours about the size of the ransom (they wanted more), thus delaying the move. (*Alliance* had disappeared again and was not part of the negotiations.) Agreement was eventually reached, and the squadron entered the firth. But headwinds from the west rose to gale force, the squadron had to turn around and sail with the wind back out of the firth, and the plan was abandoned.

Jones had a backup plan: raid Newcastle-on-Tyne (a bit farther south) and cut off London's winter coal supply. The crew of the *Richard* was all for it, and *Richard* sailed close enough to shore to see houses. But the captains of *Pallas* and *Vengeance* balked (again), Jones feared they would desert if he attacked, and he was not willing to risk the raid alone (although *Richard*'s crew, to their credit, was; they had come to like and trust Jones). So Newcastle, too, was spared.

The aborted raids were not without consequence. Jones's squadron had been sighted numerous times during the cruise; his reputation (Whitehaven, St. Mary's Isle) preceded him. Talk of his circumnavigation of the British Isles was spreading, the size of his fleet magnified in the retelling. Sir Walter Scott, writing some years later, was probably correct when he said that Jones's "three trifling sloops or brigs" were "scarce fit to have sacked a fishing village," much less the capital of Scotland.[32] But their presence in the Firth of Forth nonetheless struck fear and terror in the hearts of the local Scots. Alarm and panic grew. Along the coast, women, children, and valuables were being moved inland. Militias were mustered in anticipation of a landing. Letters were sent to the Admiralty, demanding protection. At Kirkaldy, as Jones's squadron entered the firth, a local clergyman sat on the beach and prayed God to turn the winds and blow the scoundrel Jones out to sea.[33] Benjamin Disraeli (the future prime minister), trying to articulate the terror that was felt, would later write, "The nurses of Scotland hushed their crying infants by the whisper of his name."[34]

Jones continued southward, past Scarborough, toward Flamborough Head, eluding British naval vessels in search of his fleet, capturing several more prizes along the way. On the morning of September 23, 1779, off Flamborough Head, *Pallas* (which had gotten separated) and *Alliance* (which had left two weeks before) reappeared and rejoined *Richard* and *Vengeance.*

Battle Off Flamborough Head; Capture of *Serapis*

Some lives build slowly to a single moment of glory or shame. Jones's was such a life, and Flamborough Head was such a moment. On the afternoon of the twenty-third, Jones saw in the distance, off Flamborough Head, a fleet of forty-one sails. He learned from pilots of pilot boats captured earlier in the day that it was a British convoy from the Baltic, escorted by the fifty-gun frigate *Serapis* and the twenty-gun sloop of war *Countess of Scarborough.* Jones knew the importance of Baltic convoys: they were major suppliers to the British navy. He also knew he would have to take or sink the two escorts, if he was to interdict the convoy.

"There is no doubt," writes Morison, "that *Serapis* was a newer, faster and more nimble frigate than *Richard;* and in fire power, owing to her far greater number of eighteen-pounders, she was definitely superior."[35] *Bonhomme Richard,* by contrast, was a slow vessel, much slower than Jones had wanted. But what it lacked in speed, it made up for in durability. It could, in Evan Thomas's words, "withstand heavy blows."[36] Heavy blows it was about to be dealt.

At four o'clock *Richard*'s gunners and seamen took up their battle stations. At five drums began to roll as Jones issued the general order to prepare for battle. At six—sunset—Jones signaled *Alliance, Pallas,* and *Vengeance* to form a line of battle. All three ignored the order. *Richard* would have to fight *Serapis* alone. And so it did. (Ultimately, *Pallas* would engage and defeat the *Countess of Scarborough.*)

It was a battle, fought in moonlight at close quarters "with unremitting fury" (Jones's words), vicious and bloody. *Serapis* gained the upper hand several times—so much so that, at one point, Captain Pearson of *Serapis* shouted to his adversary, "Has your ship struck?"—meaning "Have you raised the white flag? Are you surrendering?"—to which Jones famously replied, "I have not yet begun to fight."

Flamborough Head is a promontory of chalk cliffs just south of Scarborough, 450 feet top to bottom, jutting into the North Sea. Crowds from Scarborough and other nearby towns had gathered on the cliffs to watch, attracted by rumors of the impending battle and the sound of gunfire. We do not have any eyewitness accounts from the cliffs, but even from the distance of their vantage it must have been a sight: two ships maneuvering against one another in the moonlight, firing repeated broadsides, the explosion of struck guns and gunpowder, flames and smoke enveloping the carnage. Jones, nothing if not a brilliant tactician, determined that his only chance for victory was to ram *Serapis* and lash *Richard* to it, thereby preventing *Serapis* (because of too close quarters) from further firing its twelve- and eighteen-pounders and enabling Jones's marksmen, strapped to *Richard*'s topsails, to fire down onto *Serapis*'s deck, killing all who did not retreat below. This was done, and it had its intended effect: *Serapis*'s deck was cleared, a grenade tossed from *Richard*'s mainsail struck the combing of *Serapis*'s upper hatchery, fell between decks, and ignited gunpowder that had spilled from cartridges abandoned by *Serapis*'s powder monkeys scurrying for cover, resulting in a dreadful explosion that killed or wounded dozens of the enemy's crew huddled between decks. *Serapis* surrendered.

Not, however, before *Alliance,* under command of Captain Landais, entered the fray and began firing—at *Richard,* not *Serapis!* There were three separate broadsides, killing several of *Richard*'s crew and further damaging the American vessel. It was not an accident. Landais, though he later pretended otherwise, saw it as an opportunity to rid himself of his nemesis, Jones. Fortunately, the *Alliance* intervention was too little, too late: Jones and *Richard* survived, and victory went to the Americans.

Captain Pearson of *Serapis,* despite his surrender, did have one consolation: the ships of the Baltic convoy that he was escorting had found safety under the guns of Scarborough Castle and were unharmed.

The carnage on both sides was extensive, the bloodiest naval battle of the War of Independence. It had lasted about four hours. The American side suffered 150 killed or wounded. British casualties were 50 to 100 killed and 68 wounded.[37] *Richard,* though it had withstood heavy blows long enough to ensure victory, could not be saved. After trying to do so for two nights and a day, Jones ordered it abandoned, and it sank into the North Sea at eleven on the morning of the twenty-fifth.

The British, when they learned of the battle, dispatched a large squadron to find and capture Jones. It reached Flamborough Head on the twenty-eighth and, assuming Jones would try to escape to the north and west (as he had done on his prior cruise, after capturing *Drake*), headed that way. But once again, Jones eluded capture, this time by heading south toward Holland (aboard *Serapis,* flying the American flag), while his pursuers searched in the opposite direction. He arrived safely at the Dutch island of Texel on October 3, 1779, with two prizes—*Serapis* and *Countess*—and 500 prisoners.

He was born to command. A Cossack sailor known only as Ivak, who served under him, said as much: "I have never seen such a person, sweet like a vine when he wished, but when necessary, like a rock. . . . One movement of his hand you obey like a commanding voice. It seems that some people are created to command."[38] At Flamborough Head, the genius of Jones's command—his preparation, his courage—was on full display, and the victory gained there was a signal achievement.[39] Fame and glory followed. France welcomed him with laurel wreaths and open arms. "The cry of Versailles and the Clamour of Paris," wrote John Adams, "became as loud in the favor of Monsieur Jones as of Monsieur Franklin, and the inclination of the Ladies to embrace him almost as fashionable and as strong."[40] King Louis XVI invested Jones with the rank of chevalier in the Order of Military Merit and presented to him a gold-hilted sword inscribed, in Latin, with an appreciation for his valor. He was inducted into the Lodge of the Nine Sisters, the most prestigious Masonic lodge in France, whose members included the leading intellectuals, artists, and politicians of the day (Voltaire and Franklin among them). The Nine Sisters commissioned Jean-Antoine Houdon, France's most important portrait sculptor (and a Nine Sisters member himself), to do a bust of Jones. He was the guest of honor at countless dinners and parties. When he took his seat at the opera, all stood and applauded.

> An American officer was yesterday at the opera, in company with Dr. Franklin's grandson. They sat in a front box. The pitt paid great attention to him. But between the acts the name of Paul Jones having passed from mouth to mouth, great applause resounded immediately. The officer to whom they were addressed, could not mistake their object. He rose and thanked the public several times. It was Commodore Paul Jones himself, whom the pitt and boxes received in this distinguished manner. At going out, the passage were crowded with multitudes, who wished to have a near view of him, and their applause continued till he got into his coach.[41]

But if Flamborough Head was the pinnacle of Jones's achievement, it was far from the only example of his preparedness and courage, as this chapter has sought to demonstrate. James Fenimore Cooper, writing in 1846, made the point as well as any: "All the cruises of the man indicated forethought, intrepidity, and resources. Certainly, no sea captain under the American flag, Preble excepted [commander of American naval forces in the War of 1812], has ever yet equaled him, in these particulars. . . . His deeds were no more than the proper results of the impulses, talents, and native instincts of the man."[42]

3

THE MANTLE OF FORGETFULNESS

> Worn out with the fatigues of arduous service, at the untimely age of 45, alone in a foreign land, he surrendered to death, the only foe to whom he ever lowered his colors. By some strange and unaccountable fatality he was covered immediately with the mantle of forgetfulness. In all the annals of history there is not another case in which death has caused the memory of so conspicuous a man to drop at once from the height of prominence to the depth of oblivion.
>
> —Address of General Porter, April 24, 1906

THE FLAME THAT BURNS TWICE as bright burns half as long. The glory of Flamborough Head and the adulation of Paris could not be sustained without more heroics. There would be none. John Paul Jones would never again lead America in battle.

For ten years he wandered: Philadelphia, Paris, New York, Copenhagen, Petersburg, Warsaw, Amsterdam, Paris again—mostly in pursuit of elusive commands and overdue prize moneys. This decade of wandering was not without accomplishments. He commanded, briefly, two American vessels: first *Alliance* (survivor of Flamborough Head) in the Bay of Biscay to search for British merchantmen and then the sloop of war *Ariel*, in which he made his return to America.[1] Congress commended him for his service, directed that a gold medal be struck and presented to him to honor his "valor and brilliant services," and appointed him to command the Continental navy's first ship of the line, *America*, under construction at Portsmouth, New Hampshire.[2] The *America* appointment in particular was significant recognition. Congress had refused to confer on him the rank of rear admiral, apparently fearing the negative effect it would have on fellow naval officers who were senior to Jones. To be given command of America's premier warship, over those same officers, was sufficient recompense. However, it, too, would prove ephemeral. Lacking funds to complete construction, Congress gave the vessel to the French a few months later, thus ending Jones's command before there was any ship to sail.[3] In any event, the American Revolution was coming to its end; the need for naval heroes had abated.

Jones still had prize moneys to claim—for himself, for his crew. He pursued these vigorously from each of America, Denmark, and France, eventually recovering a portion of sums due from America and France but not Denmark. More than money, he craved more glory. With the blessing of Thomas Jefferson, he accepted a commission as rear admiral in the Imperial Russian Navy and commanded a Russian fleet in the Liman of the Dnieper against the Turks, winning two key battles and again displaying consummate strategic and tactical skills. Unfortunately for Paul Jones, his political talents did not match his military ones. He became embroiled (through no fault of his own) in the intrigues of Catherine the Great and her lover Potemkin and was relieved of command, falsely implicated in a major scandal, and forced to leave Russia in shame.

Now (1789) commandless, forty-two years old, and in declining health—apparently the consequence of two recent bouts of pneumonia—he roamed the Continent again for a number of months, by letter and intermediaries beseeching the empress to reinstate his Russian command, visiting acquaintances in Alsace, meeting up with the Polish hero of the American Revolution General Tadeusz Kociuszko, chasing a commission in the Swedish navy, imagining retirement on a small farm in Pennsylvania. He tried putting his name again in the consciousness of former backers, corresponding with the likes of Ben Franklin and General Washington, hoping they might make use of him. But the elderly Franklin died, and Washington was preoccupied with his recently assumed duties as first president of the United States.

Unsuccessful in his efforts to find work and financially strapped, though not broke, Jones returned to Paris in the spring of 1790 and rented rooms at 42 rue de Tournon, near the Palais de Luxembourg. He died there two years later, on July 18, 1792, between five and eight at night, alone, facedown on his bed, feet to the floor.[4] His body was discovered in the evening by Gouverneur (first name, not a title) Morris, American minister to France, who had been with Jones in the afternoon to supervise the making of his will. Morris rushed off to dinner after the will signing but later returned with his mistress and a local physician to check up on Jones. Cause of death was probably kidney failure. John Paul Jones was forty-five years old.

We can hope that Jones found peace, if not fulfillment, during his last years in Paris, though the record is not reassuring in this regard. Both Paris and Jones had changed since his last residence there. The French Revolution raged; the monarch and aristocracy that once feted him were now preoccupied with survival. Jones himself, aging and sickly, had lost his luster. Salons that once competed for his attention now turned him away: arriving at midnight to attend a masked ball at the home of a wealthy individual named Cappadocia, he was "informed that the House was full." To some, he had become boring and irrelevant, a figure of ridicule, to others tragic. The pompous, self-absorbed Gouverneur Morris, who Jones thought was a friend, wrote repeatedly and dismissively in his diary entries like the following: "Paul Jones calls and gives me his Time but I cannot lend him mine." "Paul Jones calls on me. He has nothing to say but is so kind as to bestow on me the hours which hang heavy on his Hands." More hauntingly, Thomas Carlyle, also in Paris at the time, wrote: "In faded naval uniform, Paul Jones lingers visible here; like a wine-skin from which the wine is all drawn. Like the ghost of himself! Low is his once loud bruit; scarcely audible, save, with extreme tedium in ministerial ante-chambers; in this or the other charitable dining-room, mindful of the past. . . . Poor Paul! hunger and dispiritment track thy sinking footsteps: once or at most twice, in this Revolution-tumult the figure of thee emerges; mute, ghost-like, as 'with stars dim-twinkling through.'"[5]

It was put to Morris (probably by Colonel Samuel Blackden and Jean-Baptiste Beaupoil, two friends of Jones who had been with him in his final days and who had witnessed the will) that a proper funeral should be arranged, one befitting an American naval hero of Jones's stature and accomplishments. But Morris nixed the idea, perhaps fearing he would be personally stuck for the cost, given America's strapped finances. He instructed Jones's landlord to bury him "in the most private manner, and at the least possible expense."[6] Afterward, he justified his parsimony this way: "I had no right to spend on such follies either the money of his heirs or that of the United States. . . . I have since had reason to be glad that I did not agree to waste money of which he [Jones] had no great abundance, and for which his relatives entertain a tender regard."[7] Thus did America's ranking plenipotentiary in France consign to a pauper's burial the remains of John Paul Jones.

Morris's burial instruction did not sit well with Colonel Blackden. He reported the instruction to Pierre François Simonneau, a political functionary from Jones's local district, and asked if Jones might be entitled to a state burial in the city's Protestant cemetery. Simonneau, a fan of Jones, was incensed. He presented Blackden's request to the French Legislative Assembly (then in session) and, amid applause, excoriated Morris for the insult to Jones. He offered to pay the expense of a public funeral himself if America would not. The assembly approved Jones's burial in the Protestant cemetery and authorized a delegation of twelve legislators to attend the funeral. Simonneau then took charge, put up the considerable sum of 462 francs from his personal funds to cover the expense, and had Jones's remains placed in a lead coffin, to preserve them for easier removal later, should America one day change its mind and wish to reclaim its hero.[8]

The funeral was held on July 20. Those attending, besides the assembly delegation, included the aforementioned commissary Simonneau, Colonel Blackden, and former French officer Beaupoil, as well as several others from America and France.[9] Minister Morris was not among the mourners, giving as his reason that he had a dinner engagement.[10]

The time of the funeral was fixed by the assembly, which determined it would suit the twelve deputies to attend at six o'clock. Sometime between six and seven, the deputies arrived at Jones's house. (Whether they arrived on foot or in carriages is not known; although it was customary to walk a funeral procession, the assembly had instructed that each deputy "might go on foot or in a carriage, just as he pleased.")[11] They were preceded by two huissiers and escorted by horse guards. The lead casket was brought from the house to the street and placed on a wagon, and then the cortege moved slowly from the rue de Tournon, past the Pont Neuf, into the street leading to St. Eustache, and thence onto the boulevard by the rue St. Martin, arriving an hour and a half later at the Protestant cemetery.[12]

The only known, attributed eyewitness account of the graveside ceremony—that of Thomas Waters Griffith, an American visitor to Paris who had met Jones for the first time at Gouverneur Morris's in April—says there was no priest or funeral service, only "a few soldiers" who "fired a volley of muskets in honor of the naval hero over his grave."[13] But this is inconsistent with contemporary newspaper reports, which state that the Protestant minister of Paris, M. Marron, delivered a eulogy. That there was a eulogy seems the more likely since Marron was in charge of the Protestant cemetery and would have been expected to preside over the service and to speak. Perhaps the lateness of the hour caused the reading of the eulogy to be put off. Or perhaps Griffith could not hear it or could not understand what was being said. Whatever, Marron's eulogy was printed verbatim by the press a few days later. As was customary at the time, it both celebrated the life of the deceased and used that life as an example to rally mourners to the cause of the French Revolution. In the eulogy, Marron called Jones "one of the first heroes of American liberty," adding, in a nod to the Revolution, that America's liberty was "the glorious prelude to our own." Invoking a famous motto of the Revolution, he asked rhetorically, "What homage more flattering can we render to the manes of Paul Jones, than to swear upon his tomb 'to live free or die'?" He continued in this vein for several more sentences. Then, summing up, he concluded, "[France] is in danger. Who among us would not pour out his blood for her defense? Be partakers then in the glory of Paul Jones, imitate him in that contempt of danger, that noble heroism, which, after having astonished the present generation, shall remain the unchangeable object of veneration for ages to come."[14] Marron could not know that the veneration he reasonably anticipated should follow Jones's death would in fact be deferred for many decades.

The British press reported Jones's death with condescension and disparagement. It had as little regard for Jones as it did for the French Revolution. The confluence of Jones's death in Paris and the fast-spreading Revolution was an opportunity to score points against both with one blow. London's *Evening Mail,* for example, in a piece published a week after the funeral, said it was "not surprised" to find that a legislature that had honored the "most unworthy" figures in French life (once even applauding the presence of a prostitute in its chambers) would "attend the funeral of the noted Paul Jones, who last week departed life in Paris." Jones was, harrumphed the editors,

> a man of mean birth, and without education; naturally ferocious in his mind, and when possessed of power, savage and cruel, to a degree of barbarity. He deliberately shot one of his men with a pistol, for saying, that he thought they must strike; . . . he knew and dreaded the fate that awaited his being taken by the English. . . . Fate, however, sent her mandate, and commanded him out of this life; and had not the National Assembly of France brought his memory into notice, he might have sunk into oblivion without remark. To be honored by them is to be despised by the rest of the world. Their praise is censure—their virtues are vices![15]

The *European Magazine,* though more succinct, was no less scathing: "Lately, at Paris, the notorious Paul Jones, of infamous memory, attended to his grave by a deputation of the National Assembly. This disgraceful fact, though true, will hardly be believed by posterity, as this wretch, a Scotchman by birth, could be considered in no better light than a thief endeavoring to avail himself of plunder while a house was on fire."[16]

The American press was respectful but brief; the memory of Jones in his adopted land had already dimmed. The *Boston Gazette* reported simply, "Died. In Paris, July 18, the celebrated American John Paul Jones. The Assembly sent a deputation to attend his funeral. It was objected, that he was a Calvinist, but the objection was overruled." The *Maryland Gazette* wrote, "Paul Jones died a few days ago in [Paris], in the utmost poverty. Col. Blackden was obliged to raise a small sum of money, by way of subscription, in order to bury him." Several American papers, reporting Jones's death, seemed to regard him more as a deceased French hero than an American one. "The appointment of a deputation of the French National Assembly to accompany the funeral of Paul Jones, is a remarkable instance of their desire to reward virtue and merit, as well as their respect for their country. Paul Jones was an enemy to Great Britain, and, no doubt, a warm friend of liberty!"[17]

And then John Paul Jones was forgotten.[18] Biographers and historians have speculated as to the reasons for this forgetting. Was it Jones's character flaws and personal scandals? Was it the deliberate work of his enemies in high places? Did his nonnative birth make him less of an American and less important? Perhaps the hostility of the English press was to blame? Or maybe Jones's aggressive fighting style did not fit well with America's defense-oriented naval strategy in the early years of the Republic? We will consider each of these possible explanations below.

Character Flaws and Personal Scandals

James Fenimore Cooper, a thoughtful and sympathetic biographer, writing in the mid-nineteenth century, says that there was "something in the personal character of Jones that weakened his hold on his contemporaries." Alexander Mackenzie, Cooper's contemporary, elaborated on this theme. "The glaring defect of Paul Jones's character, and the foundation of many others," he wrote, "was his abounding vanity." "No hero, indeed, ever sounded his own trumpet more unremittingly or with a louder blast. This absorbing vanity led him to claim for himself the whole glory of his victories. In all his elaborate reports of his engagements, except indeed during his Russian campaign, where the slight passed upon his officers became a reflection on himself, he is the hero, and the sole hero, of his own tale."[19]

"Haughty and intractable," "ambitious of distinction and glory to the utmost extreme that this feeling can be carried," his "natural arrogance" and "impatience of control" predisposed him "to trample on opposition and resist any interference with his plans." The "slightest obstruction in his path, the least injustice, real or fancied, rendered him frantic; instead of quiet remonstrance, he resorted at once to furious denunciation, and too often succeeded in making an enemy for life." He had as well "a taste for luxury, display, and profuse expense" (character defects all, according to Mackenzie) and was a notorious philanderer.[20]

The record supports the reality of these alleged character defects. There can be little doubt, for example, that Jones was exceedingly vain and that his self-promotion and denigration of others were often relentless. Contact with him engendered, even among his most devoted supporters, impatience and fatigue. Ben Franklin, a fellow Freemason, genuine admirer, supporter, and friend (recall that Jones named the *Bonhomme Richard* in Franklin's honor), had more than enough after seeing a note Jones sent Franklin's secretary, blaming Franklin (among others) for Jones's loss of command of *Alliance* (in 1780), even though Jones himself was largely to blame.[21] "Hereafter," he wrote Jones, "if you should observe an occasion to give your officers and friends a little more praise than is their due, and confess more fault than you can justly be charged with, you will only become the sooner for it, a great captain. Criticizing and censuring almost every one you have to do with, will diminish friends, increase enemies, thereby hurt your affairs."[22]

Similarly, Jones's thin skin sometimes got him in trouble and turned those who were, or might otherwise have been, predisposed in his favor against him. This was the case early in his career, for example, with Commodore Esek Hopkins, the officer responsible for giving Jones his first command and who had gone to Jones's defense after Jones, during the second cruise of *Alfred,* got in trouble with the owners of a Rhode Island privateer when he discovered deserters hiding on their vessel and arrested two dozen of their crew in retaliation. But those were good deeds past. By the beginning of 1777, Jones was without a ship and chafing for a new command. The Marine Committee ordered Hopkins, in early February, to give Jones a fleet of five ships (*Alfred, Columbus, Cabot, Hampden,* and *Providence*) for the purpose of capturing British territory in the Caribbean, British warships off the coast of Florida and at the mouth of the Mississippi, and slavers making for the West Indies from Africa. Jones received his copy of the order on February 19 but Hopkins not until February 28. Jones twice wrote Hopkins during this interval, saying that he wished to sail immediately. But Hopkins was not yet in a position to comply, not only because he himself had not yet received the Marine Committee's instruction but also because the designated ships were not then available: *Alfred* was damaged and needed at least six weeks to repair, *Hampden* was already at sea, and *Columbus* and *Providence* had no crews. Moreover, Hopkins had received credible and disturbing reports about Jones's handling of crew and prize money while captain of *Alfred* the previous year, reports he was obliged to share with the Marine Committee before engaging Jones in a further command.

When Jones did not receive an immediate response from Hopkins to his two letters, he wrote the commodore a third one that was frantic, insulting, and insubordinate ("I . . . demand your hearty and complete concurrence with me in the outfit [of these five vessels]" and the like) and that almost cost him a court-martial. It did not; in the end, it was the elderly Hopkins who got sacked for reasons unrelated to Jones, but the confrontation with Hopkins is illustrative of Jones's penchant to turn on his supporters too quickly and too vehemently when he perceived slights, real or imagined.[23]

Scandals involving disgruntled crewmen (such as the Tobago incident) and women also plagued Jones throughout his life. Jones was a notorious philanderer and ladies' man. He frequented prostitutes. He pursued, and was pursued by, women of the highest rank—often married women, including (to name a few of his better-known liaisons) Dorothea Dandridge, granddaughter of a governor of Virginia and future wife of Patrick Henry ("Give me liberty or give me death"); Madame Le Ray de Chaumont, wife of Jacques-Donatien Le Ray de Chaumont, a wealthy French merchant, major supplier of the American Revolution, and Jones's principal financial backer; the young wife of James Moylan, a personal friend of Jones who had provided shelter to him after his return to France from Flamborough Head; and the comtesse de Nicolson, wife of Count Murray-Nicolson and brother of William Nicolson, Jones's captain of marines aboard *Ariel.* "Delia" (Jones's nickname for the comtesse de Nicolson) nearly went mad with longing after a torrid five days with Jones in 1780 at a secluded inn downriver from L'Orient. "Dear Jones," she wrote, "if distance must separate us, what is to become of me? Mon Dieu! . . . I realize by the manifold torments of my soul that I have never loved but you and if I must be deprived of you, I feel that I shall detest my life. . . . Jones, my dear lover, pardon your unhappy Delia; forgive her weakness; remember that she adores you and will die if she loses you."[24]

Jones's pursuit of yet another aristocratic lady, Madame comtesse de Lowendahl (she painted a small miniature of him that was used to identify his corpse when his grave was finally found), was followed in detail in the London gossip columns. At least one of his affairs—that with Madame T (the widow of an Englishman named Townsend)—was rumored to have produced a son. Most damaging of his sexual scandals was probably the last one—the Russian one. Jones's military successes in the Liman of the Dnieper on behalf of Russia in 1788 were quickly appropriated by his commander in chief, Catherine's lover Grigory Potemkin, and by the ineffectual Russian naval commander Prince Nassau-Siegen. They took full credit for the victory and promoted themselves shamelessly at the expense of Jones. Potemkin rid Jones of his command (Jones's removal included three days' traveling in an open boat in foul weather, from the Liman to

Kershon, during which trip he contracted the pneumonia that fatally weakened him) and then secured his expulsion from Russia by contriving a rape charge against him. The rape charge arose out of what seems to have been consensual sex Jones had with a young woman in St. Petersburg, possibly a prostitute. The young woman's mother then accused Jones of rape. She later admitted she was paid by "uniformed" personnel to make the accusation; the young woman's husband as well as the clergyman to whom the mother first reported the alleged rape both doubted the charge. Jones, of course, vehemently denied it. But the damage was done. The charge was consistent with Jones's reputation as a philanderer, and Jones was forced to flee Russia in shame to avoid criminal charges. The incident, moreover, received press coverage elsewhere in Europe and harmed Jones's reputation. The French (again) came to his rescue. His most intrepid defender was France's ambassador in St. Petersburg, the count de Ségur, who wrote numerous letters to fellow diplomats and others, refuting the charge. De Ségur's refutation was also distributed to the press, and eventually the scandal died down.

It is one thing to admit, even lament, the existence of unsavory character traits, another to attribute national amnesia to them. Many legendary commanders and heroes have had oversize egos and thin skins and suffered scandals, yet they were not forgotten—not, certainly, on the scale of Jones. That character flaws and personal scandals were not the cause of America's forgetting Jones may be reasonably inferred from actions the American government took only weeks before his death. We saw that throughout his career, Jones had a special regard for imprisoned American sailors and a special passion for seeking their release: for example, the second cruise of *Alfred* to free American prisoners from the coal mines of Cape Breton; the failed kidnapping of Lord Selkirk, whom Jones intended to ransom for prisoners; the trade for captive Americans in England that he engineered with captured British sailors from *Drake*. Several years before he returned to Paris, Jones learned that a number of American merchant seamen had been captured in the Mediterranean by Barbary Coast pirates and were being detained by the dey of Algiers in wretched conditions. He wrote a number of letters to Thomas Jefferson and others, urging that effort be made to free them, either by military action or by ransom. Finally, in 1792, as word spread that only thirteen of the prisoners were still alive and that their circumstances were dire, Congress authorized negotiations with the dey. Jefferson, then secretary of state, recommended Paul Jones for the job, and President Washington agreed. On June 1, 1792, Jefferson wrote to Jones, advising him of the appointment: "Sir, The President of the United States having thought proper to appoint you commissioner for treating with the Dey and government of Algiers, on the subjects of peace and ransom of our captives, I have the honor to enclose you the commissions."[25] The letter did not reach Paris until several days after Jones's death, therefore too late for him to act on it or savor the honor it represented. But the letter demonstrates that, inflated ego, thin skin, and scandal notwithstanding, Jones was still remembered respectfully by important people when he died. Some other, or additional, reason than character flaws and scandal must be sought to explain Jones's disappearance from the national memory.

Enemies in High Places

Throughout his naval career, Jones had enemies in high places who tried to thwart his advancement. Did they extinguish his memory? Biographers identify four enemies in particular who regularly opposed Jones: Samuel Adams, Arthur Lee, Richard Henry Lee, and Captain James Nicholson. Sam Adams was the Massachusetts patriot who helped organize the Boston Tea Party; he signed the Declaration of Independence, was a delegate to the Continental Congress until 1781, and later served as governor of Massachusetts. Arthur Lee, a Virginian, was one of the three original American commissioners in Paris during the early years of the Revolutionary War (along with Ben Franklin and Silas Deane). Richard Henry Lee, Arthur's older brother, served in the Continental Congress and was the delegate who made the motion to declare independence. James Nicholson was the highest-ranking captain in the Continental navy.

The animosity of Adams and the two Lees was in part driven by their intense dislike of Franklin, whose early and consistent backing of Jones turned them against Jones. They may have had other motives as well. As early as 1777, they were scheming to thwart Jones. Sam Adams persuaded the authorities in his home state to make Pierre Landais, the French naval officer who detested Jones and had fired on Jones rather than *Serapis* during the battle off Flamborough Head, a citizen of Massachusetts, and Richard Henry Lee (at his brother Arthur's urging) persuaded Congress to make Landais a captain in the Continental navy and give him command of *Alliance.* Morison says the Lees wanted to "build up Landais as a naval Lafayette and rival to Jones." When the *Bonhomme Richard* squadron was put together, Arthur Lee wrote Adams that it was "shameful and illegal" to give Jones command, alleging it was all a scheme by Le Ray de Chaumont (the pro-American French aristocrat with close ties to Franklin and the French navy, who obtained French financing for the squadron) and Jonathan Williams (Franklin's nephew) to make money for themselves.[26] After Flamborough Head and Jones's triumphant return to Paris, Arthur Lee maneuvered to restore to Pierre Landais the command of *Alliance* that Jones had revoked for insubordination. Then he and Sam Adams conspired to have Jones investigated by Congress for alleged malfeasance in delivering munitions and uniforms from France to the Continental army. (Jones was exonerated.) After the war, Arthur Lee (by then a member of the Treasury Board) went after Jones for his expense accounts.

Captain Nicholson was motivated by jealousy. He had secured his first-rank captaincy based on political connections, not merit, and his naval career, once he was appointed, was a bust. He ran *Virginia* aground while trying to escape the British blockade of Chesapeake Bay and then abandoned ship in a panic in his pajamas to avoid a British warship bearing down on his stranded vessel, leaving his junior officers and crew to fend for themselves. Not long after, he lost *Trumball* in an engagement with HMS *Iris.* In 1782, when Captain Nicholson learned that Congress was planning to give Paul Jones the rank of admiral as well as command of *America,* he mounted a frenzied but effective opposition, savaging Jones for his womanizing and pleading that elevating Jones to admiral would insult all the captains senior to Jones on the captains list. Congress, as we saw, backed down from making Jones an admiral but stuck to his appointment as commander of *America.*

Clearly, there were those who had both motivation and power to harm Paul Jones. But if Jones had enemies in high places, he also had friends there, among them some of the best-loved, most powerful men in America, including (besides Benjamin Franklin) George Washington, Thomas Jefferson, and even John Adams, all four of them founding fathers, three of them future presidents of the United States. Few have had such illustrious backers. And their backing was not mere expediency; they all possessed genuine admiration and affection for Jones. We have already seen that Franklin and Jefferson interceded frequently on Jones's behalf. Franklin,

Jefferson, and Washington all kept personal copies of Houdon's bust of Jones. After Flamborough Head, Washington wrote warmly to Jones:

> Whether our naval affairs have in general been well or ill conducted, would be presumptuous in me to determine. Instances of bravery and good conduct in several of our officers, have not, however, been wanting: delicacy forbids me to mention that particular one which has attracted the admiration of the world, and which has influenced the most illustrious monarch to confer a mark of his favor, which can only be obtained by a long and honorable service, or by the performance of some brilliant action.
>
> That you may long enjoy the reputation you have so justly acquired, is the sincere wish of,
>
> Sir, your most obedient and very humble servant, George Washington.[27]

Jefferson was equally supportive. In 1784, in letters to James Madison and James Monroe advocating that the United States should build up its navy to stand up to the Barbary pirates, he wrote, "I am of opinion [John] Paul Jones with half a dozen frigates would totally destroy their commerce; not by attempting bombardments as the Mediterranean states do . . . but by constant cruising and cutting them to pieces by piecemeal." In a letter to another correspondent several years later, he said of Jones, "I consider this officer to be the principal hope of our future efforts on the ocean."[28]

Some ambiguity attaches to Jones's relationship with John Adams, but that, too, seems on balance to have been a positive one. Adams, who served two diplomatic assignments in France (from April 1778 to June 1779, with Franklin and Arthur Lee, as one of three American ministers, replacing Silas Deane, and then again from late 1779 to 1780), saw a good deal of Jones there. His early impressions are cautious, even wary, but cognizant of Jones's talents. "This is," he wrote in his diary after a dinner with Jones, "the most ambitious and intriguing [in the sense of scheming rather than interesting] officer in the American navy. Jones has art and secrecy, and aspires very high. You see the character of the man in his uniform, and that of his officers and Marines, variant from the uniforms established by Congress,—golden button-holes for himself, two epaulettes,—marines in red and white, instead of green."[29] In 1782, when Adams learned of Jones's appointment as commander of *America,* he wrote approvingly:

> The command of the *America* could not have been more judiciously bestowed, and it is with impatience that I wish to see her at sea, where she

> will do honor to her name. Nothing gives me so much surprise, or so much regret, as the inattention of my countrymen to their navy: it is a bulwark as essential as it is to Great Britain. It is less costly than armies, and more easily removed from one end of the United States to the other. . . . Indeed, if I could see a prospect of half a dozen line-of-battle ships under the American flag, commanded by Commodore Paul Jones, engaged with an equal British force, I apprehend the event would be so glorious for the United States, and lay so sure a foundation for their prosperity, that it would be a rich compensation for a continuance of the war.[30]

Ambiguity arises because Adams was also put off by Jones's vanity; he once said Jones was "leprous" with it, but then again, Adams said the same thing about the vanity of America's other great Revolutionary War naval officer, John Barry.[31] Late in life, Adams also complained about "emigrants" and "foreigners of the south" like Jones and Barry being called the father of the American navy, instead of a homegrown New England sailor, but this hardly constitutes evidence of an intention to erase Jones's memory from the national consciousness.[32] In the end, Adams was a strong advocate of naval power, and he appreciated naval talent, including that of Paul Jones.

Further down the chain from Franklin, Washington, Jefferson, and John Adams, Jones had other important friends and patrons as well who intervened at critical moments for his benefit, among them Joseph Hewes of North Carolina, a member of the Continental Congress's first Naval Committee; Robert Morris of Pennsylvania (no relation to Gouverneur Morris), a founding father, chief financier of the American Revolution, member of the Marine Committee, and the navy's first "agent of marine" (head of the Continental navy); and John Langdon of New Hampshire, a delegate to the Continental Congress and shipping magnate.

In sum, Jones's enemies were sometimes able to slow Jones's career and, on occasion, thwart his advancement, but they were never able to stop him. His more powerful friends and patrons were always there, ultimately, to intervene on his behalf. Moreover, Jones's principal enemies—Sam Adams, the Lee brothers, Nicholson—did not, in most cases, survive Jones long enough to damage him posthumously even had they wanted to. Arthur and Richard Henry Lee passed away in 1792 and 1794, respectively, and Sam Adams in 1803; Nicholson died in disgrace in 1804. Contrast this with the longevity of Jones's most powerful supporters: although Franklin died before Jones, Washington outlived both Lees by several years; John Adams and Thomas Jefferson survived until 1826, a quarter century longer than Sam Adams and James Nicholson. There was not time or opportunity for the most intrepid enemies to disparage Jones after his death and no evidence that they did so. They are not the reason Jones was forgotten.

Foreign Born

Some have suggested that the fact Paul Jones was not native born prejudiced America against him. A mid-nineteenth-century North Carolina newspaper, for example, hinted at such an explanation: "Had Paul Jones been born within the limits of the United American Colonies, or been a native of France, he would perhaps have risen to a greater height of authority than he did in either country." John Adams, many years after Jones's death, complained that "emigrants" (what we now call "immigrants") such as captains Paul Jones and John Barry (the former born in Scotland, the latter in Ireland) had taken credit for hoisting the first American flag and receiving the first British surrender, when such merit properly belonged to "New England sailors, officers, and men."[33] (He meant John Manly, the captain who captured *Nancy* in 1775, discussed below. Interestingly, Manly may have been foreign born as well—in England—although he was a long-time New England resident.) Adams's brief rant seems more prosectional than anti-immigrant; Adams was, after all, a staunch supporter of Jones during Jones's life. Moreover, there were many foreign-born persons who assisted the American Revolution who were warmly remembered thereafter, among them such famous names as Alexander Hamilton, Thomas Paine, and Lafayette. Jones's foreign birth seems a weak explanation for his disappearance.

English Press Hostility

James Fenimore Cooper raised the subject of personal character as a possible explanation for Jones's disappearance from the American memory after his death ("There was something in the personal character of Jones that weakened his hold on his contemporaries"). But Cooper preferred another explanation: the English press. "The power of England, in the way of opinion, has always been great in this country," he wrote, "and it is probable the discredit that nation threw on the reputation of Jones, produced an influence, more visible in its results than in its workings, on his standing even with those he had so well served." Others have sounded a similar theme. Sherburne, Jones's first serious American biographer, writing in 1825, more than a generation following Jones's death, says, after asserting that Jones has been misrepresented by earlier writers as a "plunderer, a pirate, cruel and unprincipled," "The venal British press and British antipathies have been the source of this defamation."[34] The editors of the *Charleston Mercury,* in an 1846 tribute to Jones (as we shall see in the next chapter, by 1846 the memory of Jones was reawakening), agreed:

> The most heinous wrong done to Paul Jones, is found in the popular notion of his character, which seems to have been borrowed from the coarse slanders of the British press, at the time he frightened the Isles from their propriety, and put Mistress Britannia in a paroxysm of terror and rage. For half a century he existed in the popular mind as little better than a successful ruffian—a big ferocious savage, with a diabolical eye, whose voice in battle was that of an enraged tiger, whose soul exulted in killing men, sinking ships and burning towns. The friend, correspondent and companion of Franklin, a ruffian! The idolized hero of the Court of Versailles, a savage! Never was there a more rascally caricature.[35]

There is much here worth considering, though the record reveals a more nuanced and complicated story. From the raids of *Ranger* through Flamborough Head to Jones's death and beyond, the British press routinely called Jones a "pirate" and the ships he commanded mere "privateers," thus denying him the dignity of his naval commission. The royalist press went further, using terms like *savage, convicted murderer,* and *dark assassin.*[36] This, for example, after the capture of *Serapis,* falsely accusing Jones of barbarity and murder:

> Paul Jones, or *John Paul,* which is his real name, is a man of savage disposition;—He was for many years a commander of a coastal vessel, in which time he committed many barbarities upon his crew, for some of which he has been tried by the laws of his country:—but one in particular will forever stamp his character as a dark assassin. Between Whitehaven and Bristol, he took a dislike to one of his crew, and meditated revenge, which he performed as follows:—One evening upon deck, he behaved with more than common civility towards him, and calling him aside to do something of the ship's duty,

> the unsuspecting man went, when Jones desired him to lay hold of a rope, which was out of his reach; Jones then desired him to stand upon a board; (the board having been so balanced, as a small weight would overturn it) which he did, when he fell into the sea and was drowned.—Thus he got rid of an innocent man without being suspected his murderer.[37]

There were dissenting voices in the English press (England had its sympathizers with the American cause). For example, in the midst of reports of English atrocities in North America, including the torching of Fairfield and Norwalk, another paper wrote, "Some people are surprised why Paul Jones and his squadron, have not burnt the towns on the Northern Coast which he has visited. True, he had it in his power; but they ought not to be surprised at it. Paul Jones is a pirate indeed, a plunderer, but he is not a Barbarian; he does not hold his commission from the Administration of Britain, and therefore has no order to ravage and lay waste its dwellings of the innocent."[38] Even the purveyors of the dark-assassin story managed the following in a subsequent installment:

> Merit loses half its lustre in a man who is supposed to be engaged in a bad cause, his bravery is said to flow from despair, and his bold perseverance is termed perverse obstinancy. This is verified in Paul Jones, whose late gallant behavior would have been extolled to the skies, if his bravery had been exerted in our service, but as he fought against us, we cannot find in our hearts to allow him any merit at all. Justice, however, requires, that while we execrate the principles of him who fights against his country, we should not rob him of those merits which we see him possess as a man, in a very eminent degree.[39]

The fact remains that the depiction of Jones as a savage was much the more prevalent one and persisted to the time of his death, as the report of his passing by a London newspaper, quoted earlier in this chapter, illustrates. In the popular press and chapbooks, too, and in the crude illustrations accompanying their stories (the captain's shirt carelessly flung open, lurid tattoos adorning his brawny chest, a gleaming cutlass clenched between his teeth, his sash bristling with pistols), Jones was consistently portrayed as a ruthless buccaneer—adventurous, daring, dauntless, but thoroughly the rogue.[40] This distortion became gospel in the years after Jones's death, as publishers cashed in on the story line, inventing out of whole cloth as they went along numerous characters and outrageous events that reinforced the main theme. It all made for a good read.

A fine example is the anonymous *Life, Travels, Voyages, and Daring Engagements of John Paul Jones, Containing Numerous Anecdotes of Undaunted Courage,* copied from English chapbooks and published by different American publishers at different times during the early years of the nineteenth century.[41] Here are some excerpts:

> After committing an infinite number of excesses in the neighborhood of his patron's residence, he attempted to seduce, (and but too successfully succeeded), the virtue of three young women of some respectability; two of whom soon after became pregnant.—But the evil did not stop here; it appears he was resolved upon completing the wretchedness of his victims, and placing his villainy beyond the possibility of a doubt; for it was no sooner known by Paul that the young persons were in a thriving way, than he endeavored, by his artifices, and insinuations, to prevail upon each of them to form an acquaintance with a wealthy farmer, for the sole purpose of making him father of the unfortunate and innocent offspring!—And it is a fact generally accredited, that he completely succeeded in this abominable design.
>
> He came to London, and . . . engaged in a criminal intercourse with the mistress of a notorious brothel . . . who assumed his name, and passed under the character of his wife.—The woman being seized with a fit of apoplexy, she expired, while he was examining some accounts in a parlour adjoining to her bedroom. He no sooner discovered her situation, than he searched her pockets, and taking her keys, secreted all her ready money and some other valuable effects, amounting in the whole to about three hundred pounds, and then absconded with his booty.
>
> He then conceived a violent attachment to gambling . . . but his unfair practices involved him in frequent contentions and incessant quarrels. His money being nearly exhausted, he then found means to procure the command of a small smuggling vessel; and after some heavy depredations committed on trading ships of these kingdoms, he went to the coast of Spain.[42]

And so on. The contours of the *Life, Travels, etc.* narrative after Jones enters service in the American cause bear more relation to reality; we read about real American flag salutes, real ships, and real battles. Instances of Jones's courage and bravery are recounted. But the details are sometimes wrong, including, for the purposes of this book, the circumstances of his death: according to *Life, Travels, etc.,* after returning to Paris in the early

1780s and receiving prize moneys due him from the court of France, Jones returned to America to purchase "a small estate at Kentucky; and after living in great splendor some considerable time, died in the summer of 1801, aged 52 years and 8 months."[43]

British prints and illustrations, reproduced in America, reinforced the pirate image. Nathaniel Fanning, who served with Jones on *Bonhomme Richard* and was in London about three years after Flamborough Head, remembered seeing there, both at a print shop and in a coffeehouse, a life-size image of Jones murdering three of *Richard*'s crew (there was no such murder): "He was represented with twelve pistols, six upon each side of him, secured in his girdle, and three men were represented before him in a kneeling posture. On the same picture one appeared to be shot dead, and falling at the feet of Jones, and he presenting a pistol in each hand to each of the other two." The frontispiece of an early chapbook depicts Jones, "the English corsair," shooting a Lieutenant Grub during the fight with *Serapis* when Grub supposedly tried to surrender *Richard* to *Serapis*'s Captain Pearson (in reality, there were no Grub and no such shooting). Another frequently reproduced illustration, titled "Paul Jones the Pirate," shows a wide-eyed, bearded Jones on deck in the midst of battle, cutlass in one hand, pistol at the ready in the other (a second pistol tucked in his belt), hat and front cloth both adorned with skull and crossbones.[44]

Similarly, English ballads of the period, while sometimes celebrating Jones's courage and daring, also sounded the pirate theme, as in the following excerpt from "Another Song of Paul Jones," sung to the tune of "Ye Jacobites by Names":

> You've all heard of Paul Jones, have you not? Have you not?
> How he came to Leith Pier, and he filled the folks with fear;
>   And he filled the folks with fear, did he not?
> He is a bold outlaw, is he not? Is he not?
> He is a bold outlaw; he has joined America
>   To destroy his country a'—has he not?
> The French king does him uphold, does he not? Does he not?
> The French king does him uphold; he robs for British gold;
>   He is a pirate bold, is he not?
> He took the Serapis, did he not? Did he not?
> He took the Serapis, though the battle it was hot;

But a rogue and a vagabond is he not? . . .
He is a murderer, is he not! Is he not?
He is a murderer, for he killed his Carpenter;
He killed his Carpenter, did he not?[45]

Publications like the anonymous *Life, Travels, etc.* provide support for those nineteenth-century Jones biographers, such as Cooper, who claim that the English caricature of Jones was absorbed into the American memory and imagination during the several decades immediately following Jones's death in Paris. Did such caricature also cause our national amnesia? Surely, it was a contributing factor. By so obscuring the historical figure, it suppressed any memory of the real John Paul Jones.

Changing Naval Strategy

Changing American naval strategy provides an intriguing explanation for Jones's disappearance from public notice, as an alternative to the ad hominem ones so far considered. At the onset of the Revolutionary War, it was not clear that America would even have a navy. During protracted debate on the subject at the Continental Congress, more than one delegate thought it the "maddest idea in the world." For starters, it was terribly expensive, and the colonists were short on money. But there were other objections, too. Edward Rutledge of South Carolina, for example, worried it would "ruin the character, and corrupt the morals of our seamen [and] make them selfish, piratical, mercenary, bent wholly on plunder."[46] Moreover, the overwhelming strength of the British navy presented a seemingly unbeatable foe. In the American theater alone, the British had already deployed ninety-plus warships, including a dozen or so ships of the line and dozens more frigates and smaller vessels.[47] There was no hope that an American navy could mount a serious challenge to this superior force.

There was, however, a supporting role that an American navy could play in the greater struggle: the interdiction of British weapons and supplies to its army in America and, where possible, the capture of such matériel for use by the Continental army. Indeed, General Washington had already launched a small navy of his own to do just that. Shortly after taking command of ground forces in Cambridge, Massachusetts, in July 1775, he chartered and armed several fishing schooners and small merchantmen, manned them with local soldiers, and sent them to harass British supply lines off the coast of New England. Together with American privateers operating in the same waters, this motley collection of makeshift vessels succeeded in capturing a number of prizes—including, notably, the ordnance storeship *Nancy* with a cargo of two thousand muskets and several tons of ammunition.[48]

Ultimately persuaded by those who advocated for a navy—men like John Adams, Silas Deane, and John Langdon—Congress in October 1775 voted to establish a small navy. This included setting up a Naval Committee to manage the navy's affairs, the purchase and arming of several vessels, the commissioning of captains, and the promulgation of rules. The purpose of the American navy was as described above: to wage war on British trade, not on the British navy per se. As we saw in chapter 2, the early cruises of John Paul Jones along the Eastern Seaboard of the United States and in the Caribbean were in service of this end.

As the war progressed, two additional strategic objectives were pursued: the projection of American naval power against the British Isles for economic and psychological impact and the establishment of American naval superiority in very limited but critical circumstances.[49] Regarding the former, as we saw, John Paul Jones was both a key proponent and the principal executor of this goal. Regarding the latter, it was fully achieved only once—by the French navy (not the American navy) at the battle of Chesapeake Bay—when Admiral Compte de Grasse successfully blocked the Royal Navy from supporting General Cornwallis, thus directly facilitating Washington's victory over Cornwallis at Yorktown that ended the war.

The American navy had its successes during the war, given the confines of its strategic objectives: it (together with the privateers) captured many British merchantmen, and Paul Jones terrorized the British Isles, captured British prizes within sight of the British coasts, and diverted Royal Navy vessels that might have deployed elsewhere to pursue Jones and protect the homeland. Nevertheless, after the War of Independence was won, the question arose whether the navy was still needed. The consensus was no—or, at the very least, that it was not affordable. The navy was disbanded and not reestablished until 1794, two years after Jones's death.

Paul Jones was, of course, a key victim of this abandonment. These were the years he wandered Europe and waged war for Russia. But the real blow to his memory, it can be argued, came later, when the American navy was reconstituted. For now, the key point is that the primary strategic objective of the new United States Navy was as limited as that of the disbanded Continental navy: to protect American commerce and facilitate trade, not to project power or wage war. It was not even to protect the coast of the United States; that job belonged, principally, to the army and the state militias and was implemented utilizing a string of coastal forts. There would be brief periods when the strategy was expanded to accommodate exigencies—the War of 1812 and the Civil War, for example. But the navy's primary mission was mostly to facilitate trade. This mission did not suit the memory of Paul Jones; or, rather, the memory of Paul Jones did not suit this mission. Jones was a warrior, not a policeman ("I wish to have no connection with any ship that does not sail fast; for I intend to go in harm's way"). The new navy, by and large, was a navy intent on staying out of harm's way. Jones was not a model for such an enterprise. For the purposes of American naval strategy, there was not any need to remember him.

Ambassador Porter in his commemoration address invoked, charmingly, the metaphor of the admiral being covered by a "mantle of forgetfulness" soon after his death. He then asserted, "In all the annals of history there is not another case in which death has caused the memory of so conspicuous a man to drop at once from the height of prominence to the depth of oblivion." There is a touch of melodrama here. Nonetheless, it is true that Jones was swiftly and largely forgotten. In May 1796, only four years after Jones's death, a Rufus Putnam, acting on behalf of the directors of a land-development outfit called the Ohio Company, began publishing notices in newspapers throughout America and Europe, seeking the legal representatives of someone by the name of John Paul Jones. Mr. Jones, the notice said, owned five shares (5,867 acres) in a tract of land northwest of the Ohio River. The company was prepared to issue a deed upon application and proof of being the representatives or legal heirs. A New York editor of one of the papers in which the notice was printed speculated that the deceased on whose behalf a representative was being sought might be the Paul Jones, originally named John Paul, who had distinguished himself in the American Revolution. If so, then the editor believed the gentleman was survived only by a sister and her children, of Dumfries, Scotland. "The family were residing there about three years ago, and had made a recent application at Paris, for some property belonging to Mr. Jones, which was retained by the national convention."[50]

The foregoing editor notwithstanding, John Paul Jones had indeed been mostly forgotten a mere four years after his death. Some combination of his character flaws and scandals, powerful enemies, foreign birth, English press hostility, and the diminished role of the navy in postcolonial American military strategy conspired against his memory. Being wifeless and childless, he lacked an inner circle of loving advocates who might otherwise be counted on to press his case for attention. His heirs—*two* sisters he had not seen for a number of years (the editor had gotten the number of sisters wrong) and some nieces and nephews—were, initially at least, more interested in his money than his memory; their energy was directed at pursuing claims due his estate, not securing his place in history. In addition, the fact that Jones spent so little time in America after the War of Independence (visiting his adopted country only twice, briefly, between 1780 and his death in 1792) and died and was buried on foreign soil was surely relevant. France was far away. America was turned inward, focused on building a new nation. "Out of sight, out of mind" is a powerful memory suppressant.

4

THE SEARCH FOR JOHN PAUL JONES, PART 1

> I at length started one day and went down to Arbigland. . . . Whilst there among the ruins [of the cottage where John Paul Jones was born], it was with pain that I reflected that the only monument to that great man was here, just crumbling away. . . . Lafayette had been lauded with wealth and fame, while the name Paul Jones is now seldom mentioned.
>
> —Lieutenant Andrew Pinkham, *Journal,* 1831

THE SEARCH FOR THE HISTORICAL Paul Jones—his memory, his birthplace—preceded by a number of years the search for his grave. It is, to begin with, a tale of two paper trails: one that starts in Philadelphia, the other in Paris, both leading, after much kerfuffle, to the printing presses of New York several decades after Jones's death.

Jones had bequeathed his estate (mostly claims for pensions, prizes, and salaries against various governments, but also debts owed by a former business partner, shares of stock in several enterprises, some cash and personal effects, and, importantly for our purposes, his papers) to his two sisters, Janet Taylor and Mary Ann Louden, both of Dumfries, Scotland, and their children, ten devisees in all.[1] The papers were the principal source of information regarding Jones's outstanding governmental claims, and therefore a valuable resource from that perspective, sufficient for the heirs to want to preserve them. No one seems to have given thought to the possibility that they also had intrinsic value—certainly historical, possibly monetary. There were two bundles: the Philadelphia papers and the Paris papers.

The Philadelphia Papers

On December 9, 1782, John Paul Jones, then in the United States, collected from Congress $20,705.57 net, owed him for salary and expenses accrued since the beginning of the war. He gave most of this to his friend John Ross in Philadelphia, to invest on his behalf.[2] The next year, following his appointment by Congress as prize agent for Europe and before his return to Paris in August, he also left certain personal papers and effects with Ross, for safekeeping, including some personal correspondence. He may have added items in 1787 as well, during his last trip to America.[3]

Sometime after Jones's death, possibly in late 1792 or 1793, but more likely 1797, the heirs directed that the books and papers should be removed from Mr. Ross to the custody of Robert Hyslop, a merchant in New York who was known to the family (he had emigrated from Scotland) and with whom there is reason to believe Paul Jones himself had lodged for a time while visiting New York. Whatever the precise timing of the family's directive, it is clear that on July 25, 1797, Janet Taylor on behalf of herself, son William, and daughter Janette gave a power of attorney to Hyslop to recover for the heirs money owed Jones by Americans and property belonging to Jones in America. Hyslop issued a receipt for the documents two weeks later. The documents included, besides evidence of various unpaid claims and property belonging to Jones, "a number of letters, accounts, journals, log-books, &c, with various other papers, supposed to be of no value." In the receipt, Hyslop promised to account to the heirs for any property he recovered or payments he obtained. Thereafter, on at least one occasion, he applied for settlement of several of the claims.[4]

Robert Hyslop died in September of the following year, apparently of yellow fever.[5] His trove of John Paul Jones papers then fell into the hands of a baker—Robert's brother John (some accounts say cousin), who was also his executor. The baker neglected them, they were forgotten for many years, and they were not rediscovered until 1824. The occasion for their rediscovery was one of those "stranger than fiction" episodes. In the most dramatic telling of it, a man by the name of George A. Ward happened to be passing by the baker's shop in lower Manhattan when he spied, through a window, a letter to General Lafayette, signed by John Paul Jones. He inquired within, was given temporary custody (and told there were many more letters where that came from), verified through correspondence with Lafayette (who happened to be visiting America at the time) that the Paul Jones signature was genuine, and acquired the entire collection for himself.

It may not have happened quite this way, but certainly along lines akin to it. A report of Ward's discovery was published in a New York newspaper on July 30, 1824, and widely reprinted:

> John Paul Jones. A letter addressed to this distinguished hero was accidentally discovered in a Baker's shop in the city, a few days since, which induced the examination of several chests of old manuscripts, when upwards of 700 papers were found, such as drafts of his official communications, and letters to the most distinguished persons of the age, and their letters to him, from the year 1775–'83—many are in the hand writing of Franklin, Hancock, La Fayette and John Adams, which prove beyond doubt their authenticity. We understand that the gentleman whose perseverance recovered them from destined destruction, has handed them to the author of the Pilot [James Fenimore Cooper], with a view to the publication of a part, by Mr. Wiley.[6]

The identity of the "persevering gentleman"—George A. Ward—was also reported a few weeks later.[7] All of this is relevant to our story and the ensuing fuss, because of what Ward did with his find.

What Ward did was in response to a notice posted in various East Coast newspapers in October 1824, including New York. The notice, authored by John Henry Sherburne, registrar of the United States Navy, announced Sherburne's intention to publish an authentic journal of Paul Jones's cruises. The journal belonged to Elijah Hall, Sherburne's father-in-law and Jones's lieutenant on *Ranger.* The forthcoming publication, according to the announcement, would also include correspondence between Hall and Jones as well as the Navy List for 1776–80 (that is, the names of all Continental navy ships, where built, rates, commanders' names, and the like, information that the registrar of the navy was particularly well placed to compile). As thus conceived, it was not meant to be a biography, or "life," of Jones. However, during the next three months, the project expanded; by the end of January 1825, prospectuses began appearing in the DC press and elsewhere advertising a 350-page "Life" of Jones by John Henry Sherburne that would comprise, besides a "Biography," an "appendix of letters and documents illustrative of the life and actions of the Chevalier." The change in scope was due to George Ward. He apparently saw Sherburne's October notice, wrote him, and offered up his recently acquired collection of Jones papers for use in the proposed publication. That, at least, is how Sherburne told the story. There is an alternative, more sinister, explanation: that Sherburne, after reading about Ward's discovery, published his notice for the express purpose of luring Ward to offer up his find so that he—Sherburne—could publish a much fuller life of Jones. For present purposes, it is sufficient to know that Sherburne got access to all of Ward's documents, expanded the work as a result, and published *The Life and Character of the Chevalier John Paul Jones, a Captain in the Navy of the United States, during Their Revolutionary War*, in the summer of 1825.[8]

Despite the title, it was not, strictly speaking, a biography. Rather, it was a loose collection—not very well organized—of letters, lists, and congressional pronouncements culled from the Ward collection, U.S. government records, and letters provided to Sherburne by notable Jones correspondents, including Thomas Jefferson. (Curiously, it did not include the *Ranger* journal originally promised.) It also included an introductory essay, a concluding essay, and brief textual commentary among the papers. The reviewers, while appreciative that something significant had been done to rescue Jones from prior miscaricatures, were dismissive of the work as serious biography or history. The following from a review in a New Hampshire newspaper is typical:

> I feel much obliged to Mr. Sherburne for the publication of his book; not so much in consequence of its literary merits, as because it will tend to arrest from obloquy and oblivion the character and achievement of a man altogether worthy of being remembered. . . . As to the general merits of the work before me, it appears to me, that its claims to the appellation assumed for its title, are not well founded—because it exhibits in no adequate degree the life and character of Capt. Jones. From it we learn very little concerning that great man until he entered the American navy, in 1776. At which time he must have been nearly thirty years of age. It is equally silent concerning the four last years of his life.[9]

Sherburne's *Life,* for all its flaws, was the first serious effort in America since Jones's death in 1792 to retrieve the historical memory of the Revolution's great naval hero. There was interest in the work outside America as well. A young Benjamin Disraeli, future prime minister of England, was tasked by the London publisher John Murray to edit an English version of the source materials collected in Sherburne's *Life* and to write an introductory biography of Jones for that book, which Disraeli did. The Murray edition was published in London in 1825 under the title *The Life of Paul Jones, from Original Documents in the Possession of John Henry Sherburne, Esq., Register of the Navy of the United States.*[10]

That John Henry Sherburne should have been the vessel for all of this was not serendipity. He was a descendant of the illustrious Sherburne family of Portsmouth, New Hampshire, that had immigrated to America in 1632. Apart from his connection to Elijah Hall (Jones's lieutenant on *Ranger*) and his being a navy man himself, Sherburne's paternal aunt Mary had been the wife of Portsmouth's John Langdon, an important backer of the Continental navy and a big Jones supporter during Jones's life. Sherburne's father, a colonel in the Continental army, had corresponded with Jones (the family kept a letter Jones sent Colonel Sherburne in 1783). John Henry must, therefore, have been exposed to talk of Jones and anecdotes of his cruises while growing up. He was as likely an American as any to start the search for the historical Paul Jones.

The Paris Papers

There was a second bundle of personal papers that Jones kept with him in Paris, larger than the bundle he left in America with John Ross. These papers were at Jones's Paris apartment when he died. Gouverneur Morris had them sealed, along with Jones's personal effects, as was the custom of the day. Early in 1793, Janet Taylor, Jones's eldest sister, traveled to Paris to claim sums owed Jones by France and to retrieve the papers and personal effects. An article published in 1826, several decades after the trip, says she was accompanied by Mark Louden, husband of her younger sister, Mary Ann.[11] There are also contemporary newspaper accounts that suggest someone went with her, but there is no direct evidence it was Louden, although it is reasonable to suppose he—or some other male—did so: Paris was a dangerous place at the time, and it would have been reckless for an eighteenth-century English woman to make the journey alone. In any case, on March 17 Taylor addressed the National Convention (successor to the Legislative Assembly) and stated her claim.[12] Apparently, liability was acknowledged. However, before payment could be effected, the political situation deteriorated, and Taylor had to leave Paris for England. She took all of Jones's Paris papers and personal effects with her. She got out just in time. Three days after she left, the proprietor of her hotel was arrested and his effects seized. A gentleman acquaintance and an Irishman who had served as her valet de place were guillotined.[13]

As noted earlier, by the terms of Jones's will, his entire estate was devised to his two sisters and their children. Janet Taylor had two children living at the time of Jones's death, a son and a daughter, both minors. Mary Ann Louden had two living daughters by a first marriage and two sons and two daughters by a second. Legally, therefore, the estate should have gone three-tenths to Janet's side of the family and seven-tenths to Mary Ann's side. Apparently, though, the sisters agreed that Jones's Paris papers should be divided equally between them. At least, that is how the *North American Review* (1826), several decades later, reported it. According to the *Review*, a "division of the effects and papers was immediately made, by a gentleman appointed for the purpose, with the mutual consent of the parties, who bound themselves to abide by his decision. This gentleman pursued an extraordinary course in regard to the papers. He portioned them out in two parcels, by weight and measure, just as they happened to come to hand, without regard to their value or connexion." It seems that the anonymous author of this article (probably Jared Sparks, editor of the *Review*, or Gulian Verplanck, a frequent contributor) obtained information for it directly from the family (both became friends of Janet's daughter after she came to America in 1830 and may have corresponded with her when she was in Scotland) and that therefore this delightful story can be credited, even though we have not been able to find independent corroboration. That some sort of division took place may be inferred from a letter many years later from John Lowden (one of Jones's nephews on the Louden side of the family who emigrated to America; the new spelling was apparently an American adoption) to Sherburne, stating that a certain document said by Lowden's cousin Janette Taylor to be then in her possession had been in his father's house "not many years ago" and must therefore have been copied by Taylor.[14]

The Paris papers apparently remained in Dumfries, unattended, in the Taylor (and perhaps Louden) households for some years. Janet Taylor died in 1817. Custody of the papers, or at least the Taylor part, passed to Janette Taylor (Janet's daughter, Jones's niece), a spinster. Janette was described some years later by a reporter who interviewed her as a person "rather under the middle size" and "incline[d] a little to *en bon point.* Her manners are agreeable, and the bright twinkle in her dark eye bespeaks great energy and vivacity."[15] Your author, after reading a number of pages of Miss Taylor's correspondence and other writings, has formed a vivid impression of his own: that of a P. L. Travers–type character (of Mary Poppins fame) as portrayed by Emma Thompson in the movie *Saving Mr. Banks*—which is to say, an accomplished woman of considerable talents, witty, sharp-tongued, self-righteous, tenacious in the extreme. At some point, presumably after her mother died, she resolved to clear her uncle's sullied name by seeking publication of the papers and writing a "true account" of his life and character. In this she seems to have been motivated as much by wounded family honor as by the prospect of royalties. In any event, she did sort the papers and sent off a letter to the New-York Historical Society, dated March 29, 1820, offering them for publication. The papers, she said in the letter, comprised correspondence with "all the eminent characters connected with the American revolution," including Washington, Jefferson, Franklin, Adams, the duke de la Rochfoucalt, and Lafayette. There was also a memoir of Jones's life as well as an account of his campaign in Russia—three large octavo volumes in all. She would, she said, have published them in England had money been her object. But the papers contained "some bitter reflections against the British Government" that it would have been necessary to "suppress," thus "injuring" the work. Better, therefore, to publish in New York, since her principal motive was to "exhibit [her] uncle's character in a just point of view," not make money. Could the society let her know if there was any bookseller in New York willing to publish the papers "and what I may expect for them"? She must insist, however, upon one thing: "that they are not to be garbled, but are to be given to the world *just as they are,* without either *adding* or *diminishing.*"[16]

The New-York Historical Society could not afford to publish the papers itself but did cause notice of the work's existence to be circulated, and Miss Taylor was apparently induced to send over to America, for inspection by prospective booksellers, a copy, or excerpts from a copy, of the manuscript.

Miss Taylor engaged an agent, who solicited on her behalf in the following terms:

> TO BOOKSELLERS. Memoirs of the late Paul Jones and his correspondence with the Executive of that time; with an account of residence in Russia, for three years: written by his niece in Scotland,—it will comprise 4 vols. The manuscript is offered for sale on her account. Apply Wm. W., No. 189, Water st. It is dedicated to the officers of the American Navy.[17]

Nothing came of it; as one contemporary observer put it, "The sums offered for the copy right were not, by any means, equal to the expectations of the author," and the manuscript languished.[18] What were the author's "expectations"? According to Sherburne, twelve hundred pounds. That, anyway, is what he says the agent demanded when Sherburne approached him—probably in 1825—about using Taylor's materials in his own forthcoming *Life.* When questioned publicly about whether he had "made any effort to avail himself of the valuable materials contained in the [Taylor] manuscript," Sherburne insisted that such manuscript contained mere "copies" of the first drafts of the letters, reports, and journals from which his own work was compiled, and therefore he had "no inducement to obtain by tedious process of law, or by the payment of a large sum of money, that, which, if obtained, could add nothing to the perfection of the present work, nor render more authentic the materials which constitute its excellence." Lest the reader be startled by the apparent arrogance of Sherburne's response, it should be added that the response was done anonymously, in a letter to the editor signed only "A Friend of the Navy."[19]

Having failed to find an American publisher for her work, but well aware of the criticisms and shortcomings of Sherburne's *Life,* Taylor decided in 1829 to publish her manuscript in Edinburgh and London and then go herself to America to try to close a deal for a reprint there. She arrived in New York on January 1, 1830, with all of the Paris papers in hand. *Memoirs of Rear-Admiral Paul Jones, Chevalier of the Military Order of Merit, and of the Russian Order of St Anne, &c. &c.,* in two octavo volumes, the manuscript that Taylor had left with her British publishers before boarding the boat, was issued in Edinburgh and London a few weeks later.[20]

Taylor insisted afterward that the whole American project was premised on her misunderstanding of American copyright law. Her English publishers had told her she could not, as an alien, hold a copyright in the United States. The plan, therefore, was to delay publication in Britain for a few weeks so she could make arrangements for an American reprint that would be published in the United States at the same time. For this purpose, she approached the firm of Carry & Co. in Philadelphia. She had had a copy of her manuscript printed before she left Scotland, and she now left it with that enterprise for inspection. They did not return it to her for several weeks, at which time they said they would be willing to reprint it but not pay her any compensation. So the *Edinburgh Memoir* got published in Britain without a U.S. reprint under contract.

Taylor, not willing to let Carry & Co. reprint the *Edinburgh Memoir* without compensating her, next consulted William Leete Stone Sr., an owner of the *New York Commercial Advertiser.* (Stone had been on the committee appointed by the New-York Historical Society to review her letter of 1820.) He advised her she should have a copyrighted work done for America, not just a reprint. He proposed that Sherman Converse, owner of the *New Haven (CT) Journal* ("a very enterprising man"), should be sold the copyright and that Robert Charles Sands, a young gentleman in his office, should edit the work. (Sands, besides his employment at the *Advertiser,* was a well-regarded poet and essayist, friend of William Cullen Bryant, and member of the famous Knickerbocker group of New York writers.) Taylor then met with Converse. She says Converse promised her $1,000, plus $250 for Sands, and that he would send her all the proof sheets for examination and correction. She agreed. The bargain was a verbal one, with no witnesses. It went badly. Taylor would later write that, having been in America little more than a fortnight, she knew nothing about Converse or Sands and was completely ignorant in regard to American copyright law. "I then believed that it was necessary that the Author, Editor or Compiler of a work, as well as the proprietor should be an American citizen in order to secure a copyright. Had I been as well informed then as I am now, I would not have thanked anyone for his services, much less paid for them. I could have done what was necessary myself and have taken out the copyright in the name of my nephew, who was a citizen by birth."[21]

To begin with, Converse insisted that the work should be published by subscription and made to look as if the subscriptions were for the sole benefit of Taylor herself, on the grounds that American booksellers would be deterred from publishing a competing pirate edition of the *Edinburgh*

Memoir as long as they thought the benefits of the American publication were going solely to John Paul Jones's niece, but would have "no such delicacy" with regard to Converse himself if he were seen as the beneficiary. Taylor was horrified, first because "it was not the truth" but also because in England "publication by subscription [was] considered a very mean proceeding." In the end, though, she allowed Converse to "represent the thing in his own way" because she thought there "might be something to" his theory of deterrence. Ten thousand copies were subscribed before the book was printed, at $2 per copy.

More distressing to Taylor than the subscription campaign in her name was that the proof sheets (contrary to her verbal deal) were never sent to her for examination, only the stereotyped pages when it was too late to make corrections. In her view, there was much to correct. "Mr. Sands," she wrote,

> was both a man of talents and an elegant scholar and could and I have no doubt would have made an excellent work had he been allowed time, but during the day he was employed in Col. Stone's office,—it was only odd hours he could devote to biography, and Mr. Converse hurried him so much that he blundered on without examining the documents in his hands, and without that previous reading which was absolutely necessary for his information.—The first thirteen pages were so blundered they were expunged entirely, you may perceive the work commences at the fourteenth page. . . . I became so much provoked that I threatened to appeal to the public, on which Mr. Sands tried to intimidate me by writing me that I was not aware of the force of ridicule in this country. I told him if I made myself ridiculous by endeavoring to prevent the public from being imposed upon, that, I would abide the consequences.—They then inserted in the preface that "Miss Taylor is only responsible for the authenticity of the correspondence quoted from or inserted, and in no wise for the casual observations of the compiler."[22]

Taylor was still not satisfied, so Sands wrote her a letter, pleading with her to refrain from taking her complaints public, in exchange for which he would oblige her in any way her could. Miss Taylor yielded. "I am not to be coerced," she wrote afterward, "but my feelings are very easily worked upon. I pledged him my word that I would remain silent." She then told Converse that, having consented to shield Sands from public ridicule, she could no longer expose Converse, even though his greed was, in her view, principally to blame for the fiasco. She did not, though, entirely absolve

Sands. “Mr. Sands,” she said, “for his own credit, ought to have insisted on being allowed sufficient time to discharge his duty faithfully. He was very much ashamed of his production, as well he might.”[23]

Miss Taylor also had difficulty getting paid—as did Robert Sands. Sands, understandably, refused to hand over the manuscript until he was paid, and Converse refused to pay Taylor unless she allowed him to deduct Sands's $250 from her $1,000. This did not sit well with the spinster from Dumfries. Thirteen years later, still angry, she would write in a letter to James Fenimore Cooper, “Converse, in a note, says if the work is successful he may refund me the 250 dollars but that he does not bind himself to do so, as much as to say I need never expect it.—I do not know what he calls success, he has already cleared many thousands by that book. But I could have forgiven his defrauding myself had he only done justice to the public, and not imposed on it, at a high price, a work containing more errors than pages.”[24] She was given nine courtesy copies of the book. Sands got none.

The list of persons to whom Taylor distributed her courtesy copies is an interesting one. Besides showing the high rank of her American acquaintances, it hints at a more cordial relationship with Sands than is reflected in the story so far told. The list included four military men: Benjamin Talmadge, a colonel in the American Revolution; Colonel John Trumbull, aide-de-camp to General Washington, who is mentioned in the book; Taylor's nephew William Paul Taylor, midshipman in the U.S. Navy; and Levi Woodbury, secretary of the navy. It also included two prominent literary figures, Jared Sparks and Gulian Verplanck, the former gentleman an editor of the prestigious *North American Review,* host to de Tocqueville during his 1831–32 visit to America, and future president of Harvard (Taylor had apparently been given an introduction to Sparks before she left Scotland and corresponded with him from New York about “errors” in the book), the latter a lawyer, politician, and writer who, together with Sands, was a member of the so-called Knickerbocker group of New York writers, as well as Dr. John W. Francis, whom Taylor described as a “warm friend to myself.”[25] Francis, with Verplanck and Sands, was a member of New York's famous “Bread and Cheese Club,” so named because “bread and cheese were the ballots used in voting for or against members, bread being pro and cheese being con, and a single piece of cheese decided against admittance.”[26] The three also belonged to the successor Sketch Club, which was active when Sands was doing his compilation. Others in the club included James Fenimore Cooper and William Cullen Bryant. All of this hints that Sands may have introduced Taylor around. In any event, she was good at what we would now call "networking." Rounding out her list of book donees were Benjamin T. Onderdonk, bishop of the Episcopal Diocese of New York and her pastor, and James G. King, a partner in the New York banking firm of Prim, Ward, and King, whom she described as "a very particular friend" of her brother's.

The title of the Sands book was *Life and Correspondence of John Paul Jones, Including His Narrative of the Campaign of the Liman.*[27] It was published in 1830, only a few months after Miss Taylor's arrival in America, six of its first fifteen pages "expunged entirely" (as she had demanded) because of errors, so that the work jumps from page 8 to page 14. Despite Taylor's disgust with the product, the reviews were generally favorable—more so, certainly, than Sherburne's *Life.*[28]

Janette Taylor lived a long life in America—long enough to see two additional serious biographies published about her uncle and to complain as well about "errors" that they contained: Alexander Mackenzie's *The Life of John Paul Jones* (1841) and James Fenimore Cooper's *John Paul Jones* (1843).[29] These works, together with her own *Edinburgh Memoir* (1830), Sherburne's *Life* (1825), and Sands's *Life* (1830), reset the memory of John Paul Jones both in America and in Britain, a reset that was made possible only by the fortuitous discovery of Jones's Philadelphia papers among the biscuits and bread of the baker of Dye Street and by the Paris papers plucked from the flames of the French Revolution by Janette Taylor's mother—plucked by her and preserved in Dumfries not for the purpose of salvaging Jones's memory but to help identify claims and property belonging to her and her family as heirs of Paul Jones. That the reset occurred is amply illustrated by what serious people, both in America and in Britain, began to say about John Paul Jones in the aftermath of their publication (for example, "Hereafter [Jones] will be considered, and truly, as a man of wonderful activity of mind and body, of great resource and energy, and withal of high and honorable feelings. That he had his weaknesses, is also unquestionably true; but they were the weaknesses of genius") and by the quest that several Americans undertook for tangible evidence of his life and death. These quests are the subject of the remainder of this chapter and the next one.[30] As to the further disposition of Jones's Philadelphia and Paris papers, the former were apparently returned to Ward and later acquired by the great collector Peter Force; Congress purchased the Force collection, including Jones's Philadelphia papers, in 1867 and placed them in the Library of Congress. The Paris papers have disappeared.[31]

Restoration of Jones's Birthplace

One consequence of recovering a memory of the historical Paul Jones, occasioned by the publication of the Sherburne-Taylor-Sands compilations, was the launching of a quest for tangible artifacts of that memory. In 1831 a thirty-eight-year-old lieutenant in the United States Navy by the name of Alexander Pinkham, on leave for twelve months, undertook a pilgrimage to John Paul Jones's birthplace at Kirkbean. *Pilgrimage* is the right term, because his excursion had a religious fervor to it, as will become apparent. It would end with Pinkham funding the restoration of the (by then dilapidated) cottage in which John Paul was born.

Lieutenant Pinkham was born in 1792, the year of Jones's death. His father was a ship's master on various whalers and merchantmen sailing out of Nantucket, where the family lived. At the age of fifteen, Alexander went to sea himself, as foremast hand on the whale ship *Chili.* In 1814 he joined the U.S. Navy as a midshipman and fought the British on Lake Erie during the final months of the War of 1812. For a time thereafter, he served as chief mate, and then master, on several merchant vessels before resuming his naval duties in 1822, rising to the rank of full lieutenant in 1825. He was an accomplished and well-liked officer and seaman. In 1829 he became master of America's first privately owned sail training ship, the brig *Clio,* part of the Coffin School at Nantucket founded by British admiral Sir Isaac Coffin. In that capacity, he sailed from Boston to Quebec and then to the Cape Verde Islands and Brazil. He resigned his command in 1831, obtained his twelve-month leave of absence from the navy, and embarked for the British Isles on June 2. The object of his journey—to visit, on foot, the Scottish relics of the poet Robert Burns and of John Paul Jones—had apparently obsessed him for some months or years.[32]

How Pinkham came to revere Jones and conceive his obsession is something of a mystery. Perhaps his family's seafaring history and his mother's Scottish heritage played a part. He would write in the journal he kept of his Scottish trip, and tell acquaintances he met there, that Burns and Jones were the two "heroes of my youth" and that their "works and exploits" were "the greatest single influence on my life."[33] This seems dubious—at least the Paul Jones part. We know Pinkham's father, on a voyage to London, got the boy's mother a copy of Burns's poems and that the boy, as well as the mother, was enthralled by them. Third parties attest he could recite long passages from memory; evidently, as a young man at sea, he would also read and recite Burns to his shipmates.[34] The larger part of his Scottish trip was spent visiting sites of relevance to Burns and his poetry (for example, Friars' Carse Hermitage, where Burns wrote, among others, "Tam o' Shanter" and "Mary in Heaven"), even calling on Burns's widow. So the Burns boyhood obsession is credible. (He spent considerable time in Scotland as well tracking Sir Walter Scott and James Hogg [better known by his pen name, the Ettrick Shepherd], successfully making contact with the latter author but not the former.)

There is nothing of similar weight corroborating the "Paul Jones as youthful hero" part, although a boyhood familiarity with the Paul Jones buccaneer legend may be presumed. It is tempting to speculate that some combination of the Sherburne-Taylor-Sands publications of the previous five years caught his eye (any literate navy man—Pinkham was certainly that—must have been drawn to the burst of new information about Jones) and kindled, or rekindled, his interest, as they kindled the interest of other Americans at the time. He is said to have recited some of Jones's exploits to his students on *Clio,* which would have been fresh enough in his mind had he read beforehand Sherburne's recently published *Life* or some of the articles and reviews it spawned. By the time Pinkham sailed up the Solway on a coasting vessel from Liverpool to Dumfries, he was at the railing, eagerly watching for a glimpse of the Arbigland cottage.

> What with adverse winds and calms, we were four days out on our passage. . . . As we passed up the Solway, there were pointed out to me where the Nith on which Dumfries is located and empties itself, the ruins of the cottage where Paul Jones was born. We had on board a dozen passengers. . . . I could not but admire the reverence they paid to the memory of their countryman Paul Jones, as we sailed past the ruins, before mentioned, about half mile from shore. All the passengers, young and old, the old cooks even, seemed well acquainted with his character and exploits. It was a fine day, about 4 p.m., running up [the Nith River] with a moderate breeze.[35]

From Dumfries Pinkham trekked the fourteen miles to Arbigland. He visited the churchyard where Paul Jones's father was buried, noting in his journal that John Paul Sr. had died in the same year Pinkham's own father was born (1767). He paused reverently at the grave, marked by "a plain stone plate covering a box tomb" with "a simple inscription stating the name, age, &c, 'Respected by all who knew him,' and near the bottom, 'Erected by John Paul Jones.'" He also made drawings of the ruined Paul Jones birth cottage and took measurements with his ruler, a "mackerel line with its accompanying jig and plummet that I had always carried with me, to measure the height of old castle walls not more famous in history than this wall perhaps. . . ."

> Whilst there among the ruins, it was with pain that I reflected that the only monument to that great man was here, just crumbling away—The man over whose head the stars and stripes of desponding liberty ever floated or, to use a more poetic term, ever fluttered in the breeze. Lafayette had been lauded with wealth and fame, while the name Paul Jones is now seldom mentioned. He never retreated, he never lowered his flag. Let any American visit this lonely spot and he must blush with the same feelings that possessed me at the moment. I took a fragment of stone that had fallen and put it in my knapsack.[36]

Based on our narrative to this point, the reader may have formed the impression of a physically slight, somewhat effete man. The following description of Pinkham, by an acquaintance in Dumfries, may, therefore, surprise:

> Mr. Pinkham was not only prodigiously stout, but beyond all comparison the most weather-beaten man I ever beheld. . . . [R]arely, if ever, has old Neptune had a fitter representative. . . . His age might be thirty-two or a little beyond—his height five feet ten or eleven inches; and then such a chest, neck, and shoulders! Limbs more muscular I have never seen. A single glance riveted attention and convinced you that the owner was indeed a Hercules whom it would be dangerous to tamper with in a dark night and on a lonely road. . . . Agile as powerful, his movements were totally unimpaired by fat: from the crown of his head to the sole of the foot he was one compact compound of bone and muscle, nerves of steel, and sinews of iron.[37]

Despite his prodigious physique, Pinkham was, according to the same acquaintance, a man of "gentle manners" and a "soft heart." "I never heard an oath escape his lips," the acquaintance said, "or the slightest boast as to the perils he had braved, or the honors he had won." If anything, he was "overly sentimental; and no one could have supposed, *a priori,* that a soul so refined lodged in a frame so masculine and weather-beaten."[38]

He was also fit and hearty. During his four months in the British Isles, Pinkham walked 180 miles in Ireland and 350 miles in Scotland and Wales, carrying a heavy knapsack and often sleeping outdoors.

After his visit to Arbigland, Pinkham left Dumfries for six weeks of walking in search of Burns, Scott, and the Ettrick Shepherd. He also fretted about the sorry state of the Paul Jones cottage, deciding in the end to return to Dumfries rather than make his way to London and America, as originally planned. He had an idea: Why not restore the cottage? After several failed tries, he succeeded in meeting D. H. Craik, owner of the Arbigland estate on which the cottage was located. Craik remembered playing with the young John Paul, sometimes hiking with him into the mountains and being carried on his back when he was tired (John Paul was the older of the two). Craik approved the restoration, agreed to Pinkham's proposed financing, and sent his visitor away a happy man.

Curiously, there is nothing about the restoration or the bargain with Craik in Pinkham's journal. Pinkham did, however, share details with John McDiamid, editor of the *Dumfries and Galloway Courier,* who had befriended him during his first visit to Dumfries. From McDiamid we learn that, upon returning from Arbigland and his meeting with Craik, Pinkham deposited twenty-five gold sovereigns with McDiamid to be used for the repair, to render the cottage habitable—apparently, the last of Pinkham's pocket funds.[39] (The amount, while not substantial, was enough for a respectable down payment on the restoration.) Pinkham also worked out a payment schedule with Craik for sending additional funds the following year. As for getting home, Pinkham reportedly said, "My legs will carry me through England, and once in any seaport there, I can work my way home on any sailing ship."[40]

The restoration was begun the following spring, and the house was "repaired in the most tasteful manner." Craik himself "gave freely from his own purse" to the project. The completed restoration was described as follows in a local newspaper:

> The site of the cottage is a glade in a thriving wood, on the shores of Solway, with a green in front, fancifully railed in, and tastefully ornamented with evergreens, flowers and flowering shrubs. Inside and out it is a trim cottage which may vie with similar buildings in England, and as the walls are whit-

> ened annually with the finest lime, it is become a sort of landmark to nearly every sail that enters the Solway. The widow of a fisherman who died under highly distressing circumstances, and who owes much to the humanity of Mr. Craik, tenants it rent free, and will probably close her eyes under its honored roof; and as this fact is generally known, almost every tar, in passing the spot, doffs his bonnet in token of gratitude, and says, God bless the kind Lieutenant Pinkham.[41]

As for Pinkham himself, after returning to the United States, he married Lydia Davis of Portsmouth, Virginia. They had two children, both of whom died in childhood. Janette Taylor learned of Pinkham's restoration of her uncle's birthplace and gave him as a token of her thanks a tiny miniature of Paul Jones, set in a locket of gold, painted by the Countess of Lavendahl in Paris after Flamborough Head. Pinkham did not keep the miniature for himself but deposited it with the New York Naval Lyceum.[42] He died in 1843, age fifty-one.

Relics

Renewed interest in finding the historical John Paul Jones gave rise as well to interest in things—relics—that once belonged to Jones, not only Countess of Lavendahl's miniature but also swords, flags, and spyglasses. The spyglass Jones purportedly used when he spotted *Serapis* and the Baltic convoy off Flamborough Head provides an interesting example in this regard. The spyglass was evidently given by Jones to his Philadelphia friend John Ross (the same Ross to whom he entrusted what we have earlier called his Philadelphia papers) and then given by Ross to his son-in-law Samuel Breck, a Pennsylvania merchant and politician. (Breck claimed to have crossed the Atlantic in May 1787 from Le Havre to America in the company of Jones and St. Jean de Crèvecouer.) After keeping the glass for some fifty years, Breck decided that, to honor Jones's memory, it should be "preserved by some gentleman" of the naval profession "worthy of its guardianship." He gave it to Captain S. F. Du Pont of the U.S. Navy and engraved on its sliding tube the following inscription: "This spy-glass was once owned by John Paul Jones, who gave it to John Ross, by whose son-in-law, S. Breck, it is presented to S. F. Du Pont, of the U.S.N., in token of the high esteem in which he holds the public services and private virtues of Capt. Du Pont." Du Pont, flattered, wrote Breck an effusive thank-you letter that reads in part: "I cannot convey to you my sense of gratitude for this mark of your kindness; but I feel myself undeserving of your partiality, in desiring to make me the recipient of an object associated with the professional career of so remarkable a man. I can only consider myself the guardian of it for my brethren in the naval service, who will hear of this memento with extreme interest, and will look upon it as an heirloom in the profession, to incite to deeds of daring and glory."[43]

Jones's Grave

The quest for tangible artifacts also involved ashes and bones, in connection with which Colonel Sherburne now makes a second appearance in our story. He had, since his Paul Jones compilation of 1825, resigned his position as registrar of the navy and moved on to other projects, many of them literary. He wrote poetry for journals of popular literature (poems such as "The Sleigh Ride," "Mnemosyne," "To Thee," and "The Oath"); he republished, with notes and an appendix of his own making, a history of the Adams administration written by John Wood that he claimed was "suppressed" in 1802; and he authored a number of other works, all traces of which have since been lost to history except for their titles, among them "Naval Sketches," "Etiquette," and "Osceola: A Tragedy." Sherburne also developed an interest in ocean telegraphy and cosigned, with Philadelphia lawyer Horatio Hubbell, a memorial to Congress advocating the laying of a transatlantic cable from North America to Europe. But he had not totally lost interest in John Paul Jones. In the late 1830s he became involved in the affairs of the Paul Jones estate, filing papers of administration as legal representative of John Lowden and the Lowden heirs with respect to their Danish claims. This ended badly, with Sherburne's letters of administration being revoked.[44]

For our purposes, it is another of Sherburne's later works, a travel book with the somewhat precious title *The Tourist's Guide; or, Pencilings in England and on the Continent,* published in 1847, that is chiefly of interest. Before writing *Pencilings,* Sherburne had toured Europe, including a visit to Paris and the Père Lachaise cemetery there. The following entry in *Pencilings* is about Père Lachaise:

> To stop and examine *all* the tombs in this celebrated cemetery, would require some days. . . . *La Fayette* (a name dear to every American heart)

> and his wife lie entombed in the eastern part of the city; the tomb is of plain marble, with a suitable inscription. A short distance east of this tomb, lie the remains of *La Fayette's* old and valued friend, *John Paul Jones,* late a Captain in the United States Navy, and so celebrated in the *Revolution* for his chivalric daring, naval exploits, in so often humbling the *proud flag* of England, by capturing, singlehanded, its *crack* frigates, then dashing meteor-like, through its *fleets,* unharmed, into the *British Channel,* causing its rock-bound shores to *echo* and *re-echo* with the thunder of his cannon, to the dismay of a *foe* thought to be invincible on the ocean.
>
> This lamented naval hero, who may be ranked as the *Washington of the Atlantic,* died in Paris on the *12th of September,* 1792, of water on the brain; and although a *Calvinist,* his funeral was attended by the French National Assembly, all the foreigners of distinction, and citizens of note, of both sexes. An eloquent oration was pronounced over his tomb by the late celebrated orator, *M. Marron,* one of the leading influential members of the National Assembly.
>
> I little dreamt, while engaged in writing the life and character of this *naval* hero, for the purpose of having *his name* enrolled among the *defenders* of American liberty and independence, which had been neglected for near half a century—or, while writing the biographical sketch of *La Fayette,*—that the day would arrive when I should stand three thousand miles from my native land, in a foreign clime, between the sacred remains of these gallant twin champions of liberty.[45]

This entry is interesting for two reasons. First, it previews Sherburne's interest in the grave of John Paul Jones, an interest he was about to act upon with considerable fanfare. Second, it is astonishingly misinformed about the details of Jones's death and funeral—astonishing, at least, coming from Jones's first serious biographer. For example, Sherburne had gotten Jones's date of death wrong in his 1825 compilation (the date of death was July 18, 1792, not September 12, 1792), and he gets it wrong again here, despite the fact that later biographers such as Robert Sands provided the correct date and irrefutable proof of it. Sherburne, it seems, never read these later biographers. Also, the funeral was not the lavish affair he makes it out to be, and M. Marron was not a "celebrated orator" or "one of the leading influential members of the National Assembly," merely the proprietor of the Protestant cemetery where Jones was interred whose duty it was to preside over funerals there. Most troubling, for a man who would soon announce his intention to bring Jones's remains back to America, he seems not to know anything about where Jones was buried—or, for that matter, Lafayette. Standing in Père Lachaise, he makes it sound as if he can point to Lafayette's tomb on one side of him and Jones's on the other, whereas neither of them was buried in that cemetery! What is going on?

As early as 1845, Colonel Sherburne had begun lobbying the secretary of the navy for permission to bring Jones's remains back to America. In 1847 and 1848, he corresponded about it with the American minister in France, and in January 1851 he petitioned the navy secretary again. On January 30, the secretary responded favorably, informing Sherburne that "an order has this day been issued to the commander of the Frigate St. Lawrence, directing him to receive at Southampton, the remains of the late John Paul Jones, to be transported to New York." Sherburne was concerned that the order did not expressly direct the commander to allow Sherburne himself on board, and so he wrote the secretary again, seeking clarification. The secretary was losing patience. "The Department," he replied, "does not deem it necessary to issue the order asked for, as it presumes there will be no difficulty in the case."[46]

Satisfied, Sherburne ratcheted up publicity for his forthcoming trip and triumphant return. An unidentified correspondent he describes as a "distinguished author in Philadelphia" promised "a most glorious reception, an honorable and public internment [for the remains.] As soon as we learn that you are about to start with them, so soon will we prepare for a public demonstration, which will be enthusiastic." Newspapers across the country began reporting the movements of the *St. Lawrence* and of Sherburne. This, for example, from the *Boston Daily Atlas* of April 1: "[It] has been announced that the frigate St. Lawrence was to proceed to France, before her return from Southampton, for the purpose of bringing home the remains of the celebrated Paul Jones. Col. Sherburne, of New York, by order of the government, goes out to Europe by the next Collins steamer for Liverpool, to superintend the exhuming of the remains and their safe conveyance to this country."[47]

Unfortunately, no one had thought to inquire whether Sherburne actually knew where Jones was buried. He did not.[48] (Readers of Sherburne's *Pencilings* might have sounded a warning, but perhaps there were not many of them.) By June it became clear the mission had failed; this, too, was duly reported. "The Paris journals announce that Col. Sherburne, deputed by the United States Cabinet to convey the remains of Commodore John Paul

Jones to America, has been unable to discover the grave, and abandoned the search."[49]

Was it all just a publicity stunt to sell books? A second edition of Sherburne's 1825 *Life* was due to be published in June, with several pages of new material (including Sherburne's correspondence with American officials about retrieving the remains from Paris—but still containing the wrong date of death). No one questioned his good faith.

There were, though, questions about the mission itself—and second-guessing whether Jones had even been buried in Paris. A Boston newspaper complained, "This business of removing bones and ashes of distinguished men is unworthy the thought of government. If honor is to be paid to Paul Jones, let it be to his immortal, not his *mortal* part."[50] A shipmaster from Leith, writing to the *Times* of London, testified that the remains were in Russia, not France; he had often seen the headstone there:

> Sir—I notice, from your paper of yesterday that the Americans have been unsuccessful in their search at Paris for the remains of the redoubtable Paul Jones. I think had they examined the Strangers' Burying-ground at Cronstadt they would have met with more success. Some time after his attempt to land here he went to Russia, and got an appointment in the Russian navy; but, in consequence of the remonstrances of the other officers of the fleet, he had to resign, and was allowed a small pension by the Empress. He shortly after died, and was buried as above stated. I have often seen the stone which was erected over his grave.[51]

The shipmaster's letter aroused public debate about whether Jones had really been buried in Paris and whether his remains could ever be recovered. The consensus reached during the summer of 1851 was that the shipmaster was mistaken—internment had been in Paris, not Cronstadt—but that the grave had been desecrated and the bones removed to the Catacombs and there intermingled irretrievably with those of a million other nameless souls.[52] The Paris correspondent for the *Times* reported it this way:

> A friend of mine, duly authorized to investigate the matter, after visiting in vain, all the Ministerial *bureaux* in Paris, by a careful and patient inspection of the records of the Prefecture, and a subsequent reference to the *Moniteur,* has established to a certainty that the death of the remarkable person in question occurred in Paris; that his body was interred in the Protestant burial-ground then existing to the rear of the Hotel Dieu; that the piece of

> land devoted to such purpose was afterward sold, and that all the bones were collected and thrown into a common pit (or, perhaps, the catacomb). The documents, or authentic copies of them, for substantiating these facts, are in the hands of the gentleman alluded to, and in due time will be published. I should add that the *Moniteur* corresponding in date to the entry found in the archives of the Prefecture corroborates in all particulars what has been stated.[53]

On July 14, 1851, in a final report to Secretary of the Navy William Graham, Sherburne himself endorsed this conclusion.[54] Perhaps the author of *Pencilings* was humbled by his failure to find Paul Jones's grave. In August 1851, he petitioned the Common Council of New York City to set aside a suitable small place in City Hall Park for the erection of a monument to the memory of Jones.[55] The petition was denied. Sherburne also advocated that a first-class frigate should be named for Jones, but this, too, was ignored.[56]

5

THE SEARCH FOR JOHN PAUL JONES, PART 2

> You know the frigate *St. Lawrence* was to bring to the United States the remains of Admiral Paul Jones. The failure was owing to the unbecoming steps taken therefor. In point of fact, the remains are in a leaden coffin in which the Directory of France caused them to be interred, and were not disturbed by the national decree that broke up several cemeteries. They remain covered by a building, and are now fifteen feet below the surface. If our Congress choose to give some money to get them they can be soon in our Capital Cemetery.
>
> —American correspondent in Paris, November 17, 1851

THE READER WILL KNOW, BECAUSE we began our story at its end, that there existed an alternate narrative to the consensus with which we concluded chapter 4 about what happened to the remains of John Paul Jones after Colonel Sherburne failed to find them. The consensus had it that the graveyard where Jones was buried was, like a number of other Paris cemeteries, dug up during the French Revolution and its contents transferred to the mass grave of the Catacombs; therefore, the bones were gone forever, and Sherburne's search was doomed to failure from the start. The alternate narrative, summarized in the above passage from the letter of an American correspondent in Paris in 1851, told a different story: the graveyard had been covered by a building, not dug up, and Jones's coffin was there for the taking, fifteen feet below the surface.[1] This alternate narrative lay dormant for fifty years, until an American ambassador to France, Horace Porter, revived and pursued it. How Porter came to his resolve to search for the lost grave of John Paul Jones, and the details of that search, is the subject of this chapter.

Horace Porter is a fascinating story in his own right.[2] He was born in Huntington, Pennsylvania, in 1837 of a well-to-do family in the iron business. His father, who was active in state politics, served as governor of Pennsylvania from 1839 to 1845. The young Porter aspired to a military rather than political career. He graduated West Point in 1860, third in his class; was commissioned second lieutenant in June 1861; and served with distinction in the Civil War, earning the Medal of Honor for bravery in the battle of Chickamauga. He came to the attention of General Ulysses S. Grant and was Grant's aide-de-camp during the last year of the war. Porter was present at the surrender ceremony at Appomattox and gave Lee the pencil Lee used to make corrections in the terms of surrender—a pencil that Lee returned to him and Porter proudly kept.[3] Porter and Grant would remain close for the rest of Grant's life, with Porter continuing to serve Grant for a number of years after the war, first as aide-de-camp to then peacetime General Grant during Reconstruction, from 1866 to 1869, and then as personal secretary in the White House to President Grant, from 1869 to 1872. (It was Porter who alerted Grant to Jay Gould's effort to bribe administration officials and corner the gold market.)

Porter resigned from the army in 1873 and became a railroad man, including vice president of the Pullman Palace Car Company; president of the New York, West Shore, and Buffalo Railroad; and president of the St. Louis–San Francisco Railway. He was in business for twenty-five years, serving as a director in fourteen railroad companies and financial institutions. He was also active in many clubs and civic organizations. When General Grant died, Porter spearheaded the campaign to raise money for Grant's Tomb on Riverside Drive in New York City and spoke at the dedication ceremony. He was a popular orator and after-dinner speaker as well as a prominent resident of New York City. President McKinley appointed him ambassador to France in 1897, a post he held for eight years and during which time he conducted the search for Paul Jones's grave.[4]

That a new search for Jones's grave should have been tried at the end of the nineteenth century is not itself surprising. That Horace Porter would be the instrument for that search is less obvious. As to timing, the last decade of the nineteenth century witnessed the first sustained shift in American naval strategy since the Revolution—from protection of American commercial interests to defense of the Western Hemisphere and projection of American power.[5] The deeds of John Paul Jones—he who raided Whitehaven and St. Mary's Isle, plundered British shipping within sight of British coasts, and defeated *Drake* and *Serapis* in British waters—were more relevant to a navy tasked with projecting national power than facilitating commerce. Consistent with this shift in strategy, favorable writing about Jones began accelerating: books, articles, fiction, plays.[6]

As to Porter, there is nothing obvious in his résumé to account for his obsession. Colonel Sherburne, we have seen, was a navy man linked to Jones in important ways, among them his father-in-law's service as Jones's lieutenant on *Ranger* and his own father's personal correspondence with Jones. Cooper and Mackenzie were also navy men. Janette Taylor was Jones's niece, heir, and custodian of his Paris papers. Porter had no similar connections to the commodore. He was an army man. Porter's paternal grandfather, Andrew Porter, had served briefly as captain of the marines on board the Continental navy's *Effingham,* but this commission was soon abandoned for a commission as an artillery officer, in which capacity the grandfather served with distinction at the land battles of Princeton, Brandywine, and Germantown. A cousin of Porter's (also an Andrew, also an army man) was married to a Biddle (a distant relation of Commodore Biddle of the Continental navy), but this connection seems too remote to explain anything. Porter himself had little to say on the subject of his motivation. The following, written in 1905 after his efforts were successful, is the only occasion:

> Upon assuming charge of our embassy in Paris and finding myself among the old landmarks, which are still honored there as recalling the many historic incidents in the sojourn of Paul Jones in that brilliant capital, I felt a deep sense of humiliation as an American citizen in realizing that our first and most fascinating naval hero had been lying for more than a century in an unknown and forgotten grave, and that no serious attempt had ever been made to recover his remains and give them appropriate sepulture in the land upon whose history he had shed so much luster.[7]

This has a bit too much of the set piece about it to be convincing, at least to this reader.

Porter's daughter, Elsie, wrote an affectionate memoir of her father after his death.[8] She was close to her father, frequently standing in for her mother at diplomatic events in Paris as her mother's health declined. Were there more to tell—that is, if Porter had more to say on the subject—the daughter might be expected to know it and report it. But there is nothing in the memoir of her father regarding his motivation to search for Jones's grave, beyond his own published explanation. Therefore, it is left to the rest of us to speculate.

One intriguing clue, or possible clue, can be found in Porter's published account of his year as Grant's aide-de-camp, *Campaigning with Grant.* There Porter tells of a visit that Secretary of State William Seward made to Grant's camp on July 23, 1864.[9] Porter took notes. The talk was about naval matters. Seward discussed how the *Trent* Affair in 1861 had led to an almost complete breakdown of U.S.-British relations.[10] He also discussed the recent battle between the USS *Kearsarge* and the CSS *Alabama.* The *Alabama* was the most feared commerce raider of the Confederate navy. From 1861 to 1864, it captured sixty prizes around the world, even sinking a Union warship. Union warships had pursued it, unsuccessfully, for years. Finally, on June 19, 1864, the *Kearsarge* encountered *Alabama* in the English Channel, near Cherbourg, and engaged it. After one hour of fierce combat, the *Alabama* surrendered and then sank—one of the greatest Union naval victories of the Civil War. Fifteen thousand Frenchmen witnessed the battle from the cliffs above Cherbourg. The captain and crew were lauded for their tactics and bravery.

The analogy to Flamborough Head, though not perfect, was there: two evenly matched warships, the American vessel in Europe far from home waters, a brave and talented American sea captain deliberately putting himself in harm's way, thousands of spectators watching from the nearby cliffs. Porter, commenting in *Campaigning,* called the *Kearsarge*'s Captain Winslow "a man after Grant's heart in audaciously pursuing the *Alabama* and forcing it to fight."[11]

The same could have been said of Paul Jones, another brave captain from an earlier era intent on going in harm's way.[12] Porter may not have made the Paul Jones–Grant connection that evening in the field listening to Seward's account of the sinking of the *Alabama* or years later in his private study compiling his notes of the evening; certainly, there is no indication that John Paul Jones was mentioned. But when Porter did start to think about Jones, whenever that was, the thought that he, too, was "a man after Grant's heart" must have surfaced. That Porter retained a lifelong interest in *Alabama* is evident. His brother, William, a Pennsylvania Superior Court judge, was a member of the Court of Alabama Claims, and we know from Porter's biographers that he took great interest in those claims and their resolution by the Treaty of Washington with Great Britain in 1871.[13] At the dedication of Grant's Tomb in 1897, Porter cited the *Alabama* settlement as one of Grant's achievements.[14]

Porter's interest in naval affairs, despite his being an army man, can be further discerned from a variety of other incidents and sources. He often spoke at events and dinners honoring the navy and naval personnel, including a dinner at Delmonico's for Theodore Roosevelt in 1887 at which Porter toasted "the army and navy" and a dinner in 1893 for Admiral Hopkins and officers of the British naval fleet. He was on the Naval Parade Committee that organized the massive Columbus Day parade in New York to celebrate the four hundredth anniversary of Columbus's discovery of America. In January 1897, before his ambassadorial appointment, he helped establish, and was elected first president of, the National Defense Association, a civilian group whose goals, according to the *New York Times,* read like "an agenda for both the War and Navy Departments," including "protection of America's coasts, establishing more fortifications and coastal defenses, assisting the Navy reserve program, and pressing Congress to appropriate money to support those objectives."[15]

Porter was also a very public promoter of Revolutionary War commemoration. He belonged to the Sons of the American Revolution and served for a time as its president general. The group's explicit goals included promotion of research about the Revolution; acquisition and preservation of records of individual service in the war, including documents, relics, and landmarks; marking the scenes of Revolutionary achievement by appropriate memorials; and celebrating the anniversaries of key Revolutionary events.[16] Porter attended, and frequently spoke at, dinners and events sponsored by the group and its counterpart, the Daughters of the American Revolution. Not infrequently, the Continental navy and John Paul Jones were discussed at these events. For example, at an anniversary dinner celebrating the Boston Tea Party, at which Porter gave a speech titled "The Teachings of the American Revolution," Porter also heard Secretary of the Navy Hilary Herbert recount Paul Jones's exploits in the North

Sea.[17] At another Sons banquet Porter attended, honoring Rear Admiral Bancroft Gerardi, Chauncey Depew, one of Porter's best friends, compared Gerardi's heroism and naval genius to that of Paul Jones.[18] Shortly after becoming ambassador to France, Porter established a French branch of the Sons of the American Revolution.

Porter was also a fierce promoter of American-flag reverence, a common theme of patriotic fervor in the early 1890s that was frequently linked to Jones because of the key role he played in obtaining early recognition of the flag. Betsy Ross's grandson, for example, sent a letter to the *New York Tribune* in 1893 that was featured by that journal under the title "First United States Flag: Story of Its Making and of the Flag Used by Paul Jones." The so-called John Paul Jones flag (the original American flag under which Jones sailed with the authority of Congress) was unfurled at the Chicago World's Fair on July 4, 1893, to great fanfare and before huge crowds. Porter's own flag enthusiasm was on display a year later, at Dobbs Ferry, New York, at the laying of a cornerstone for a monument honoring the spot where Rochambeau's forces joined Washington's on the march to Yorktown and where Washington planned the Yorktown campaign. Porter gave an address at the ceremony in which he said that the American flag should "float perpetually over every public building and every schoolhouse in the land" and "never be hauled down." He said the country's "rallying cry" should be: "If any man attempts to haul down the American flag, shoot him on the spot."[19] On July 4, 1901, Porter supervised the flying from the Eiffel Tower of the largest American flag ever made.[20] Although he never (to this author's knowledge) mentioned Paul Jones explicitly in his flag orations, Porter must have been aware of the connection.

As the Dobbs Ferry cornerstone laying also illustrates, Porter was a dedicated monuments man; he believed passionately that heroes like Grant should be commemorated and remembered and that one important way of sustaining their memory was to erect a monument in their honor. His deep involvement with Grant's Tomb (called Grant's Monument at the time), from conception to financing to dedication, was a testament to this belief. He must have been aware that Jones was a worthy candidate for such honor as well; Jones's was one of eighteen names, including Grant's and Lincoln's, that had been put to Congress in 1896 for funds to erect a monument.[21]

None of the above "explains" Porter's decision to search for Paul Jones's grave. But it constitutes abundant "circumstantial" evidence that his predisposition was well suited to such an undertaking.

The Search Begins

From time to time, the U.S. legation in Paris received inquiries from the public about Paul Jones. They received several such inquires in the fall of 1898, probably incited by Dewey's decisive victory over the Spanish Navy at Manila Bay earlier that year. These included a letter dated November 25 from Charles Landis, congressman from Indiana and brother of future baseball commissioner Kenesaw Mountain Landis, addressed to his fellow Hoosier at the embassy Consul General J. K. Gowdy. Landis wanted to know where John Paul Jones was buried. Gowdy did some research and then responded to Landis on January 2, 1899. "There are in the catacombs bones representing six million people. After all the research I have made I very much fear that the remains of John Paul Jones lie in the Catacombs, but have learned nothing positive to that effect. I am still trying to get some information, if possible, and if I succeed will write you at once. I learned from his biography that 'his remains were placed in a leaden coffin, for the convenience of their removal in case the United States should ever claim them for burial,' but unfortunately our Government never did so."[22]

In June Henry Vignaud, the embassy's first attaché, also received an inquiry about Jones's grave. This time the question came from the secretary of state, John Hay. President McKinley had gotten a letter from a Civil War veteran (now a lawyer) in western New York, asking the president to initiate a search for Jones's grave in Paris in order that his remains, if identified, "may be brought home" or, at the least, "the spot where he was laid to rest may be so designated so that on the next Memorial Day loving hands can cover it with flowers." The correspondent speculated that Jones may have been buried in the same cemetery as Lafayette. McKinley forwarded the request to Hay, who forwarded it to Vignaud. Vignaud replied that he did not know where the grave was, but for sure it was not in the same cemetery with Lafayette.[23]

At this point (June 1899), Ambassador Porter became involved. He knew both Hay and McKinley well. Perhaps he calculated that if the president and the secretary of state were interested in Jones's grave, he should be too. Possibly Gowdy and Vignaud had briefed him on earlier inquiries they had received and alerted him to the growing interest in the topic. Maybe, just as he said afterward, in the magazine article quoted above, he felt a deep sense of humiliation that America's "first . . . naval hero had been lying for more than a century in an unknown and forgotten grave." There was, in any event (as we cataloged earlier), much in Porter's temperament and background to predispose him in favor of wanting to find the lost grave of a hero and to repatriate the remains. Porter resolved to "undertake personally a systematic and exhaustive search for the body." He organized an investigative team, headed by embassy second secretary Colonel Arthur Bailly-Blanchard, and committed a substantial sum from his personal finances to fund the search. His team included, at the suggestion of embassy naval attaché Lieutenant William Sims, a well-regarded French antiquarian named Albert de Ricaudy, who was much in the news at the time because he had recently concluded, successfully, a similar search for the remains of Robert-Jacques Turgot, noted French economist and comptroller general of finance from 1774 to 1776.

Porter began his search by trying to verify the city, date, and cemetery where Paul Jones was buried. In an age when hundreds of eighteenth- and nineteenth-century newspapers, journals, and government documents have been scanned into databases that can be easily accessed by keyword searches on a computer done from the researcher's desk, it may be hard to imagine the difficulty of such an undertaking at the time Porter was doing his investigation. Even the "consensus" about these things identified at the end of the prior chapter—or, rather, the memory of such consensus—would have been lost in the intervening half century and therefore be difficult to reconstruct. Porter and his investigative team were thorough. They read all of the writings about Paul Jones that they could obtain, including official documents.[24] As leads developed, they pursued them in numerous archives and libraries, both public and private. By way of illustration, one of the key clues eventually connecting Jones to the Saint Louis cemetery apparently came from a chance finding in the archives of the Church of the Oratory in Paris. It involved the discovery of a voluminous correspondence of the cemetery's gatekeeper with the Ministry of Foreign Affairs, the municipality of Paris, and the city's Protestant Consistory, seeking (unsuccessfully, as it turned out) payment of back salary.[25] The research work was summarized, although not cataloged, in a report that Porter submitted to President Roosevelt.[26]

It seemed clear enough from the available evidence that Jones had been buried somewhere in Paris (the shipmaster's sighting in Cronstadt notwithstanding). However, there was one correspondent of Porter, who had lived in Scotland as a child, who insisted he had seen John Paul's gravestone in the Kirkbean churchyard, near Dumfries. Porter, with his customary thoroughness, wrote the rector of the Kirkbean church to inquire. The rector wrote back that the stone there was that of the father, John Paul Sr., not of the admiral, and that it had been erected for his father by John Paul Jr.—in other words, the marker Alexander Pinkham had visited and described during his 1831 walking tour of Scotland. Porter was satisfied that Paris, and only Paris, was the venue to be searched.[27] (Apparently, the shipmaster's sighting at Cronstadt had disappeared from public memory; Porter seems not to have been aware of it.) There was some disagreement about the date. Sherburne, even in the second (1851) edition of his biography, stated that the date of death was September 12. There were also stories that Jones had not been buried right away; rather, his body was stored temporarily—at least several weeks, perhaps years—and then thrown in a potter's field.[28] All of the available documentary evidence, however (contemporaneous journal accounts, the National Assembly edicts, Colonel Blackden's published letter to the heirs about the circumstances of Jones's death), pointed clearly to July 18, 1792, as the date of death and July 20 as the date of burial. Porter would eventually confirm the dates when he found a copy of Jones's death certificate.

The Cemetery

Verifying the cemetery was an altogether different, and more complicated, undertaking than verifying the city or dates of death and burial. There were several candidates, multiple theories, and much less hard evidence. Popular belief had it that Jones was buried at Père Lachaise. This was what James Fenimore Cooper initially thought, before Janette Taylor corrected him. It was apparently what Colonel Sherburne thought, if what he said in *Pencilings* is to be believed. It is certainly what the famous French novelist Alexandre Dumas père said in his widely read *Capitaine Paul.* And it is what Michaud's authoritative *Biographie universelle* (2nd ed.), published in 1858, said. There was a fatal flaw, though, in this theory: Père Lachaise was not opened until 1804, twelve years after Jones's death.

A few thought Jones was buried at Picpus, where Lafayette and his wife were interred. But this was more farfetched than Père Lachaise. Picpus was owned by the Catholics (many of those guillotined during the Terror were buried there, including the Carmelite nuns immortalized in Poulenc's opera). Jones, a Protestant, could not have been buried there.

The earlier fitful research of Gowdy and Vignaud did not advance the search. Gowdy's discovery from the biographies that Jones was evidently buried in a lead casket would become important, but only later, after the cemetery was identified. None of the biographers named Saint Louis cemetery as Jones's place of burial. All of the credible evidence, though, suggested that Jones was buried in a cemetery for foreign Protestants.[29] However, before Ricaudy and Porter could say which one, there was some anti-Protestant history to sort through. In 1620, several years after revocation of the Edict of Nantes, Louis XIV had issued a decree prohibiting the burial of Protestants anywhere in France, whether native or foreign. Thereafter, Protestants had to be buried secretly, in cellars or on private land belonging to the embassies of Protestant countries such as England, Holland, and Sweden or in Catholic cemeteries, with the complicity of the gatekeepers of those cemeteries.[30] Finally, in 1720, responding to lobbying by the Dutch ambassador to France, it was decreed that a place should be set aside for the burial of foreign Protestants. Saint Martin's cemetery was established for that purpose, in the suburbs, near Saint Martin's gate. Saint Martin's cemetery might, therefore, have been a prime candidate as the site of Jones's burial—except that it had been closed in 1762.

Normally, there would exist a registered certificate of burial for the deceased. There had been such a certificate for Jones, but the register, together with other municipal archives, was in an annex of the Hôtel de Ville (the Municipal Building), on Victoria Avenue. In May 1871, the Commune set fire to this and other government buildings, destroying all of the records contained therein.[31]

There was one copy of Jones's burial certificate in existence, made and published by the French antiquary Charles Read in 1859 in a French magazine called *La Correspondance Littéraire.* Indeed, there were even English translations, published by *Russell's Magazine* in 1859 and *Atlantic Monthly* in 1890.[32] Neither Ricaudy nor Porter knew about the Read copy of the burial certificate, or the translations, when they began their search. They eventually found them.

The burial certificate did not, in so many words, identify the Saint Louis cemetery by name, but it did say that John Paul Jones was buried July 20,

1792, in "*the* cemetery for foreign Protestants" (emphasis added), the article *the* strongly implying there was only one such cemetery in existence at the time. (The commentary accompanying the *Russell's* translation, though not the *Atlantic Monthly* one, even stated that "the" cemetery for foreign Protestants was located "in the street Hôpital St. Louis"—a significant further clue.) Porter also got hold of a 1781 decree not only reconfirming establishment of the Saint Martin cemetery in 1720 but also revealing it was replaced by Saint Louis cemetery in 1762 when Saint Martin closed; there was even continuity of caretakers between the two cemeteries—a "Corroy" was custodian of both cemeteries, and the position had passed from father to son. Thus, it became relatively clear that the Saint Louis cemetery was the only cemetery for foreign Protestants in existence in 1792. Moreover, Porter sensibly inferred that, even if there had been at the time more than one cemetery for foreign Protestants, M. Simonneau, the commissary who had formal responsibility for burying foreign Protestants in his section of Paris (hence Blackden's appeal to him for permission to bury Jones) and who had personally paid for the burial, would have made sure Jones was buried in the most prominent of the Protestant cemeteries, that is, the Saint Louis cemetery.[33]

In fact, Porter's exhaustive research did not turn up any cemetery for foreign Protestants existing at the time of Jones's death other than the Saint Louis. Porter also learned that M. Marron, the preacher who had reportedly presided at Jones's funeral, was pastor of a church called the Church of Saint Louis and that the parishioners at that church were always buried at Saint Louis. He even found Marron's church minute book—but the four pages that would have covered the date of Jones's funeral had been torn out! Apparently, a M. Coquerel, also pastor at that church, was an enthusiastic collector of papers relating to Protestantism in Paris; upon his death, his heirs had sold the four missing pages to the Society of the History of Protestantism. Porter found the four pages in the society's library. They were pertinent, confirming Marron's role in Jones's funeral (as reported by Blackden and others).[34]

Charles Read, in his 1859 article, stated categorically his conviction that "the cemetery for foreign Protestants" referenced in Jones's burial certificate was the Saint Louis cemetery, long since abandoned, situated at rue L'Hôpital Saint Louis, now Granges-aux-Belles, and that Paul Jones was buried there. He reaffirmed this in his 1887 article. Porter would conclude the same with equal conviction: "After . . . researches in every possible quarter that could furnish information on the subject, the fact was clearly and incontestably established that the Saint Louis Cemetery was the only burial ground in Paris for foreign Protestants at the time of Paul Jones's death; that he was not interred in any other cemetery; and that Charles Read was perfectly correct in his opinion that the Admiral had positively been buried in the cemetery of Saint Louis."[35]

One oddity, never explained, is that Consul General Gowdy seems to have been engaged in a parallel identical search for Jones's grave at precisely the same time that Porter and Colonel Bailly-Blanchard were engaged in theirs. Gowdy described his search to an interviewer in 1905.

> I . . . had long cherished a desire to find the coffin of the famous hero, and I had been working on it prior to the investigations set on foot by Gen. Horace Porter [this, presumably, a reference to the research Gowdy did as outlined in his letter to Congressman Landis dated January 2, 1899]. I hired the services of two bright men to prosecute the search but each worked independently and neither knew of the other's employment.
>
> One day one of my agents came to me with a beaming face and said that at last his labors had been rewarded and that he had found the grave beyond all doubt. And sure enough he had, but not quite soon enough to win the glory, for only the day before one of Ambassador Porter's employees had made the identical discovery.[36]

What, exactly, was going on? Was Gowdy acting with Porter's knowledge? Had Porter set up a Team B? Or was Gowdy acting on his own, perhaps out of jealousy or resentment that Porter had deputized Colonel Bailly-Blanchard to run the search, not Gowdy? Gowdy would describe his parallel search, in similar terms, in another letter to Landis several years later. He then assured Landis (was he merely being defensive?) that "General Porter and myself always worked in perfect harmony in everything. To General Porter is due the credit of finding the body of the greatest Naval Hero of his day, John Paul Jones."[37]

Condition of the Site

Porter visited the site of the abandoned cemetery, in what he called "an uninviting section in the northeast corner of Paris," at the corner of rue Granges-aux-Belles and rue des Écluses Saint Martin. As it turned out, there was an old map of Paris, by Verniquet in 1791, that precisely marked the spot. The area was now known (1899) as "le Combat" (the Combat Zone), because it had been a popular venue for dog- and cockfights. It was covered with buildings "of an inferior class," among them a laundry, apartment house, stable, and barn. Gradually, Porter pieced together a description of the cemetery and a history of the property since Jones's burial there in 1792. He was aided by documents discovered in the archives of the prefecture of the Seine that provided an exact plan and description of the cemetery.[38]

The Saint Louis cemetery had consisted of two parts: a courtyard, 130 by 90 feet, fronting on rue des Écluses Saint Martin, where the entrance was located, and a larger garden with fruit trees in the rear, 120 by 130 feet, fronting on rue Granges-aux-Belles. The garden, divided by crosswalks into four sections, was 8 feet below the courtyard, accessible by a staircase. It was there in the garden that foreign Protestants were buried. (Beginning in 1777, native Protestants could be buried in the courtyard.) A wall 6 to 9 feet high had surrounded the cemetery.[39]

The cemetery was officially closed early in 1793—not, though, before a Paris mob, three weeks after Jones's death, attacked the Tuileries Palace and killed a number of Swiss guards trying to protect the king and queen. The guards were buried at Saint Louis in a common grave. The custodian, who leased the property after it closed, and then the new owner (the developer), who bought it from the government in 1796, continued to allow some burials there until 1805.[40] In all, about five hundred bodies were interred there, Jones's being among the last one hundred.[41]

For a while after the cemetery closed, the property was used as a garden, the "moldering bodies of the dead fertilizing its vegetables." Still later it became a dump. Dogs and horses were buried there, and its soil was "soaked with polluted waters from undrained laundries." A contractor for removing night soil stored his carts there. Eventually, several buildings were constructed, as mentioned above.

Whether Jones Was Moved

Porter's first task after locating the site of the former Saint Louis cemetery and confirming that Jones had indeed been buried there was to verify that the remains of the persons buried there had not been removed. The reader will recall the consensus that emerged following Sherburne's failed attempt to find the grave in 1851: that Jones had been buried in a cemetery for foreign Protestants, but that his bones (along with those of the others buried there) were later removed to the Catacombs and mingled with the ashes and bones of other countless dead. (This had been Consul General Gowdy's initial conclusion.) The theory was plausible. By the middle of the eighteenth century, Paris's principal graveyard—the Cemetery of the Innocents adjacent to Les Halles (the city's largest market)—had become a source of pestilence and infection. In 1785 the government closed the Innocents and ordered that its contents be transferred to a series of limestone quarries that undergirded the city, these quarries being the remnants of the mines from which the stones that built Paris were extracted. In 1788 it was further decreed that the remains of all other Paris cemeteries should be removed to the quarries as well (that is, to the Catacombs of Paris, as the quarries came to be called). These removals continued until 1814.

The issue was whether the Saint Louis cemetery had been one of those subject to the removal decree of 1788. It was not. Although it was located within the boundaries of the city of Paris at the end of the nineteenth century when Porter made his search, it had been a suburban venue in 1788 when the removal decree—applicable only to the city of Paris—was issued. Porter was also able to verify, from the detailed registers of the Catacombs, that none of the bodies buried at Saint Louis had ever been transferred to the Catacombs.

There remained the question of whether bodies might have been removed to somewhere else. Further research indicated that this had happened only once. The remains of a Lady Alexander Grant had been exhumed and sent to England in 1803, with the permission of the authorities. There was no record of any other removal.[42]

There was one other possibility to consider: that an unauthorized exhumation had occurred. It was alleged by some that the Revolution's armies had dug up lead caskets like Jones's and converted them to bullets. Porter did not think this likely. "The French," he said, "have a profound respect for the dead and the sacredness of places of burial"; they would not have done such a thing. Moreover, there were plenty of lead objects in public places more easily accessible for taking—statues, busts, water pipes—yet none of these had been touched. Finally, the cost of digging up a lead casket was more than the price of buying bullets. In sum, the lead-caskets-for-bullets theory was highly improbable.

Satisfied that Jones's remains must still be there, under the buildings on the land of the former Saint Louis cemetery, Porter now faced the challenge of negotiating with the current owners for the right to excavate.

Negotiations

One of the curiosities of Porter's otherwise thorough report of his search is that it makes no mention of M. Albert de Ricaudy, the eminent Paris antiquarian and editor of *L'Echo du Public* Porter retained who conducted much of the actual research just described and who should be credited with the key findings establishing Saint Louis as the cemetery where Jones was buried. There was a reason for this omission, and it was not that Porter wanted to steal credit for himself. (In fact, in a preliminary report that he sent Secretary of State Hay on November 9, 1899, Porter did fully credit Ricaudy.)[43] The problem was that Ricaudy went public with his findings behind Porter's back. Possibly Ricaudy was receiving supplemental payments from the *New York Tribune;* a *Tribune* reporter accompanied him during part of his work. Or maybe he just wanted fame. Ricaudy published a short summary of his findings on October 28, 1899, in his own journal, *L'Echo du Public,* and gave a long interview about his work and findings to the *New York Tribune* reporter. The *Tribune* published the story (datelined Paris, October 28) on November 12, 1899. The unwanted publicity spurred rumors of fantastic prices that Porter and his government would pay for access to the property, thereby pricing the project out of reach and sabotaging Porter's efforts to secure rights from the current owners to dig at the site of the former cemetery. Porter was furious. He masked his fury in the report—and punished Ricaudy by not mentioning his name—but his anger is apparent: "I was about to open negotiations quietly with the proprietors and tenants who occupied the property with a view to purchasing the right to enter upon the premises and make the necessary excavations in order to explore thoroughly the cemetery, when unfortunately the news of this intention became publicly known through the indiscretion of persons who had been consulted on the subject."[44]

There was more. Ricaudy, it turned out, had gone and acquired from the current owner and tenants an option, good for two years, to buy the property himself! Porter learned this when he set about trying to negotiate access—and found himself having to negotiate with Ricaudy.[45] Thus, not only was Ricaudy responsible for the exorbitant pricing, but he also stood to benefit from any deal that Porter made. He had, though, been too clever by half. Porter suspended negotiations, "to let the excitement subside" and Ricaudy's two-year option lapse. It would be another five years before he resumed them.[46]

The five-year hiatus was not entirely quiet. To begin with, Porter refused to pay Ricaudy, resulting in Ricaudy filing a claim against the United States.[47] There was also confusion about whether anything identifiable of Jones would be left to find, wooden coffins being known to deteriorate rapidly; somehow, it was lost sight of that Jones had been buried in a lead casket. A low-intensity debate ensued about whether the better course was to excavate the site in the hope of finding remains and returning them to America or level it and turn it into a memorial park honoring Jones.[48] In the fall of 1903, Consul General Gowdy offered a one-thousand-dollar reward "to any one who will find his grave. The registers of most of the cemeteries were destroyed during the Commune. Hence the difficulty." He challenged the United States to supplement his reward.[49] But then he added, "Our investigations thus far lead us to believe that Paul Jones is buried in a small cemetery in the Rue Ecluse St. Martin, near the St. Louis Hospital. The cemetery is now built over with small cottages."[50]

At about the same time that Gowdy was offering his reward, a reader of the *New York Herald* complained in a letter to the editor that Jones's memory had been shamefully neglected. The U.S. government, he wrote, had been aware of the grave's exact location in Paris for several years but had "never taken any action toward having his ashes brought to this country and a suitable monument erected in his honor." The letter came to the attention of Secretary of the Navy William Moody, various patriotic organizations began lobbying the secretary to acquire the Paris land containing Jones's remains and to search there for them, and on October 9, 1903, President Roosevelt wrote to Ambassador Porter, asking him for a status report and recommendation. Porter replied on October 20, detailing what had transpired since his last report to Secretary Hay in 1899. He confirmed that the chances were "more than even" that Jones was buried in a lead coffin at the site of the former Saint Louis cemetery and that it was unlikely the coffin had ever been moved. He estimated it would cost $180,000 to $200,000 to buy the property, plus an additional "considerable sum" to remove buildings and make excavations—a "large sum [for] a project based entirely upon conjectures, though backed by strong circumstantial evidence." There was speculation in the press that Moody would seek an appropriation from Congress for the project, but nothing happened.[51]

Porter, though, did restart the project, undertaking what he called "long and tedious negotiations" with the owner and tenants of the former cemetery site (by this time, Ricaudy was out of the picture) before finally securing options from them in writing that allowed Porter to enter the premises for three months and do excavations. In exchange for the right to explore the abandoned cemetery by means of subterranean galleries to be dug under the buildings, Porter promised, in addition to payments, to repair any damage to buildings, to indemnify any victims of disease caused by "foul emanations from the disturbed soil," and to restore the property to its original condition when the project was done. Porter reported the result of his successful negotiations to Secretary Hay, President Roosevelt sought a modest appropriation from Congress ($35,000) to fund the excavation, but Congress balked, and so Porter undertook the excavation using his personal funds.[52]

The Excavation

The excavation began on February 3, 1905. It was conducted by M. Paul Weiss, chief engineer of the Municipal Department of Paris. Initially, the biggest challenge was the looseness of the soil. The eight-foot drop from the cemetery's courtyard to its garden had long since been leveled with landfill sufficiently compact to support the buildings constructed upon it but not firm enough to support the shafts and galleries to be dug. They had to be lined and buttressed by heavy timbers. In addition, drainage was bad, and there was much water to contend with. Walls of one building were badly damaged. Further, as Porter would not so delicately describe it, "Slime, mud, and mephitic odors were encountered, and long red worms appeared in abundance."[53]

The plan called for sinking five shafts at strategic locations, to a depth of approximately eighteen feet, and then to construct "galleries" (tunnels) outward from the shafts, in every direction, from which "soundings" could be taken. "Soundings" meant shoving long iron rods, fabricated for the purpose, from one gallery to another, so as to strike (sound) any lead coffin between them, thereby determining the location of all lead coffins buried at the site. Both day crews and night crews were employed. It was proved from the first shaft dug that the remains in the cemetery had never before been disturbed and that there were likely only a few lead coffins there, because skeletons were systematically encountered lying about a foot apart, often in two layers, sometimes in three. This meant, as a previously discovered inspection report of the cemetery had implied, that most of the dead buried at Saint Louis were poor and that they had been interred in communal trenches rather than individual graves. It also meant there would not be many lead coffins to be found, as they were used only by affluent families who could afford them. (There would not be many wooden coffins either, as they would have deteriorated.)[54]

The first quadrant searched, the one to the front right (northeast) of what would have been the original cemetery entrance, contained a mass of skeletons, in three layers, with no order to them: some lying faceup, others on their sides, some lengthwise, others crosswise. These were, evidently, the remains of the Swiss guards, hurriedly tossed from carts, without coffins, into a mass grave, as depicted in a contemporary drawing by Béricourt.[55]

On February 22 a lead coffin—the first one—was discovered under the former courtyard. It was not well preserved. The outer wooden coffin in which it had been encased was almost gone, and the head of the lead coffin itself had been severed by some earlier violent blow that also separated the skull within from the rest of the skeleton. It was surmised that a barrel had been sunk in the ground (one was found nearby the coffin) to drain water from the courtyard and that during excavation to install the barrel, the coffin had been struck and broken. There was a copper identification plate on the lid of the coffin—so brittle that part of it crumbled when it was picked up. The inscription could not be read because of corrosion. Porter engaged a local firm that specialized in restoration of old objects to try to recover the inscription. They succeeded. The coffin contained the remains of one M. E. Anglois (presumably an Englishman, identified only by his initials), died May 20, 1790. Not Jones.[56]

A second lead coffin was discovered on March 23 and a third on March 31, both in the southwest quadrant near the west wall and close to the former walkway that divided north from south. Each of the two lead coffins, like the first one, was shaped like a mummy coffin (typical for the time), "widening from feet to shoulders with [a] small round top to fit the head." The inscription plate on the former coffin was easy to read: Richard Hay,

Esq., died January 29, 1785. There was no inscription plate on the latter, but it was "much superior in solidity and workmanship to the others." Some fragments of the wooden coffin in which it had been placed were still on the side, near the feet; otherwise, the wooden container coffin had totally deteriorated or been removed. An attempt was made to open this third lead coffin, but the foul odors in the gallery were so overpowering that the attempt was postponed until the gallery could be linked to another for ventilation. This was done, and coffin number 3 was then opened on April 7—though not without difficulty: the lid was so firmly soldered, it could not be easily pried off.

Coffin number 3, when opened, smelled of alcohol, but the alcohol had mostly evaporated, apparently through a pick hole in the lid and a crack near the foot of the coffin. Evaporation, though, had been slow, impeded by the hard black earth that covered the holes, so the contents were still well preserved. The body, covered with a winding sheet, was firmly packed with hay and straw. It measured, roughly, the presumed height of Paul Jones. Porter had provided each member of the search team with copies of Jones's congressional medal, showing his bust in profile, the copies having been struck from the original mint that Porter found in Paris.

> Half a dozen candles were placed near the head of the coffin, and the winding sheet was removed from the head and chest, exposing the face. To our intense surprise, the body was marvelously well-preserved, all the flesh remaining intact, very slightly shrunken, and of a grayish brown or tan color. The surface of the body and the linen were moist. The face presented quite a natural appearance, except that the cartilaginous portion of the nose had been bent over toward the right side, pressed down, and disfigured by its too close proximity to the lid of the coffin. Upon placing a medal near the face, comparing the other features and recognizing the peculiar characteristics—the broad forehead, contour of brow, appearance of the hair, high cheek bones, prominently arched eye orbits, and other points of resemblance—we instinctively exclaimed, "Paul Jones!" and all those who were gathered about the coffin removed their hats.[57]

Those gathered about the coffin were, besides Porter (he had left standing instructions with the crew that whenever a lead coffin was discovered, he should be notified at once so he could come and personally supervise the search for an inscription plate and otherwise oversee the identification effort), Colonel Bailly-Blanchard (second secretary at the embassy who was Porter's immediate deputy on the project), M. Weiss, M. Géninet (the superintendent of the work), the foreman, and several workmen. The delay between the coffin discovery and the opening had allowed time for a full complement of hatted witnesses to assemble.

Why the coffin holes, the searchers asked, and why no inscription plate? The answer to both questions seemed to lie with a corpse found immediately above the lead coffin: the digger of the upper grave had struck the lower coffin with his ax, making a pick hole in the lid, and then had made off with the inscription plate as a relic or because of its intrinsic value. Alternatively, perhaps there had not been an inscription plate. The violence of the French Revolution was escalating just as Jones died. He was buried only two days after his death. It may have been the case that no engraver could be found at that time. (The crack at the bottom of the coffin was probably caused by the weight of accumulated dirt at that spot after the wooden coffin encasing the lead one had rotted away.)

The lead coffin with what were thought to be the remains of John Paul Jones was transferred the next night, quietly, to a laboratory at the École de Médicine, where two well-regarded professors of anthropology were engaged to examine the body further to determine if it was really Jones. They pronounced that the corpse was Jones. (The forensics will be discussed in the next chapter.) In the meantime, the digging and soundings at the former cemetery site continued. On April 8, a fourth lead coffin was found bearing the inscription Georges Maidison, English gentleman and secretary to the British ambassador, died August 27, 1873, age thirty-six years. A fifth lead coffin—the last found—was discovered April 18. It did not have an inscription plate. However, it contained the skeleton of a man well over six feet tall, much taller than John Paul Jones. "There were discovered in all," summarized Porter, "five leaden coffins in the cemetery. Four having been easily identified, reasoning upon the principle of elimination led to the conclusion that the other must be the coffin sought."[58]

Spreading the News

Porter cabled the State Department on April 14, before the fifth lead coffin was discovered, that he had found Jones's remains. The department made Porter's cable public, and newspapers across the country began reporting the find, mostly in celebratory terms. Congratulations poured in to Porter. On the seventeenth, Secretary Francis Loomis cabled back that the government would send a naval squadron sometime in June to bring back the remains. Porter arranged for the body to be put back in the original coffin and encased in a second casket that could be hermetically sealed and transported to America. To be more precise, a larger second lead casket was procured and lined with a bed of sawdust. The original coffin lid was placed in the bottom and next to it the original casket. The body was treated with preservatives and put back in the original casket on top of the original winding sheet, oiled silk, and cotton. Certain relics were put in the casket as well, including a glass jar with specimens of the hay and straw that had constituted the original packing. The lid of the second casket, with a large glass plate cut in it to permit viewing, was then soldered shut. This second casket was placed in a third coffin made of oak. The outer oak coffin had eight silver handles and a lid secured by sixteen silver screws.

On April 20, the coffin was taken from the École de Médicine to the American Church of the Trinity on avenue de l'Alma and covered with an American flag. Ambassador Porter, First Secretary Vignaud, Second Secretary Bailly-Blanchard, Consul General Gowdy, and chief engineer Weiss witnessed the transfer. The coffin remained at the church until July 6, when it was turned over to Admiral Sigsbee, amid much pomp, as described in chapter 1.

Porter was not quite finished. For some time, he had wanted to visit the rooms at number 42 rue de Tournon, where Jones died, but the addresses on that street had changed, and it was no longer clear whether the building still existed and, if so, which one it was. This time Porter engaged the services of M. Taxil, chief surveyor of the city of Paris. M. Taxil determined that number 42 was now number 19. The notary who drew up Jones's last will and testament had said in the preamble of the document that Jones's apartment was on the "first floor above the entresol" (mezzanine), that is, on the third floor; number 19 was the only building on the street with a mezzanine.[59]

Porter and Colonel Bailly-Blanchard visited number 42 (now number 19) on July 4, 1905. The street, once fashionable, was still home to several "persons of distinction." Porter was charmed by a sign on the ground floor:

"Lessons in fencing, boxing, and the use of the singlestick." He wrote, "This proffered instruction in the several arts of fighting in the house in which Paul Jones resided, coupled with the fact that the underground station close to the cemetery where his body reposed is called 'Combat,' looks as if fate had determined that he should everywhere be identified with signs of conflict and struggle, whether in life or in death."[60]

Cottage on the Arbigland Estate, parish of Kirkbean, Scotland, where John Paul Jones was born July 6, 1747, and spent his early childhood. The slightly taller section at the back, overlooking Solway Firth, was added as part of Alexander Pinkham's 1830s restoration. NH 48634 courtesy of the Naval History & Heritage Command.

Rue de Tournon, Paris, in 1906. Luxembourg Palace is visible at the end of the street. Jones rented an apartment at number 42 (now number 19) during the last years of his life (building at left, third level, front windows on the near side of the balustrade). He died there on July 18, 1792, age forty-five.

Courtesy of HathiTrust, from Commission du Vieux Paris, *Communications relatives à la découverte et à l'identification des restes de l'admiral Paul Jones* (Paris: Impr. Municipale, 1906). Digitized by Google.

Engraving depicting Jones as a pirate, probably first published in England in the late 1770s or 1780s.

NH 48746 courtesy of the Naval History & Heritage Command.

Right profile of a bust of Jones by the French sculptor Jean-Antoine Houdon, modeled in 1780. Thomas Jefferson, like others who knew Jones well, called the bust "an excellent likeness."

NH 48628 courtesy of the Naval History & Heritage Command.

Frontispiece and title page of Robert Charles Sands's *Life and Correspondence of John Paul Jones* (1830), one of the first serious biographies of Jones, based on letters and manuscripts belonging to Jones's niece Janette Taylor, retrieved from Paris by her mother during the French Revolution.
Philadelphia Rare Books and Manuscripts Co. (PRB&M).

Alexander Pinkham, depicted here in a painting by William Slain, was an American naval officer who visited the ruins of Jones's birth cottage in 1831, was appalled by its condition, and funded its restoration.
Photo courtesy of the Coffin School Trustees, Nantucket.

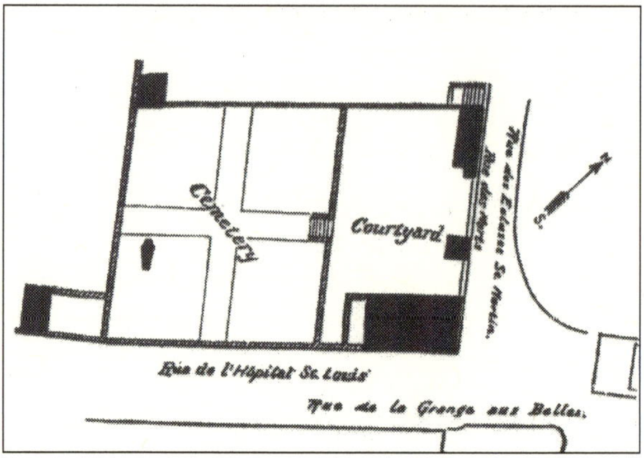

Map of Saint Louis cemetery, where Jones was buried, showing street names from 1792 when Jones was interred and 1905 when the grave site was rediscovered, from *Commemoration at Annapolis* (1907). Buildings in 1905 are shaded dark. The location of the lead coffin believed to be Jones's is marked.

Courtesy of Sons of the American Revolution, South Coast Chapter.

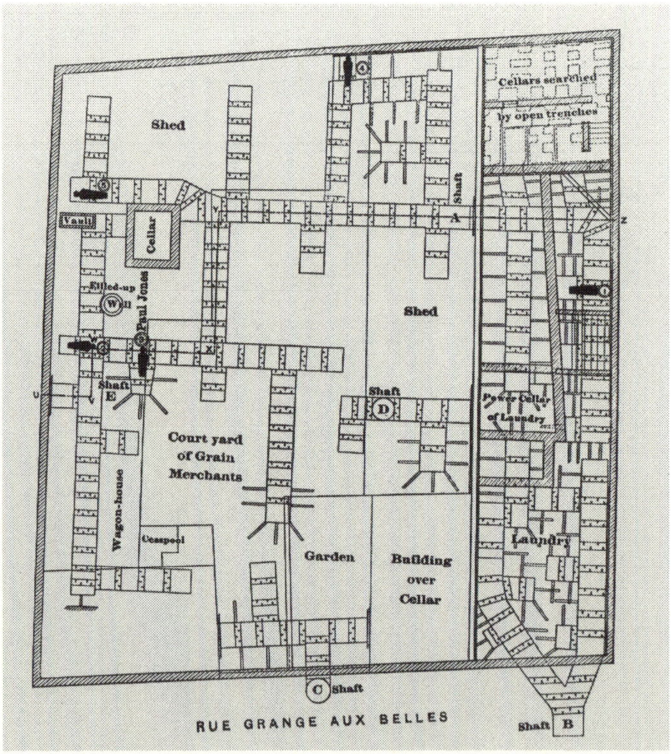

Plan of the shafts sunk and galleries excavated in 1905 under the buildings covering the former Protestant cemetery during the search for Jones's coffin, from *Commemoration at Annapolis* (1907). Black coffins mark the locations of the five lead coffins that were found.

NH 78752 courtesy of the Naval History & Heritage Command.

View of buildings that covered the Saint Louis cemetery site in 1905, seen from rue de la Grange-aux-Belles, with shaft C at left and shaft B at right. The buildings (*left to right*) are the grain merchant, the laundry, and the apartment house.

NH 78742 courtesy of the Naval History & Heritage Command.

Ambassador Porter (*left*) and other dignitaries, underground, at the spot where the lead coffin believed to contain Jones's remains was discovered.

S-021.01 courtesy of the Naval History & Heritage Command.

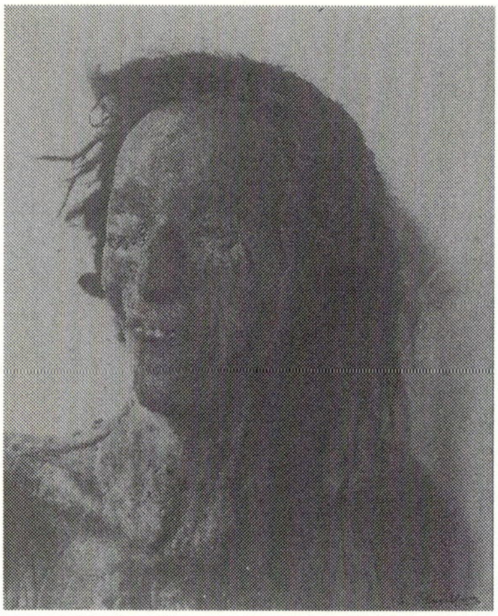

The head of the corpse believed to be Jones, surprisingly well preserved, photographed on April 11, 1905, four days after the coffin was first opened.

Paul Weiss Papers, Special Collections & Archives Department, Nimitz Library, U.S. Naval Academy.

Houdon bust of Jones (*front view*) from the Trocadéro Museum in Paris, used to identify the corpse as that of Jones.

NH 48632 courtesy of Naval History & Heritage Command.

Overlay of photographs of the Houdon bust and the corpse's head, a novel forensic technique at the time, demonstrating a remarkable similarity between the two.

NH 48749 courtesy of Naval History & Heritage Command.

French artillery caisson, bearing the coffin of John Paul Jones through the streets of Paris, July 6, 1905 (from a contemporary French postcard).

Paul Weiss Papers, Special Collections & Archives Department, Nimitz Library, U.S. Naval Academy.

Jones's flag-draped coffin on the afterdeck of the tug *Standish* as it neared Annapolis on July 23, 1905, following transfer of the coffin from the USS *Brooklyn*, the battleship that brought the coffin from France to U.S. waters. An honor guard surrounds the coffin.

NH 48600 courtesy of the Naval History & Heritage Command.

President Roosevelt arriving at the Naval Academy Armory for the commemoration ceremony, April 24, 1906. Courtesy of the Library of Congress, LC-DIG-ppmsca-36234.

Exterior view of the new Naval Academy Armory, 1905, in which the commemoration ceremony was held. Courtesy of the Library of Congress, LC-DIG-det-4a12581.

Speakers stand at the commemoration ceremony, overlooking Jones's casket. *Left to right:* Secretary of the Navy Charles Bonaparte, French ambassador J. J. Jusserand, President Theodore Roosevelt, Maryland governor Edwin Warfield, General Horace Porter, and Naval Academy superintendent Admiral James H. Sands.

Print Collection, Miriam and Ira D. Wallach Division of Art, Prints, and Photographs, New York Public Library, Astor, Lenox, and Tilden Foundations.

Following the ceremony at the armory, Jones's coffin was transferred in a solemn procession to Bancroft Hall, to await completion of the new Naval Academy Chapel and final burial in the crypt beneath the chapel. American and French warships can be seen in the harbor.

NH 65665 courtesy of the Naval History & Heritage Command.

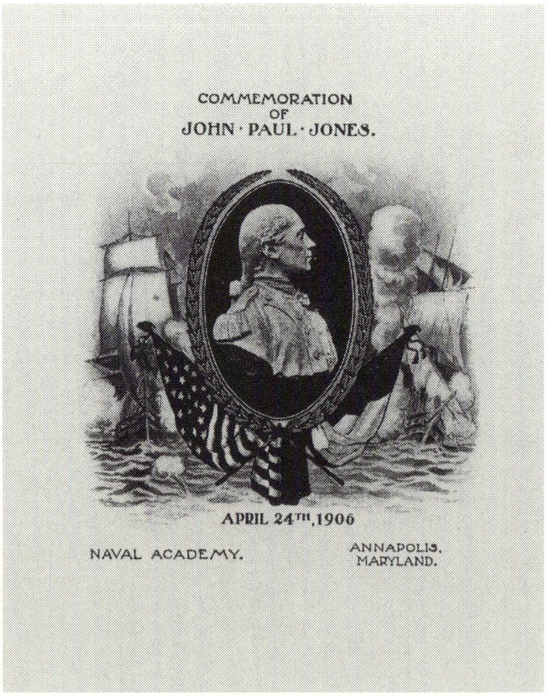

Cover of the commemoration program. The wreath was colored yellow; the American and French flags were colored in their respective red, white, and blue colors.

NH 48646 courtesy of the Naval History & Heritage Command.

President Roosevelt and William Sims on board the presidential yacht *Mayflower* in December 1907, watching the Great White Fleet depart from Hampton Roads on its world cruise. Sims, while U.S. naval attaché in Paris, helped Ambassador Porter search for John Paul Jones. Later, he was a key adviser to Roosevelt on increasing U.S. naval preparedness.

Courtesy of the Library of Congress, LC-DIG-ppmsca-36369.

The Great White Fleet steaming through the Straits of Magellan in February 1908, as depicted in a painting by Henry Reuterdahl (according to the Naval History & Heritage Command, copied during the 1930s from Theodore Roosevelt's autobiography).

NH 41657 courtesy of the Naval History & Heritage Command.

Street in Yokohama, Japan, decorated with paper lanterns and American and Japanese flags in anticipation of the visit of the Great White Fleet, circa mid-October 1908.

NH 106111 courtesy of the Naval History & Heritage Command.

Jones's final resting place, a large crypt beneath the Naval Academy Chapel, his coffin sealed in an extravagant marble sarcophagus resting on bronze dolphins and covered with cast garlands of bronze sea plants, surrounded by eight marble columns.

Courtesy of the Library of Congress, HABS MD,2-ANNA,65/1–22.

USS *John Paul Jones,* an *Arleigh Burke*–class destroyer, said to be the U.S. Navy's most sophisticated and capable warship in the world today. Its motto is "In Harm's Way."

U.S. Navy photo by Mass Communication Specialist 1st Class Jeffrey Ballge, courtesy of NavSource Naval History.

6

WAS IT REALLY JONES?

> There will ever remain a mystery as to who actually was John Paul, and whether the body to whom so much honor has been paid is that of the famous commander of the *Bonhomme Richard.*
>
> —*Atlanta Constitution,* April 23, 1913

THE EUPHORIA FOLLOWING THE NEWS that Jones's remains were found and would be repatriated to America had not yet run its course when questions began surfacing about whether the body was really that of the commodore.[1] We saw in chapter 1 that the subject was much discussed on the train carrying dignitaries from Washington to Annapolis for the commemoration and that the doubting Thomases included many Frenchmen as well as Americans. There were even, it seems, doubters close to the president. Secretary of the Navy Charles Bonaparte reportedly sent an aide to then acting secretary of state Alvey Adee, seeking to have a second autopsy performed on the body in the United States, before the commemoration ceremony. Bonaparte's office was close by Adee's. Adee, in a state of agitation, jumped out of his chair and ran to Bonaparte. "Strange bellowing sounds" were then heard coming from behind closed doors. Later, Bonaparte told his aide that, on further reflection, he had decided "not to have any examination of Jones's body made at this time."[2]

Bonaparte may have had second thoughts about seeking a further autopsy, but that did not mean he did not have his doubts. In response to a reporter's question whether he believed General Porter had really found John Paul Jones's remains, Bonaparte told a story about his student days at Harvard. "Somebody started a subscription," he said, "to erect a monument over the grave of a supposed former Harvard celebrity that presumably had been long neglected. After the money had been subscribed and the monument was well under way, it occurred to some individual of an inquisitive turn to satisfy himself whether, after all, we might not be mistaken. The body was dug up and carried to Prof. Agassiz, who finally identified it as the carcass of a sheep."[3]

The doubters continued to raise questions even after the commemoration and have done so down to the present day. We therefore ask: Was the body really that of John Paul Jones? Formidable experts have weighed in on both sides. Park Benjamin, one of the doubters, framed the issue this way:

1. If you were a juror in a case of willful murder would you bring in a verdict of guilty solely on the proof of the *corpus delicti* here advanced and thereby send the prisoner to execution?
2. If you learned that a relative long since dead, whom no one living could recognize, was interred in a European cemetery, would you solely on the proof of identity here advanced accept an otherwise unknown body, go to the expense of transporting it to this country and bury it in your family plot?[4]

Let us review the evidence.[5]

This much seems unassailable: that Jones died in Paris on July 18, 1792; that his remains were placed in a lead coffin, with the intent to preserve them; that he was buried two days later on July 20, 1892, in the Saint Louis cemetery, one of the last hundred or so of the five hundred persons buried there; that the cemetery was later closed and built over; that Ambassador Porter found its exact location in the Northeast of Paris in 1899; that the remains in the closed cemetery had not in the meantime been removed to the Catacombs; that the only record of any removal was that of a Lady Alexander Grant exhumed and sent to England in 1803; that in the course of excavating the Saint Louis site in 1905, Porter unearthed five lead coffins, three of which bore inscription plates that were not Paul Jones and two of which were without any identifying plate; and that as between the two unidentified coffins, the one Porter believed was Jones's smelled of alcohol and contained a body that was outwardly very well preserved, whereas the other did not smell of alcohol and contained the skeleton of a very tall person.

The Excavation

Could there have been additional lead coffins that Porter did not find? The answer depends on how thoroughly the site was searched. Engineer M. Paul Weiss, in his report of the excavation, says the cemetery "was almost entirely explored; 25 meters of shafts, 245 meters of galleries, 178 meters of soundings were excavated."[6] "Almost entirely" means "not completely." After lead coffin number 3 (the alleged Jones coffin) was discovered on March 31, the workmen continued to dig for several more weeks, while the tunnel leading to coffin number 3 was ventilated, the coffin itself was moved to the School of Medicine, and various forensic investigations of its contents were performed. During this time, lead coffins numbers 4 and 5 were discovered. Work was stopped toward the end of the third week of April, when the forensic investigators reported their conclusion that the corpse in coffin number 3 was that of John Paul Jones. At that point, how much was left to excavate and sound? Weiss does not say. The map of the shafts sunk and the galleries excavated, included with Ambassador Porter's final report, shows that much of the site was indeed excavated and sounded, but not all of it.[7] Therefore, one cannot rule out the possibility that had the excavation work continued, more lead coffins might have been found. That said, the most thoroughly excavated sections of the site—near the northeast wall (where the entrance from the courtyard was located) and the southwest wall (farthest from the courtyard entrance, where coffin number 3 was found)—were the two most likely sections in which to search for a coffin that was among the last one hundred burials, since the earliest burials probably began near the courtyard entrance and worked their way to the southwest or vice versa, either way putting the Jones coffin closer to one of the extremes than in the middle.[8]

The Straw Packing

Coffin number 3 was opened for the first time on April 7, 1905, when it was still at the cemetery. "As soon as the lid was raised," wrote engineer M. Paul Weiss a few weeks later, "the minute precautions that had been taken when the body was placed in the coffin became apparent. The body was packed in hay and straw and appeared ready to be transported a long distance."[9] And not merely "packed," but tightly packed in all the interstices around the body, "so as to render the corpse completely immovable in its coffin."[10] So immovable, in fact, that in order to remove it from the coffin a few days later for the autopsy at the School of Medicine, pincers had to be used.[11] "The sole fact of the careful packing," said Weiss, "was a serious presumption leading to the supposition that one was in the presence of Admiral Jones."[12]

Colonel Blackden had written to Jones's sister several weeks after the funeral that the body of John Paul was put in a lead coffin, "that in case the United States, whom he had so essentially served and with so much honor to himself, should claim his remains, they might be more easily moved."[13] Blackden did not mention any alcohol preservative or straw packing, but both would have served the purpose Blackden gave for using a lead coffin. The tightly packed straw would protect the body from shocks caused, say, by the rolling of a ship transporting it across the sea.[14]

The Houdon Bust

The fact that the corpse in coffin number 3 was so well preserved meant that a visual identification might be possible. But what did Paul Jones look like? We saw in chapter 2 that one of the many honors conferred on Jones following his victory at Flamborough Head was induction into France's most prestigious Masonic Lodge, the Lodge of the Nine Sisters in Paris, a group whose membership included luminaries such as Voltaire and Franklin, and that the Nine Sisters commissioned Jean-Antoine Houdon, France's foremost portrait sculptor, to do a bust of Jones. Sculpted in 1780, the bust was uniformly acknowledged by those who knew him to be a very close likeness indeed. Metra, writing shortly after the bust was cast, said, "All Paris admires the bust of the famous Paul Jones, the resemblance of which is striking" ("le buste du fameaux Paul-Jones, dont la resemblance est frappante").[15] James Madison wrote that the bust was "an exact likeness, portraying well the characteristic features." Jefferson pronounced it "an excellent likeness."[16] The Houdon bust of Paul Jones would become an important tool in the identification of the remains in coffin number 3, for two reasons: it was the model for the portrait of Jones engraved on the medal that the grave diggers used to identify Jones as the corpse in the coffin, and it was used for comparison by the forensic team that examined the corpse at the Paris School of Medicine. We discuss these visual identifications in the following two sections.

Visual Identification: The Gold Medal Portrait

We saw in chapter 5 that Porter gave copies of Jones's congressional medal, with a portrait of Jones engraved on one side, to the workmen excavating the cemetery site. The medal had been awarded to Jones in 1787 for "valor and brilliant services" in capturing *Serapis.*[17] Thomas Jefferson, then America's minister to France, to whom Congress delegated the task of procuring a medalist—someone to design and engrave the medal (France was at the time the premier venue for such work)—chose Augustine Dupré, medalist to the king of France. Dupré modeled his engraved portrait on the Houdon bust. (Jones got word ahead of time that he would be getting the medal. Never shy, he approached a French medalist friend, Jean-Martin Renaud, and sat for a series of sketches by Renaud. Dupré, however, preferred the Houdon bust to the Renaud sketches.) The mold, or die, used to cast the medal was preserved at the Hôtel de la Monnaie in Paris and was presumably the die that Porter found and used for the reproductions he made for the crew.

When coffin number 3—still in the tunnel—was opened, those gathered around it compared what they saw to the portrait on the medal and exclaimed that the corpse was Jones. Granting that the portrait on the medal, based as it was on the Houdon bust, was a good likeness of Jones, and granting, too, that the corpse was remarkably well preserved on the outside—the photographs taken several days later show this to be so (there was even a full head of hair!)—and Porter tells us the corpse looked even more lifelike when the coffin was first opened, before it was exposed to air, even so, identifying a 113-year-old corpse by visually comparing it to an engraved portrait on a small gold medal strains credulity.

There was, however, a further visual identification made, one based on a comparison with the Houdon bust itself. There were also comparative measurements made of the corpse and bust.

Visual Identification and Measurements: The Houdon Bust

Ambassador Porter provided his forensic team at the School of Medicine with a copy of the Houdon bust, which he obtained from the Trocadéro Museum in Paris. The museum's copy was a plaster cast made by Frank Millet from the Houdon bust in the National Academy of Design in New York City.[18] Porter's forensic team, all faculty members of the Paris School of Anthropology, included George Hervé, past president of the Paris Anthropological Society and a member of the Municipal Commission of Old Paris; Louis Capitan, professor of prehistoric anthropology; Georges Papillault, assistant director of the laboratory of anthropology; and V. Cornil, a specialist in pathological anatomy. (We will review the team's credentials in more detail later.)

Professor Papillault performed a noninvasive examination of the corpse, comparing the subject's head to the bust, and observed several visual similarities:

- The implanting of the hair was "the same," with the "beginning of baldness" at the temples.
- The forehead was "rather straight," the skull "rounded, with pronounced frontal bumps."
- The cheekbones were "prominent and massive."
- The root of the nose, unlike that of many others, "[didn't] recede behind the frontal plane"; the bridge of the nose was "rather thin."
- The chin was "so little prominent that the projection of the jaws" was "remarkable," the chin itself "solid, neither bifid nor pointed."

Papillault then made a series of comparative measurements on the head and the Houdon bust, with the results shown in table 1. "The dimensions of the bust," Papillault concluded, "are exactly those of the corpse. The comparison is therefore easier than if the bust had been of a reduced size. [The] measurements offer an approximation really extraordinary. Two experienced anthropologists measuring a same subject would often make as great differences."[19]

TABLE 1

	BUST CM	HEAD CM
Length of face from root of hair to chin	19.5	19.5
Length from root of hair to subnasal point	12.7	12.9
Length from subnasal point to chin	7.5	7.4
Length of upper lip	2.4	2.5
Length of lower lip and of chin	4.6	4.6
Minimum width of forehead	10.4	10.2

An identification of the corpse as Jones, based on a comparison of head and bust measurements, requires one to assume that the bust is not merely a likeness of Jones but also an anatomical duplication. This assumption has been vigorously challenged—among others, and most exhaustively, by art historians Charles Henry Hart and Edward Biddle in their 1911 study of Houdon.[20] Hart and Biddle concede that the bust was a wonderful likeness of Jones and also that it was "life-size." But they do not accept that the bust's measurements are an exact measurement of the head represented, thus rejecting the notion that the measurements of the bust done by Papillault can be useful in any way for purposes of comparing to the cadaver.

> The consensus of opinion of the most eminent of American sculptors which the writer has obtained, is against the measurement of a bust as being accepted as the exact measurements of the living head reproduced, as the true artist makes but little moment of measuring and is likely to vary in his work from the measurements of nature, exaggerating parts, either *plus* or *minus*, to produce a desired effect. The truth is that the sculptor seeks to express character and general lifelikeness, not the mathematical measurements of the subject, and therefore, while Houdon unquestionably was very exact, he may have been also very inaccurate; consequently, to take a work of art to prove a scientific fact seems, to say the least, most unscientific.[21]

The Hart and Biddle critique assumes that Houdon did not make precise measurements of his subjects' heads. They cite the testimony of other sculptors who say they do not do so, that the job of a sculptor is to render "character and lifelikeness," not anatomical duplication. More recently, a senior curator at the National Gallery of Art cautioned, "Sculptors, especially great ones, don't usually obey the actual proportions."[22] It turns out, though, that Houdon was unusual in this regard; he *did* measure. And not only measure; he often made life masks of his subjects. "Houdon," says Louvre curator Guilem Scherf, "employed a rigorous system of measurements using calipers." He "even took impressions from the faces of the living . . . and of the dead."[23] Thus, for example, Houdon used life masks for sculpting Voltaire and George Washington, in the case of Washington making a special trip to the United States for that purpose.

Professor Nikki Rogers and several colleagues have also pointed out that Houdon described himself first as an "anatomist" and only second as an artist. "In his letter requesting nomination for the Legion d'Honneur award in 1803, he claimed, 'the constant occupation of my whole life has been the study of anatomy applied to fine arts.' . . . Indeed, his reliance on scientific method using compass measurements of angles and distances between anatomical points on the face led many of his contemporaries to regard him as unimaginative and uninventive."[24] To be sure, the fact that Houdon often made precise measurements of his subjects' heads and used life masks to guide his sculpting does not mean he did so in the case of Paul Jones. It also does not mean that, even when he measured, his portraits were anatomically precise. (One critic suggests that the measurements may have been mere showmanship.)[25] But Houdon's practice of measuring is sufficiently suggestive to rule out any summary dismissal of his having done so for his bust of Jones.

Park Benjamin, another early critic of Papillault's bust comparison, rejects the comparison for a different reason—that it is too exact. According to Benjamin, the very similarity between the measurements of the cadaver and bust proves that the cadaver is *not* Jones!

> Five of [Dr. Papillault's six measurements] are vertical from forehead to chin, and while as between body and bust none vary more than two or three millimeters, two (from line of hair demarcation on the forehead to chin-point, and from mouth-opening to chin-point) are precisely the same! . . . If a bust which gives only the contour of a living face which has become reduced (to quote Dr. Papillault) to "a skeleton covered with tissues, in this instance hardened with alcohol," why does not the coincidence logically prove not identity, but non-identity? For, if the hard, woody integument now measures the same as the bust, manifestly if it were changed to living tissue its measurements should be different from those of the bust. Measurements which are the same when two objects are in different physical conditions may well prove to be entirely different when the objects are in like physical condition.[26]

Benjamin's critique may seem logical, but it lacks understanding of anthropometry, the methodology employed by Papillault for doing his measurements. "Anthropometry," to quote Professor Rogers again, "is based upon measurements between stationary landmarks, and are most frequently bony landmarks or margins between facial structures. This allows replicable measurements to be made despite changes in soft tissue due to age or illness. . . . While it is possible that trichion (tr), labeler superiors (ls), and stomion (sot) could have been affected by changes in the hairline and skin plasticity due to aging, illness and preservation, it is unlikely that an experienced anthropologist such as Dr. Papillault would have measured distorted features."[27] In short, it is perfectly possible that anthropometric measurements of a corpse's head could be similar to such measurements taken on the subject twelve years earlier, prior to the subject's death, notwithstanding aging, illness, and tissue deterioration in the intervening years.

Composite of Bust and Head Photo

Evidently, neither Hart and Biddle nor Benjamin was aware of the composite print that was made, overlaying a print of the Houdon bust and the photo of the cadaver's head from coffin number 3. At least, neither commented on it. It was published in Stewart's 1907 *Commemoration* compilation.[28] The technique of using overlays, now common in forensic science, was novel for Porter's time. To an untrained eye, the match is remarkable. To the eyes of four professionals, "The position of the mouth, teeth, eyes and zygomatic processes of the cheeks of the corpse and Houdon bust conform well," even though the photograph of the corpse was taken after it was exposed to air for three days, and the lips therefore are "unnaturally contracted."[29] The composite does not prove that the cadaver in coffin number 3 is Jones, but it is consistent with such identification.

The Dutch Sketch

Mrs. Reginald (Anna) De Koven, one of Jones's early-twentieth-century biographers, says a "M. de Steurs" of the Dutch Embassy in Paris made a sketch of Jones "immediately after the coffin was opened" and that it "revealed a physiognomy strikingly resembling the well-known and often-recorded features of Paul Jones." She also referred to the sketch in an earlier interview with the *New York Times,* stating there that the sketch was in her possession, that it was made "before the air had affected the face," and that it was "so like" the Houdon bust that "it goes to strengthen the belief that the body was really that of Paul Jones."[30] The artist's name is spelled "de Stuers" in the *Times* article. Could De Koven be referring to Victor de Steurs, the Dutch art historian who also did several portrait drawings during his life? Or was "M. de Steurs" merely an embassy employee?

Regardless, there is no known copy of the sketch and no other mention of a drawing having been done. Indeed, none of the official reports mentions any individual by such name having been present when the coffin was opened or at the autopsy. Given these circumstances, little evidentiary weight should be given to the purported sketch.

Ear and Nose

Before quitting the subject of the Houdon bust and comparisons to the body in coffin number 3, one further similarity and one alleged anomaly need to be addressed. The similarity concerns the ear, the anomaly the nose. According to Papillault, Professor Hervé, who apparently oversaw the forensic examinations but did not author any report, observed "a very peculiar characteristic of the cartilage of the ear . . . which seemed entirely identical on the bust and on the body."[31] This was apparently a reference to the shape of the lobe of the ear.[32] It is not clear why Papillault attributes the observation to Hervé without himself endorsing it. Does that mean he saw it differently? Unclear. Perhaps he did not see the same similarity, or perhaps it did not strike him as peculiar. Porter, though, included Hervé's observation in his report as further proof of identification. Unfortunately, the referenced peculiarity is not obvious from the bust, the photo of the head does not show the ear, and no one made a sketch.

The nose presented a special problem. The cartilaginous portion was bent over to the right and pressed down, severely distorting the shape. Porter's explanation for this was that the corpse's hair, when gathered in the linen bag at the back of the head, had raised the head so high that the lid of the coffin flattened it, pressed it to the right, and distorted it. Whatever the cause—Porter's explanation was certainly plausible and is consistent with the fact that the head itself, when the coffin was opened, was turned slightly to the right despite the firmly packed straw—the bent nose made comparison to the Houdon bust difficult.

Papillault makes the following observation regarding the cadaver's nose: "The root of the nose does not recede behind the frontal plane, as is often the case. The bridge of the nose is rather thin, the root somewhat narrow." Then, comparing his observation to the Houdon bust, he says, "Seen in profile, the nose is of an undulating form on the bust. . . . This form depends a great deal on the cartilage. The bony part of the nose, however, is quite compatible with it."[33] Hart and Biddle were derisively critical of this observation. They insisted, based on their examination of the photograph of the body taken April 11 and later published in the journals, that the nose of the cadaver was precisely the opposite of what Papillault said. "The photograph shows that the nose of the man buried in the exhumed coffin was 'terribly arched and aquiline,' to use Cowper's expression in 'The Task,' from the root, a pronounced Roman nose, almost Semitic in its convexity; while the most casual glance at the Houdon bust of Jones will show the nose there to be 'concave from the root and enlarged to the tip,' almost a pug nose, or perhaps, in its thickness at the nostrils, more like the nose of the negroid races."[34]

Hart was so exercised about this particular point that he even wrote Porter about it in July 1905. Porter replied with his explanation about the raised head and the coffin lid, adding, "At the angle which the photograph was taken the nose appears Roman or aquiline, instead of straight. The anthropologists pay no attention to the cartilaginous portions of the body in making their comparison, as these are subject to change in the best preserved body. They measure only the bony or solid structures."[35] Hart was not persuaded. He wrote back that the nasal bone, not the cartilage, was "absolutely convex from the root," whereas in the Houdon bust, "the nasal bone, from the root direct, is positively concave, beyond the possibility of a doubt. . . . Such being the case, the fact is hardly explained away by the statement that the bag containing the body's hair raised the head into contact with the lid of the coffin and changed the nose from concave to convex. Pressure from above might possibly have changed a convex to a concave, but impossible to have pushed a depressed nasal bone up from below, so as to become convex."[36]

Papillault's principal observation about the nose seems to have gotten lost in this exchange and was probably misinterpreted by Hart and Biddle: that the root of the nose "does not recede behind the frontal plane, as is often the case." This simply means, according to Professor Rogers, "that the nasal bone continues in a straight plane downward from the frontal bone." She adds—convincingly, to this reader—that "comparison with the side view of the 1780 Houdon bust is consistent with this description."[37]

Other Identifying Markers: Age, Height, Hair

In addition to giving the forensic team a copy of the Houdon bust, Porter gave them information about other of Jones's presumed physical characteristics, gleaned from the documentary record of his life—principally, published biographies to that time. The purpose was to facilitate comparison of measurements of the cadaver that were being made by Professors Papillault and Capitan with Jones's known physical characteristics. An article about the identification process published shortly afterward states that the measurements of the cadaver were done "before any other information as to the admiral's characteristics had been furnished," to "give greater surety" to the identification.[38] That is certainly how it should have been done. However, neither of the reports provided by Papillault and Capitan confirms the point, and one is left to wonder. Absent clear confirmation that information about Jones's physical characteristics was withheld until the measurements were completed, the opposite should be assumed. Thus, we assume here that the forensic team, when it made observations and measurements of the cadaver's other physical characteristics, such as height and hair color, apparently did so with foreknowledge of what Porter hoped their examination would confirm. Did having access to such information during the examination influence the findings? We will describe the findings below and then evaluate credibility in light of the process.

Professor Papillault was the person principally responsible for the noninvasive examination of the corpse in coffin number 3. He made observations and took measurements of the cadaver's external characteristics. Initially, he noted that the subject was male, not clothed except for a "fine shirt," hair gathered in a "cap of course linen," beard shaven except for a few days' growth, and the body "perfectly preserved." When the hair was removed from the cap, it proved to be remarkably long, showing a few white hairs.[39]

Age. Jones was forty-five when he died. Papillault could not, from the observed features, determine the subject's age at the time of death. However, the beard indicated a man past his youth and the white hairs someone who had attained maturity. The incisor teeth were somewhat worn, further confirming that the subject was a mature adult.

Height and Hair Color. Papillault was told Jones's height was 1.70 meters (5 feet, 7 inches), according to the documentary record. He measured the length of the corpse as 1.71 meters, assumed that the 1.70 meter measurement reported in the sources was done standing, noted that a corpse in a lying position is typically 1 to 2 centimeters longer than that of a person standing, and concluded that the length of the corpse was therefore consistent with Jones's reported height.

Regarding hair color, Papillault was a bit more circumspect. He does not actually say what the hair color should be according to the sources. He merely observes that the corpse's head hair was "dark . . . showing a few white hairs" and the body hair "somewhat more red, as the case generally is, but belong[ing] to a dark subject." He then states, by way of conclusion, that the cadaver's hair color was "brown"—which Porter, in his report, expands to "dark brown, slightly streaked with gray and thin above the temples, agreeing fully with the historical descriptions." Papillault would later write, unequivocally, that the color was brown: "I had some trouble in freeing a few locks of his hair from the matter which the embalming liquid had deposed upon them. But I could in the end put beyond doubt that his hair was brown."[40]

Neither Porter nor Papillault identified their documentary sources for Jones's physical characteristics, other than Papillault making a general reference to "memoirs of the time" furnished to him by Colonel Bailly-Blanchard. Porter does, however, elsewhere in his report, cite three memoirs for other purposes, those of Buell, Sherburne, and Sands; therefore, it is likely that one or more of these was the source of the information about height and hair color of the historical Jones. Buell, in his 1902 biography—a best seller at the time—says Jones was "five feet seven inches" tall, with "black" or "jet-black" hair and eyebrows. Sherburne says nothing about stature. Sands says that Jones was of "middling stature." Neither says anything about hair color. Taylor, in her *Edinburgh Memoir*, says nothing about stature or hair color. Therefore, it seems reasonably clear that Papillault's source for his information about height and hair color was the Buell biography.[41]

The problem is that the Buell stature and hair-color descriptions were fake—as was much else in the biography, as it turned out.[42] Buell cited three "sources" for his descriptions: a work titled "Anecdotes of the Court of Louis XVI," for which he did not provide an author; a Jones "Journal" of 1791 in which Jones was said to have described Russian "General Suwarrow" (Suvorov) as "about my stature—five feet seven inches"; and an 1826 article by a Professor Wentworth quoting Lafayette as saying Jones's hair was black. None of these works was real. Hart and Biddle exploit the misplaced reliance on Buell's forgery to good effect. After demonstrating that the "Anecdotes" were counterfeit, they dismiss Papillault's measurements of the height of the cadaver as "utterly worthless" for purposes of identifying the body as that of John Paul Jones since the purported historical measurement cited by Buell against which Papillault's was compared—five feet, seven inches—was fake. As for hair color, Hart and Biddle state—correctly in my view—that the best evidence suggests Jones's hair was reddish brown, not Porter's "dark brown," and certainly not "black," as attributed by the unidentified memoirs.

> Jones . . . preserved for us a lock of the hair of his head; and not merely a few strands, but a long coil. . . . [A]t the same time Jones sat for Houdon, he sat to the Comtesse Bourbon de la Vendahl, an accomplished amateur, for a miniature which she painted of him, and for the setting of which she doubtless wanted the lock of his hair that he sent to her. . . . That miniature, with the finely braided lock of Jones's hair in the back, around a blue enameled medallion bearing Jones's initials "J.P.J.," interlaced with gold, is in the museum of the United States Naval Institute at Annapolis, Md., and the color of the hair is reddish brown, a dark sandy, as it should be on the head of a typical Scotsman, and not "very dark brown" that anyone could possibly call black. So that as to . . . the color the hair, instead of being "identical" with that of the exhumed body, as General Porter says it is, is nothing whatever like it.[43]

The Vendahl miniature is not the only evidence indicating that Jones's hair was actually reddish brown or sandy, not black. There is a Charles Wilson Peale portrait, the only authenticated oil portrait of Jones painted from life, showing his hair to be light brown.[44] Mackenzie, perhaps relying on one or more of the foregoing, says Jones "had the kind of hair which country people call 'sandy,' but which had probably been made lighter by constant exposure to wind and sunshine."[45] Some of Jones's later biographers also cite as a source for the color sandy or brown a description by Basil Lord Daer, the Earl of Selkirk's son, who met Jones in Paris in 1791; afterward, Daer wrote a letter to his father in which he said that Jones was "not dark as I had heard."[46] But surely this is a reference to Jones's complexion, not hair color.

It may be that Papillault, struggling to conform his visual observation of a brown (or possibly reddish brown) hair color on the cadaver to the mistaken source information saying Jones's hair color was black, downplayed the source and limited his conclusion to one word: *brown.* Porter pushed "brown" to "dark brown" in his report, it would seem, for the same reason. This may lead one to question the integrity of the forensic investigation (this was Hart and Biddle's point): forensic investigators should be recording objective observations and measurements, not trying to conform them to a preconceived picture. But Papillault did in the end report an observation (brown) that did not conform to his erroneous source information but did conform (as it turned out and unbeknownst to Papillault) to Jones's actual hair color. This should give his observation additional credibility, not less.

The stature issue is more complicated. Papillault (mistakenly) thought Jones's actual height was five feet, seven inches (1.70 meters), based on a counterfeit source (Buell). His measurement of the cadaver (1.71 meters), adjusting for measurements taken in a lying versus standing position, was well within the margin of error. But the Buell figure was fake. Therefore, Papillault's cadaver measurement is meaningless, unless there exist other more reliable sources for Jones's height to which we can compare Papillault. Three of Jones's contemporaries remarked on his height. Nathaniel Fanning, a midshipman on *Bonhomme Richard* and Jones's captain of the maintop (therefore someone who had spent time with Jones), wrote in his memoirs that "Captain Jones was a man of about five feet six inches high." Abigail Adams, who met Jones briefly, said he was "small of stature." John Hancock (perhaps intending condescension rather than anatomical accuracy) called him "little Jones." Taylor, who may be quoting from a letter by a "gentleman . . . from Amsterdam" written "shortly after" Flamborough Head, says Jones was described at the time by those who saw him as being of "middling stature, stern countenance, and a swarthy complexion." Sands, quoting a "London newspaper" from February 1778 ("the date," he cautions, "may be erroneous as to the year"), says Jones was of "middling stature." Mackenzie, quoting from a "contemporary letter, published in a London newspaper of the day" (perhaps the same source referenced by Sands), also uses the term *middling stature.* Disraeli, the only other early biographer to reference height, says Jones was "short in stature" but does not provide a source.[47]

These are anecdotal, not scientific, indicators. Cumulatively, however, they suggest that Jones was probably a little less than average height for his time. What was average? There is no definitive information on average male heights in the second half of the eighteenth century. Moreover, stature varied between European and North American populations, with North Americans tending to be taller. Fanning, Adams, and Hancock were Americans, and therefore what they saw as middling or average was probably taller than what a European would see. Komlos and Cinnirella, in a study of English and Irish (not Scot) populations in North America during the *first* half of the eighteenth century, based on military records, estimate average English and Irish male heights at 1.65 meters (five feet, five inches) and 1.68 meters (five feet, six inches) respectively—*below* averages for the same period obtained from a sample of runaway indentured and convict servants in colonial North America. Komlos, in another study of the average heights of men who fought in the Revolutionary War, concludes that their average was five feet, eight inches—well above European standards.[48] It seems that "middling," seen through American eyes (Fanning, Adams, Hancock), would likely have been somewhere around five feet, seven inches, and that short of middling would have been an inch or two below that. Fanning's "five feet six inches" is certainly a plausible figure for Jones's height.

Papillault's measurement (1.71 meters), once adjusted downward 1 to 2 centimeters to account for the difference between standing and horizontal positions, would put the cadaver's standing height at five feet, six and a half to seven inches. Did Papillault "stretch" his measurement a tad to "fit" his preconception of Jones's height? We do not know, but it would have been a gross breach of his scientific ethics to do so. How one measured the height of a 113-year-old cadaver, though, was not settled science in 1905—especially where, as was the case here, the body's feet were forcibly extended when the body was originally put in the coffin. This meant Papillault could not measure from the vertex to the heel; instead, he had to measure to the anklebone and then add eight centimeters to approximate the rest of the height, eight centimeters being based on an average he had derived from measurements in an earlier study he did of one hundred Parisian males.[49] Eight centimeters is just over 3 inches. Since Jones was, if anything, less than average height, perhaps eight centimeters was not quite the right adjustment, and it should have been less. Of course, we do not know whether the turn-of-the-century average Parisian in Papillault's study was "average" relative to Jones.

The best we can say, discarding the Buell forgery, is that Papillault's height measurement is not inconsistent with anecdotal evidence of Jones's probable height and falls within any reasonable margin of error given the approximations that had to be made to adjust for standing versus horizontal positions and the forcible extension of the subject's feet in the coffin.

Style and Length of Hair. Papillault says the subject's hair had been "combed with care, in the fashion of the times, from the forehead toward the back, curled in rolls over the ears. At the back it was brought together in one mass, slightly twisted and falling naturally. Its length was remarkable; it attained 75 to 80 centimeters," that is, 30 or so inches.[50] Nothing here contradicts the Jones identification: John Paul's hair was long, and, in his later years, he combed it from the forehead to the back, as can be seen in the Houdon bust.

The Missing Body Wounds

Porter says that no wounds were found on the body in coffin number 3.[51] This is startling, if the body belonged to John Paul Jones. No wounds on a battle-tested warrior? "The question," wrote Sands, more floridly, "is whether Jones, who wrought as a common sailor, while he acted as a commander in the engagement, who lashed the ships together with his own hands, repulsed the boarders, and personally worked the only serviceable guns, was wounded in the conflict. It would seem that he must have 'borne a charmed life,' if in all his daring and seemingly rash exploits, no bullet was marked for him, and if, among crashing timbers, exploding cartridges, and flying ruins, he moved unscathed amidst carnage and destruction."[52]

Sands's answer to his question is that Jones *was* wounded. "It is known, as I am assured, that he was once severely wounded in the head, and that he underwent great suffering several times, from violent injuries received in discharging his duty."[53] The doubters have all followed suit. There is, however, no hard—or even soft—evidence that Paul Jones was in fact ever wounded. Certainly, Sands himself does not provide any, stating only that he has been "assured" he was. Were these "assurances" from Janette Taylor? She does not refer to any wounds in her *Edinburgh Memoir*. Nor does Jones himself, in any of the letters, drafts, and the like that we have in his own hand, ever mention any personal injury.

There is one sentence in Jones's papers that some have interpreted to mean that John Paul was wounded at Flamborough Head. It is from a fragment written in 1792 in which Jones recalls his meeting in Paris with M. de Sartine, secretary of the French Navy, after escaping from the Texel, where the British fleet had cornered him in 1779 after he found safe harbor there in the captured *Serapis:* "The minister of the United States accompanied me to M. de Sartine, who gave me a reception as cold as ice, did not say to me a civil word, nor even ask me if my health had not suffered from my wounds, and the uncommon fatigue I had undergone."[54] Surely, this is a comment about Sartine's bad manners, not an affirmation by Jones that he was wounded. Moreover, this is the only sentence in all of Jones's papers where there is even a hint of his having been wounded. Since Jones was not shy talking about himself and his accomplishments, it is reasonable to suppose that if he really had been wounded in battle—at Flamborough Head or elsewhere—he would have written about it proudly and at length.

Nor are there any third-party witnesses to Jones's having been wounded or to his having said he was wounded, except one anonymous correspondent—a "fellow-lodger," as he describes himself—who says Jones told him he received one small wound that was "not worth mentioning": "Paul Jones took a stand upon an Arm Chest on the quarter-deck at the commencement of the battle [with *Serapis*], which he did not quit until the end of it. . . . During the battle he received one small wound which he said 'was not worth mentioning' and he found a hole in the skirt of his coat which appeared to have been made by a musket ball. . . . This much from frequent conversations I had with the Commodore at the Hague and Amsterdam a few years after the battle."[55]

Finally, it is worth noting Sherburne's statement in his compilation that "Commodore John Paul Jones on the ocean during the American Revolution was as General Washington on the land—never known to be defeated in battle, and neither ever received a wound."[56] Porter quotes this in his report and goes on to say that Richard Dale and other officers who had served with Jones were still alive in 1825 when this was written, and none of them challenged the statement.

As unlikely as it may seem, therefore, the absence of any wound found on the body in coffin number 3 is consistent with the historical record regarding Jones.

The Autopsy

Although John Paul was evidently never wounded and enjoyed reasonably good health for much of his life, he did endure bouts of fever and other maladies. It is probable that he contracted chronic malaria or yellow fever (or perhaps dengue) either in Africa, picking up slaves, or in the West Indies, during a voyage there. As Philip Dale notes, most seamen engaged in West Indian trade got malaria in those days. We know Jones suffered cyclical fevers at Cork in 1773, a symptom typical of malaria, and that, as with malaria, these cyclical fevers recurred later in life, possibly in the summer of 1779 while outfitting *Bonhomme Richard,* certainly in Pennsylvania in the summer of 1783. In 1780, while *Alliance* was anchored near L'Orient, he became "almost blind with sore eyes." As mentioned previously, he developed a severe case of pneumonia in Russia in late 1787, traveling from the Liman to St. Petersburg, including three days in winter in an open boat, and there were other illnesses from time to time as well.[57]

Regarding his death, we know from Colonel Blackden's letter to Jones's sister that John Paul had been sick for about a year prior to his death and that in his last two months, he lost his appetite and showed signs of jaundice. Ten days before passing, his legs began to swell. The swelling progressed to his belly such that, during his final forty-eight hours of life, he could not button his waistcoat and had difficulty breathing.[58] The burial certificate listed cause of death as "dropsy in the chest," an old medical term for edema, the swelling of soft tissues due to an accumulation of fluids.[59] Today, we would regard such swelling as a symptom of whatever it was that caused Jones's death, not the cause itself.

The body in coffin number 3 was so well preserved that it was decided an autopsy should be done, to obtain whatever information possible about the subject's internal injuries, illnesses, and cause of death. M. Montpillard took photographs of the full corpse and head on April 11, Dr. Capitan performed the autopsy on April 13, and Professor Cornil studied the tissue sections microscopically. Eight organs were examined: heart, liver, gallbladder, stomach, intestines, spleen, lungs, and kidneys. They were accessed through the back and replaced when the autopsy was completed. The brain was not autopsied; Capitan assumed it was completely deteriorated because the alcohol could not penetrate it. The eight organs that were examined, though emaciated and contracted ("the organs of a patient rather pronouncedly consumptive"), were well preserved. However, the cellular elements had deteriorated badly—according to Cornil, probably due to the body not having been immersed in alcohol until a day or two after death or there not having been a sufficient quantity of it, in either case allowing partial decomposition to take place in the deeply seated organs. (Alternatively, the alcohol may have leaked before the preservative could fully penetrate.) The deterioration of the cellular elements limited the scope of the microscopic exam. The following summary of the autopsy results is based on the final reports of Dr. Capitan and Professor Cornil, unless otherwise noted.

Heart. The heart was small, contracted, the color of "dead leaves," the shrinking presumably due to the action of the alcohol preservative. But its gross and microscopic characteristics were said to be normal. One observation, though—that microscopic sections of the cardiac wall showed "some" muscular fibers "still very clearly visible"—has caught the attention of one medical reviewer. According to Philip Dale, "A heart so far gone with post-mortem changes that merely *some* of the fibers are visible cannot be said to be 'normal' in the sense that pre-mortem disease processes have been excluded."[60] True enough, but as we have seen, Capitan and Cornil included appropriate caveats at the beginning of their reports regarding deterioration of the subject's cellular elements generally. Clearly, "normal" in this context means insofar as the cellular structures could be examined.

Liver, Gallbladder, Stomach, Intestines. These organs, though also shrunken (again, a consequence of the alcohol), were pronounced normal. The "healthy" gallbladder contained bile of a pasty consistency; the intestines were empty. The cellular deterioration, though, was evidently significant. Cornil could not obtain any useful microscopic information from his sections of the liver and apparently did not try to examine the gallbladder, stomach, and intestines microscopically.

Spleen. Intriguingly, the spleen, according to Papillault, was "comparatively more voluminous than it ought to have been," given the marked contraction of the other organs. Cornil adds that there were no anatomical lesions. However, the forensic team does not speculate as to the cause of the enlargement. One medical reviewer, Dale, does. "The enlarged spleen (ague cake) was an inevitable consequence of the severe and prolonged malarial infection he had suffered on the African coast and later in the West Indies."[61] Clearly, Dale subscribes to the conclusion that the corpse in coffin number 3 was Jones. For those inclined to be more circumspect, it can at least be said that an enlarged spleen is consistent with the possibility that the subject in the coffin suffered a severe malarial infection at some point in his life. There are other possible causes as well.

Lungs. The lungs and kidneys, it turned out, were full of clues. Most important in the case of the lungs, there were pleural lesions in the upper lobes, but the stain test performed by Professor Cornil on the sectioned tissues showed no evidence of tuberculosis. This is significant because Jones was widely thought to have suffered from tuberculosis. The stain readings are reliable despite decomposition of the cellular elements because tuberculosis bacilli should have survived the decomposition and been identifiable by the staining, if there were any. Also, as Rogers notes, there is no mention in the autopsy reports of tuberculosis cavitation (bubbles) in the gross or microscopic observations of the professors, something to be expected if there had been advanced tuberculosis.[62] The subject in coffin number 3 did not have tuberculosis.

The professors attributed the pleural lesions, instead, to pneumonia, a malady Jones *did* suffer from, dating to his service in Russia. He may also have had severe bronchitis toward the end, which would be consistent with the fibrous scarring of the lesions and with reports of his hacking cough and inaudibility.[63]

Kidneys. The kidneys were small, hard, and contracted—much more reduced in size than they should have been, even allowing for the alcohol preservative. There were numerous lesions and fibrous nodules in the organs; also, the Bowman's capsules and renal arteries had thickened and were lined with sclerosis. The professors' diagnosis was unambiguous: chronic interstitial nephritis, a severe kidney inflammation that can lead to total kidney failure. Importantly, this diagnosis was consistent with the various symptoms presented by Paul Jones in his final days: emaciation, consumption, considerable swelling. None of the critics has taken issue.

The Missing Nameplate, Clothes, and Relics

The coffin, as previously noted, did not have a nameplate on it. Nor did it contain any sword, medal, or other personal effects of the deceased. The body itself was undressed, except for a "fine shirt."[64] The doubters have made much of this. According to Park Benjamin:

> Nothing is more remarkable than the total absence of identifying marks or objects in or upon the coffin. There was no plate, not a written word, no recognizable garment and not a trinket. It is necessary to believe, therefore, at the outset, that this man whose celebrity was notorious, who was the friend of many of the leaders of the French Revolution, who was honored by national mourning, and whose body it was supposed the United States would soon exhume, was nevertheless interred with no more certain marks whereby it could be known than a pauper's corpse thrust into the Potter's Field.[65]

Porter proposed two theories to explain the missing inscription. One, the digger of the later grave above Jones's, after apparently striking Jones's coffin with his pick (the reader will recall that the coffin had what looked like a pick hole in its center), dug down to the coffin, saw the plate, and removed it, either to keep as a souvenir or for its intrinsic value as silver. Or, two, there never was a nameplate because, the burial having taken place in the midst of the French Revolution with violence and chaos in the streets, no engraver could be found to do the work in the two days between death and burial.[66] Porter's alternate explanations, while plausible, are hardly dispositive. The fact remains that one might have expected a nameplate on the coffin, whether the coffin contained John Paul Jones or not. No nameplate was found. The fact of the missing nameplate does not, however, constitute evidence that the body in the coffin was not Jones.

Moreover, there are reasons other than engravers in hiding that could explain there not having been a nameplate from the outset. Perhaps the lead coffin had been encased in a (now disintegrated) wooden one on which there *was* a nameplate or other identifier.[67] Papillault speculates that maybe it was thought the coffin would be dug up and sent to America very soon, and therefore identification on the coffin was not necessary.[68] Perhaps there was a marker at the grave that was later destroyed when the cemetery was upended, or possibly, at the least, one had been commissioned or planned—thus negating any need to provide evidentiary material regarding the identity of the corpse on or in the coffin itself—but the events of the Revolution intervened. If the expectation was that America would one day retrieve the remains, it would make sense to leave the choice of uniforms, trinkets, and the like for later decision. Finally, the very decision to immerse the corpse in preservative liquid may have influenced the decision not to dress the corpse in more than a shirt and winding sheet. The goal was to pack it tightly for long-distance travel and allow the preservative to penetrate the corpse with maximum efficiency.

The Initials on the Cap

There is one final identification marker, or possible marker, to mention. Papillault says in his report that the course linen cap in which the long hair of the body in coffin number 3 was gathered had marked on it an "initial" that "in one direction is a capital P with a small loop, and looked at in contrary direction a J, the loop of which is closed, both letters constituting the initials of the Admiral."[69] If true, this would be a powerful indicator that the corpse in the lead coffin was Paul Jones. Unfortunately, the cap has disappeared, and no one took a photo or made a drawing of it. How reliable or convincing is this crucial testimony? Hart and Biddle ignored it (their focus, to be fair, was the Houdon bust). Park Benjamin dismissed it:

> The reference to a mark like a J found on the bag containing the hair, which, like J's in general, especially the script character, looked like a P when turned upside down, seems inconclusive. That any one should select so cryptic a symbol for the specific purpose of identifying the body is hardly conceivable. That Jones ever used it . . . as a monogram, there is no evidence, and a monogram that has to be turned upside down to reveal its constituent letters is not only phenomenal, but in the present instance seem to prove too much. There is no mark easier to make accidentally or, as the school copy books show, with the minimum of skill or intention than the simple J hook, and besides there is nothing to prove that the fabric having the supposed mark ever belonged to Jones or formed any part of his apparel.[70]

Papillault's report is dated April 14, 1905. Three months later, he wrote a summary of the report for the *Independent* (it was actually this summary to which Park Benjamin was responding, not the original report) in which, however, he gave a fuller account of his discovery of the initial than in the report itself. At the very start of the forensic investigation, he says,

> we had examined all the linen in the coffin, hoping to find some initials on it. But all our efforts in that direction failed. The shroud was a sheet whose ends had been cut off in order that it should fit in the coffin, so that the place

> where the mark would be was missing. The shirt, which was of fine linen, was discolored in parts by the embalming liquid, and notwithstanding all my efforts to clean it and remove extraneous matter I could discover no letters of any kind. But there remained one article which a long washing succeeded in cleaning. I refer to the linen bag which held the dry long hair of the Admiral, neatly arranged and done up in accordance with the fashion of the time. I found here a mark, whose peculiar form was significant. Looked at in one position it was a P, the loop being very small. Turned upside down it became a J. We evidently had here a monogram representing the initials of the Admiral's name.[71]

Papillault goes on to say that he actually discovered the initial only at the last moment, that is, the "very moment" he "presented" his report to a meeting with the embassy staff, the prefect of police, the prefect of the Seine, Ambassador Porter, and several scientific persons. Papillault is undoubtedly referring to a meeting at the School of Medicine on April 14 to examine the coffin and the body. The meeting is minuted in an Official Certificate of the Participants and Witnesses, dated May 19. The certificate is signed by the two prefects; Ambassador Porter; engineer M. Paul Weiss; Professors Hervé, Papillault, and Capitan (but not Cornil); and members of the embassy staff, including Vignaud, Bailly-Blanchard, and Gowdy.[72] At the meeting, Porter, Weiss, and Bailly-Blanchard confirmed that the coffin and body were those they found at the former Saint Louis cemetery and transferred to the School of Medicine for identification. Papillault and Capitan read their reports. They affirmed their conclusion that the body was that of Jones. They also placed the Houdon bust next to the body to verify the resemblance and displayed the shirt and winding sheet in which the body was wrapped for examination.

They apparently did one more thing: display the linen cap to the assembled group, because the certificate also states, "On the cap which contained his hair those present noted the existence of an initial which in one direction is a capital 'P' and in a contrary direction a 'J,' both letters constituting the initials of the Admiral."[73] In other words, the signatories to the certificate all represent that they personally saw the initial on the linen hair cap and that it read as a *J* in one direction and as a *P* when turned upside down.

There are twelve signatories on the certificate, including Papillault—all eminent figures. That is a lot of high-powered corroboration. The problem is that the timing does not quite work. If Papillault first noticed the initial only at the April 14 meeting, at the "very moment" (as he says) when he presented his finished report of the same date, then it would have been too late to include the find in the report itself. But the initial on the linen hair cap *is* described in the report. It is hard to know what to make of this timing discrepancy and whether it should have any significance for purposes of credibility. Possibly, Papillault's "very moment" was not meant to be taken literally; maybe it was just a way of saying that the discovery was made late in the investigation, as he was finalizing his report. Alternatively, perhaps the written report that he presented on April 14 was not truly final in the sense of signed and delivered; maybe he reworked it over the next few days to incorporate the hair-cap initial, but used the April 14 date because that was the date of the official presentation. (The Capitan report is undated, and the Cornil report is dated June 1, so April 14 does not seem to have been a date certain for handing over the written product.) This author is inclined to give Papillault the benefit of the doubt and ascribe the timing discrepancy to one or the other of the aforementioned explanations, because the fact remains that the many corroborating witnesses all verify they saw the initials on the cap.

As for Benjamin's criticism, it may indeed be the case that any scripted *J* will look like a *P* when turned upside down. That disposes of the *P* but not the *J*. True, there is no evidence that Jones owned an initialed linen hair cap, but that does not prove he didn't; it is likely he had a hair cap of some sort, with or without initials, in which to gather his very long hair at night. It was common enough to do so. It does not seem a stretch to imagine that such cap was also initialed.

Credibility of the Experts

Professors Papillault, Capitan, and Cornil, the principals of the autopsy team, were preeminent in their fields. All had stellar credentials. Dr. George Papillault, besides being a professor at the Paris School of Anthropology and an assistant director of the laboratory of anthropology at the École des Hautes Études, was the author of numerous scientific articles and a member of several learned societies, both in France and internationally. Dr. Louis Capitan was a professor at the Paris School of Anthropology, member of the municipal commission of Old Paris, member of the Committee of Historic and Scientific Works of the Ministry of Public Education, vice president of the French Biological Society, and president of the French Anthropological Association. He had also authored more than 250 scientific papers and articles. Dr. V. Cornil was a highly regarded microscopist and professor of pathologic anatomy at the School of Medicine.

Did the professors, despite their credentials, compromise their standards in their eagerness to prove the corpse was Jones? Hart and Biddle seem to have thought so. Samuel Eliot Morison, a large figure in modern Paul Jones studies and one of Jones's most respected biographers, also believed that "the people employed by General Porter were so eager to establish the identity that they made no correct measurement of the corpse."[74] (Morison was specifically referring to Papillault's measurement of stature. His guess was that Jones was five feet, five inches, tall, not five feet, seven.) To this admirer of Morison, the judgment seems overly harsh. While the forensic team's manifest eagerness to identify the corpse as that of Jones poses, at a minimum, a risk of unconscious bias, there is no actual evidence of manipulation. In the case of Jones's stature, Papillault explains his method of measurement, the adjustments he made (for vertical versus horizontal positions and the extended foot), and the source of his adjustment figures. The adjustments are estimates, not hard numbers; there is a margin for error. Also, Papillault acknowledges a margin for error even when two trained experts make the same measurement. In the case of hair color, Papillault says the color was brown, even though Buell said it was black. Capitan and Cornil state with certainty there was no tuberculosis, even though it was widely believed that Jones had tuberculosis. None of the three found any evidence of body wounds, even though Sands—and common sense—suggests Jones must have been wounded. These examples indicate that the professors did their examination objectively and professionally.

More disturbing, to this author at least, are some of the actions of Horace Porter—most egregious, apparently providing documents to the investigative team disclosing identifiers of Jones that should have been kept from them until after their investigation was complete, to ensure that their findings were entirely objective and would not be influenced by what Porter hoped they would find.[75]

Conclusions

No single piece of evidence, standing alone, proves that the corpse in coffin number 3 was John Paul Jones. But equally, no single piece disproves it or is inconsistent with what we know about the historical Jones; on the contrary, the evidence is consistent with the corpse being that of Jones. Cumulatively, the evidence is persuasive that the corpse was Jones. Also, as among those who have studied the evidence and the reports, those who conclude the corpse was Jones—Professor Nikki Rogers and her colleagues foremost in this group—are much more persuasive than those who conclude the contrary.

The key evidence that it was Jones is as follows. First, there is the Saint Louis cemetery where the coffin was found: we know that Jones was buried there and that the remains of the five hundred or so persons buried there were not later removed, except for an Englishwoman's. Second, there is the coffin—lead, the body preserved in alcohol and tightly packed as if to facilitate transport: we know that, anticipating the Americans might one day want to retrieve his remains and transport them across the Atlantic, Jones was buried in a lead coffin. Lead coffins were unusual. There were only a few at Saint Louis. None of the other four that was found contained alcohol or straw. The names inscribed on three of them were not Jones. Of the two without nameplates (coffin numbers 3 and 5), the corpse in coffin number 5 was much larger than Jones, while that in coffin number 3 was within the range of what we believe to have been Jones's middling or short-to-middling stature. Although most of the cemetery was excavated and sounded, not all of it was, so we cannot be absolutely sure there were not more lead coffins there. Therefore, the coffin itself is not dispositive, but it is highly suggestive. Third, the similarities to the Houdon bust are striking. The six physical measurements of the subject's head compared to the bust are similar. We know it was Houdon's practice to take precise measurements of his subjects. Of course, we do not know if he did so for Jones, and we do know that sculptors take artistic liberties. Still, the coincidence of the measurements is compelling. So is the photographic overlay of the head and bust. Fourth, other physical characteristics match what we know of Jones: the reddish brown or tan hair, the length of the hair, the absence of body wounds. Fifth, the autopsy results: the scars from pneumonia or severe bronchitis, the enlarged spleen, and the evidence of renal failure are all consistent with illnesses and diseases Jones is believed to have suffered during his life, and they are consistent with the symptoms he suffered in the last weeks of his life, including the cough and swelling. Sixth, the linen hair cap with the initial *J:* it would have been customary for Jones to use such a cap and not unusual for it to be initialed. It is unfortunate that the cap was not preserved and that there is no photograph or sketch of it. But twelve witnesses, all men of consequence, attest to it.

As for Park Benjamin's two questions: Would you convict of murder if this were the sole proof of the corpus delicti? Would you go to the expense of transporting these remains from Europe to the United States and bury them in your family plot, if this was the sole proof that the remains were those of a long-lost relative? The answer to both questions is, unequivocally, yes.

One commentator, Adam Goodheart, has raised the issue of whether a DNA test could be done. There exists at the Naval Academy Museum in Annapolis a small gold-framed miniature portrait of Jones painted by a female admirer in 1780, on the back of which, surrounding the initials *JPJ,* is a lock of brown hair thought to be that of John Paul. Goodheart asks, "If the sarcophagus were ever opened, could the DNA of the hair be compared with the DNA of the corpse?"[76] As a practical matter, of course, it seems unlikely that the relevant authorities would allow casket number 3 to be reopened once again. More important, for the writer of this book at least, further proof of identify is unnecessary: we already know beyond a reasonable doubt, based on the evidence described above, that the remains in casket number 3 are those of John Paul Jones. If a comparison were done and the DNA of the hair and corpse matched, there would still be doubters—conspiracy theorists, for starters. If they did not match, it would not prove the corpse wasn't Jones; it could be that the lock of hair belonged to someone else.

7

THE GREAT WHITE FLEET

In a time of peace, it is necessary to prepare, and be always prepared for war by the sea.

John Paul Jones, 1783

Our Marine will rise as if by Enchantment, and become, within the memory of Persons now living, the wonder and envy of the world.

John Paul Jones, 1778

THE DISCOVERY OF THE ABANDONED cemetery for foreign Protestants in Northeast Paris, beneath the laundry, grocery shop, stable, and barns at the corner of rue Granges-aux-Belles and rue des Écluses Saint Martin, and the identification of the remains in lead coffin number 3 as those of John Paul Jones effectively ended the search for Jones's lost grave. But it did not end the search for his lost memory. These searches—for the memory and grave of Paul Jones—had engaged the attention and time of many persons (some obscure, some distinguished) for more than a century, among them (as detailed in prior chapters) Colonel John Henry Sherburne, Janette Taylor, Robert Sands, Benjamin Disraeli, James Fenimore Cooper, Alexandre Dumas père, Lieutenant Alexander Pinkham, Alexander Slidell Mackenzie, Charles Read, Consul General J. K. Gowdy, embassy attaché Henry Vignaud, Colonel Arthur Bailly-Blanchard, naval attaché Lieutenant William Sims, French antiquarian Albert de Ricaudy, and, finally, most notably, Medal of Honor winner and American ambassador to France Horace Porter.

There is another name still to add to this list, that of the man who, more than any other, shaped Jones's memory for twentieth-century America—in effect, completing Jones's transition from corsair to Achilles of the Ocean and enlisting Jones one last time in the service of his adopted country. The additional name is Theodore Roosevelt.

It can be said, only half in jest, that if John Paul Jones had not existed, then Roosevelt would have had to invent him. In a sense he did. Certainly, it did not take the president long to grasp the political opportunity presented by Ambassador Porter's discovery of the Saint Louis cemetery where Jones had been buried in 1792. In the several months following Porter's January 1905 report to Secretary of State John Hay, stating that he was now ready to undertake the necessary excavations, the president made four key decisions regarding the excavation, repatriation, commemoration, and American burial of Jones's remains.

- In February 1905, Roosevelt asked Congress to appropriate funds for the excavation project, including compensation to the property owners and tenants for the right to dig there, though he couched the request in moral, not political, terms:

  > The great interest which our people feel in the story of Paul Jones's life, the national sense of gratitude for the great service done by him toward the achievement of independence, and the sentiment of mingled stress and regret felt because the body of one of our greatest heroes lies forgotten and unmarked in foreign soil, lead me to approve [Ambassador Porter's] suggestion that Congress should take advantage of this unexpected opportunity to do proper honor to the memory of Paul Jones, and appropriate the sum of $35,000, or so much thereof as may be necessary, for the purpose above described.[1]

- On May 12, at a cabinet meeting, Roosevelt ordered that a special squadron, commanded by Rear Admiral Charles Sigsbee, be dispatched to France to retrieve and return the body of John Paul Jones to the United States.[2]
- Also on May 12, Roosevelt directed that Jones should be buried at Annapolis rather than Arlington or one of the other cities lobbying for the grave site.[3]

- On July 20, Roosevelt decided there should be an elaborate ceremony of commemoration at Annapolis to honor John Paul Jones when his remains were laid to rest there. Initially, the president wanted the ceremony to take place two months thence, on September 23, the anniversary of Jones's victory over *Serapis.* But the date proved inconvenient, as the Naval Academy's midshipmen, whom Roosevelt very much wanted in attendance, would still be on annual leave. Roosevelt then acquiesced to April 24 of the following year (1906), the anniversary of Jones's second most famous capture: that of the British ship of war *Drake,* off Carrifergus, in 1778.[4]

Each of the president's four decisions was meant to serve a larger political purpose: mustering support for a more robust U.S. Navy and projecting American naval power around the globe, themes not inconsistent with views expressed by Jones himself during his lifetime. In the following pages, we will examine in more detail the uses to which Roosevelt put the evolving memory of John Paul Jones—what could be called Jones's "final deployment" in the service of his adopted country.

Theodore Roosevelt exhibited a special interest in navies and naval warfare his entire life, an interest that can be traced to his childhood. He was a sickly boy, prone to bouts of asthma that could last for days and that left him, in the words of one biographer, "sweat-soaked and trembling," dreading the next attack. Fear of asthma attacks kept him indoors, with plenty of time for toy ships and soldiers, counterpane wars, and storytelling. His mother, a southerner, had two brothers in service to the Confederacy: one, James, the Confederate agent in England responsible for construction of *Alabama* (the feared commerce raider that sank or captured fifty-seven Union merchant ships before it was itself sunk by the Union's *Kearsarge* off Cherbourg), and the other, Irvine, a midshipman on *Alabama,* rescued from the sinking ship and said to have fired its last shot.[5] (The reader will recall that, in 1864, future ambassador to France Horace Porter, then a Union officer and aide to General Grant, took notes as Secretary of State Seward discussed the sinking of *Alabama* during a visit to Grant's camp.) These exploits made for good stories, and "Mittie," Roosevelt's mother, never tired of telling them, along with many other tales of the sea, enflaming the future president's imagination. As Roosevelt himself would later put it, she told tales "about ships, ships, ships, and fighting of ships till they sank into the depths of my soul."[6]

The young Roosevelt also read many books about the sea, including Frederick Marryat's *Mr. Midshipman Easy,* a popular Victorian novel about the life of a young officer in the British navy during the Napoleonic Wars—"reveling" in it, as he later wrote—and Fenimore Cooper's nautical tales, which he particularly loved, to name a few of the books we know he read and reread.[7] Were any of them about John Paul Jones? It seems likely. The interest in Cooper—*The Pilot* and *The Rover,* if nothing else—must have taught him something of Jones. We also know, because he says so in his autobiography, that he inherited from his great-grandfather a biography of Jones (one of three books from his great-grandfather's library that Roosevelt specifically references in the autobiography). It is fair, therefore, to surmise that Roosevelt knew about John Paul Jones from an early age. His impression of Jones, though, was likely that of a corsair, not a national hero, as may be inferred from correspondence with the publisher George Haven Putnam in 1897. In response to an inquiry from Putnam as to whether Roosevelt would be willing to author a volume on Jones in Putnam's Heroes of the Nation series, Roosevelt replied, "Now, about Paul Jones. He hardly seems to me to size up big enough for a Hero of the Nation. He did have a dramatic and spectacular career; but if the series should include any American naval man it should be Faragut, as far as mark is concerned. I myself would not have time to write about Paul Jones."[8] Roosevelt would retain this impression of Jones as pirate rather than hero until after he became assistant secretary of the navy.

If the future president's interest in ships and sailing was first piqued by the many tales of the sea told to or read by him in childhood, his later focus on naval preparedness and naval power was shaped by independent study of the War of 1812 that he began during his senior year at Harvard. *The Naval War of 1812,* completed and published three years later in 1882 when he was twenty-three, is a carefully researched, well-regarded operational history of the naval aspects of that war, including detailed renderings of battles, colorful descriptions of the men involved, and keen strategic insights. It would become a textbook at the Naval War College. In 1886 copies were placed on every ship in the U.S. Navy.[9] The book's purpose, as summarized by one modern reviewer, was threefold: first, to "do justice" to "both sides" of a story that had been previously told mostly from the British perspective only; second, to refute in particular the version presented by British historian William James that "extolled English naval supremacy and denigrated American successes"; and third, using examples from the war, to illustrate what he saw as "the foolishness of skimping on naval expenditures in peacetime," errors that, according to Roosevelt, were being repeated in his day.[10]

Mention should also be made of the writings of Alfred T. Mahan, at the time Roosevelt first encountered him an obscure naval officer, historian, and lecturer at the Naval War College who would become the college's president and whose (then) recently published *The Influence of Sea Power upon History, 1660–1783* Roosevelt read over an intense weekend in 1890. Roosevelt wrote a laudatory review in the *Atlantic Monthly* in which he called Mahan's study "the best and most important . . . book on naval history which has been produced on either side of the water for many a long year." Mahan's thesis was, in essence, that the British prevailed in the eighteenth- and nineteenth-century naval wars with France and Holland because they controlled the sea, by which Mahan meant "the ability to bring to bear at any chosen place and time sufficient force to defeat any force that the enemy might mount."[11] It was a theme consistent with Roosevelt's own conclusions drawn from his research regarding the naval war of 1812.

The condition of the U.S. Navy in 1880—the year Theodore Roosevelt graduated Harvard and began his naval war research—was grim.[12] There were sixty ships on the Navy List, but only twenty-six were ready for duty. Of these, fewer than twenty were fast enough to pursue (or escape from) a fast cruiser. It was claimed that thirteen of the listed ships were first-rate men-of-war, but in fact only one, *Tennessee,* was in active service. Moreover, none of the seven navy yards then in operation had the equipment to build a first-class ship-of-war. The situation with regard to naval armaments was similarly grim: American guns were markedly inferior in power and efficiency when compared with the corresponding caliber of foreign artillery. As for personnel, the enlisted force was substantially smaller than the seventy-five hundred authorized by law; many of these were foreigners whose loyalty was open to question. By contrast, there were too many officers for the number of enlisted men, and their rank was determined by seniority only, not merit. Finally, a cumbersome pre–Civil War system of naval administration prevailed: separate uncoordinated bureaus were responsible for building guns, designing ships, supplying provisions, and so on. Secretary of the Navy William Hunt, in his annual report for 1881, summarized it this way: "The condition of the Navy imperatively demands the prompt and earnest attention of Congress. Unless some action be taken in its behalf it must soon dwindle into insignificance."[13]

During the rest of the nineteenth century, periodic efforts were made to modernize the navy. In 1883, for example, Congress authorized construction of four new steel warships, the first of which was commissioned in 1886.[14] However, these ships were, in the words of one historian, "small, slow, without armor, and lightly armed." Moreover, they were "equipped with sail as well as steam, and it remained policy that, when at sea, sail would be preferred to steam."[15] Eventually, the masts and sails were abandoned, and Congress authorized construction of ships without sails. But there persisted genuine disagreement, not only among the political class but within the navy itself, as to the proper mission of the navy—and therefore the proper number, size, and types of ships that should be built.[16] Should the goal remain, as it had been for most of the Republic's history, protection of commerce and coastal defense? In that case, focusing on cruisers rather than battleships might be more appropriate. Or was a more robust, expansionist mission now necessary? If so, the battleship would have to take center stage.

Ships, armor, and armaments were not the only issues. There were serious disagreements about personnel and training to be resolved as well. For example, should the navy continue to recruit from all over the world? Or should U.S. citizenship be a prerequisite for service? There was also the pre–Civil War administrative structure to be addressed: Could a modern navy be managed by uncoordinated bureaus inherited from the first half of the nineteenth century?

Theodore Roosevelt picked sides early and never wavered. He favored a fleet of first-class battleships, staffed by American sailors under the command of disciplined, well-trained officers ranked strictly by merit, that could take offensive action anywhere in the world and prevail. In June 1897, shortly after becoming McKinley's assistant secretary of the navy, Roosevelt gave a speech at the Naval War College, in which he famously summarized his thinking. A century had passed, he said, since Washington wrote that the most effectual means to promote peace was to be prepared for war. While we often pay "lip loyalty" to the maxim, "It has never sunk deep into our hearts," indeed "of late years many persons have refused it even the poor tribute of lip loyalty." Instead, they "prate about the inequity of war" as if that justified not taking steps that "can alone in the long run prevent war." There has "never been" a time in our history, Roosevelt continued, "when preparedness for war was any menace to peace."

> On the contrary, again and again we have owed peace to the fact that we were prepared for war; and in the only contest which we have had with a European power since the Revolution, the War of 1812, the struggle and all its attendant disasters were due solely to the fact that we were not prepared to face, and were not ready instantly to resent, an attack upon our honor and interest; while the glorious triumphs at sea which redeemed that war were due to the few preparations which we had actually made. We are a great peaceful nation; a nation of merchants and manufacturers, of farmers and mechanics; a nation of workingmen, who labor incessantly with head or hand. It is idle to talk of such a nation ever being led into a course of wanton aggression or conflict with military powers by the possession of a sufficient navy. . . . Preparation for war is the surest guaranty for peace.[17]

The theme of naval preparedness and offensive power was seemingly vindicated a year later, on May 1, 1898, at the battle of Manila, a mere ten days after commencement of the Spanish-American War. There U.S. naval forces under command of Admiral George Dewey destroyed ten Spanish warships and killed more than four hundred Spanish sailors without significant damage to any American ship or loss of a single American life. It was one of the most devastating, one-sided victories in naval history. Manila was followed two months later by an equally devastating naval victory over the Spanish at the battle of Santiago, Cuba. This time six Spanish warships were destroyed (among them several of Spain's finest), more than three hundred Spanish sailors were killed, there was no serious damage to any American ship, and only one American life was lost. The battle effectively ended the war. "Perhaps," as Kenneth Wimmel has written, "Spain was not a first-class naval power, and perhaps it was true that these two victories did not deserve to be compared with Nelson's triumph at Trafalgar or the Battle of the Nile. Maybe Dewey was not another Nelson or John Paul Jones. But in the eyes of most Americans in the summer of 1898, the millions of dollars that had been lavished on the navy and its battleships for the past decade and longer had been fully justified."[18]

At the very least, the U.S. Navy of 1900 was a much larger, more robust force than in 1880 in terms of material and personnel. There were now 256 ships built, in construction, or authorized, including 18 battleships (of which 7 were commissioned) and 35 cruisers (of which 25 were commissioned), as well as a significant number of smaller vessels, including gunboats, torpedo-boat destroyers, torpedo boats, and submarines. Most of the battleships displaced eleven thousand tons and were well gunned, carrying four twelve- or thirteen-inch guns and eight eight-inch guns. They were also heavily armored, though slow and not capable of extended cruises away from base; their purpose was still, primarily, coastal defense and operations close to U.S. shores. (Their official description was "seagoing coastline battleships.") The cruisers, displacing three to four thousand tons less than the battleships, were intended to operate singly, as raiders, harassing and destroying enemy commerce during wartime. Indeed, all of the ships in the fleet cruised singly, there were no real joint operations, and fleet maneuvers as such were largely unknown.[19]

In terms of personnel, while still understaffed, the navy of 1900 was much larger than that of 1880. It now comprised almost seventeen thousand enlisted men, of whom 68 percent were born in the United States and only 7 percent were foreign citizens. The promotion system was still defective; one had to serve many years in subordinate positions before one could be promoted to command, and there were therefore many unqualified officers among the higher ranks. In 1899 a board chaired by Roosevelt procured a law, the Personnel Act of 1899, that weeded out a number of incompetent officers. But it did not provide any method for selection and advancement based on merit.[20]

Administratively, the bureau system, in place since 1842, was unchanged. The secretary of the navy was formally in charge of the bureaus, but the tasks were too broad for effective control. There were eight bureaus: Yards and Docks, Construction and Repair, Steam Engineering, Ordinance, Equipment, Supplies and Accounts, Medicine and Surgery, and Navigation (the latter responsible for personnel and movement of ships), all save Navigation essentially civilian rather than military activities. Individual bureaus could be effective in discharging their assigned tasks, but there was no mechanism for coordinating with other bureaus. A General Board, composed of naval officers, was created in 1900 to provide a coordinating function, but it was largely ceremonial, as it had only power to recommend, not implement.[21]

Theodore Roosevelt resigned his office as assistant naval secretary shortly after the start of the Spanish-American War. He enlisted in the army; went to Cuba; commanded there a makeshift group of cowboys, miners, law enforcement officers, and Native Americans that came to be known as the Rough Riders; and with the Rough Riders helped capture San Juan Hill, one of the decisive land battles of the conflict. Roosevelt returned from war a military hero.[22] He was drafted to run as McKinley's second-term vice president, got elected, and ascended to the presidency in September 1901, following McKinley's assassination.

As president Roosevelt was not content with the navy of 1900. One reason for his discontent was a young naval attaché, William Sims, who was stationed at the U.S. Embassy in Paris from 1897 to 1900. This was the same Sims we previously encountered—the young man who persuaded Ambassador Porter to hire Albert de Ricaudy, the noted French anthropologist, to be part of the investigative team searching for John Paul Jones's grave. Sims's primary responsibility in Paris, though, was not the Jones search. He spent most of his time there gathering intelligence on European navies, especially regarding ship construction and target practice. (He was the United States' principal source of information about the Spanish Navy and its operations during the Spanish-American War.)[23] Sims was convinced that American gunnery was inferior to that of the great European navies. For example, in January 1898, he wrote to the chief of the Office of Naval Intelligence that European gun pointers were "far better than our own. . . . If we build ships of equal power and number, we should still be powerless to resist [the enemy] for the simple reason that they fire more rapidly and more accurately." The Europeans, according to Sims, were spending a lot of time and money training gunners to fire at actual targets; the Americans were wasting their annual supply of training ammunition firing at the open sea, not concerned with accuracy.[24] Sims was also critical of American ship design and construction compared to Europe.

In all, Sims wrote some eleven thousand pages of letters and intelligence reports from Paris. Roosevelt saw several of these while he was assistant secretary of the navy and was impressed. He wrote personally to Sims, praising him for the "energy, zeal, and intelligence that you have displayed in the collection of so much valuable information in so short a time, meriting in a high degree the confidence reposed in you. I am very much pleased, you have done *well;* your report and enclosures were as interesting as anything I have recently read."[25]

The battles of Manila Bay and Santiago, though, seemed to contradict Sims. The Americans there had achieved two swift, decisive victories over what was thought to be a formidable European navy. Roosevelt himself at first thought that these triumphs proved American naval superiority. In an address in 1899, he said, "In the early eighties the attention of the nation became directed to our naval needs. Congress wisely made a series of appropriations to build up a new navy, and under a succession of able and patriotic secretaries, of both political parties, the navy was gradually built up, until its material became equal to its splendid personnel, with the result that in the summer of 1898 it leaped to its proper place as one of the most brilliant and formidable fighting navies in the entire world."[26]

The indefatigable Sims persisted. Following Paris, he was assigned to *Kentucky.* On his first voyage, from Gibraltar to China Station in 1900, he conducted a thorough investigation of the battleship and concluded it was greatly inferior to the European battleships with which it was meant to compare. He wrote a report detailing various deficiencies.[27] Then in Hong Kong, Sims met Captain Percy Scott of the British fleet. From Scott he learned about the firing-practice scores achieved by Great Britain's HMS *Terrible,* scores "phenomenally higher" than any other British ship and much higher than any American ship had ever achieved. Sims was aware of recent studies, not widely reported, that the American victories at Manila and Santiago had been won not because of superior firing skills but in spite of shockingly poor American marksmanship. At Manila Dewey's ships fired 6,000 rounds at a Spanish fleet standing perfectly still on perfectly still water, yet scored only 142 hits—an accuracy rate of only 2 percent. At Santiago, under slightly less ideal, but still almost perfect, conditions, the results were even worse: 122 hits out of 9,400 rounds fired, for an accuracy rate of only 1 percent![28] HMS *Terrible,* by contrast, hit the target 80 times out of 104 shots, an accuracy rate greater than 75 percent. Yes, this was target practice, not war. But the target was only sixteen feet high by twenty feet long. It was located nearly a mile away, and *Terrible* was moving at a speed of twelve knots. Moreover, the six best gun captains averaged more than 5 hits per minute, a combination of accuracy and speed theretofore unimagined.[29]

There were several reasons for this astonishing achievement, among them better elevating gear, better telescope sights, and a better method for mounting the sights on the guns.[30] But the biggest reason was a new technique for firing the guns, developed by Percy Scott, called "continuous-aim firing." Since the time of Lord Nelson, gunners had depended on a ship's rolling or pitching to aim the gun at the target, a technique known as "firing on the weather": once the gun barrel was set at the elevation deemed necessary to carry the shell the estimated distance to the target (typically in the late 1890s, somewhere between three-quarters of a mile and a mile), the pointer looked through the gun sight and waited for the roll of the ship to bring the target within sight at the crest of the roll and then fired. This firing-on-the-weather technique had two major constraints. First, the frequency of firing depended entirely on the frequency of the roll. Second, because of the time lag between the brief moment the target would be within the gun sight and the time it took to "pull the trigger," the pointer had to guess when the target would come within sight—and make himself fire an instant beforehand. The former constraint limited the rapidity of fire. The latter constraint reduced accuracy, because the time lag varied from pointer to pointer and in all cases required guesswork. Scott's continuous-aim-firing technique eliminated both of these variables. In essence, it allowed the pointer to keep the gun sight and the gun barrel trained on the target at all times during the ship's roll. The new technique was revolutionary. As one naval historian put it, it "changed naval gunnery from an art to a science," increasing gunnery accuracy 3,000 percent.[31]

Sims wrote a report about this. Indeed, more than one. This time, he also wrote a letter directly to Roosevelt, who had just become president. In it he said, "The protection and armament of even our most recent battleships are so glaringly inferior in principle as well as in details, to those of our possible enemies, including the Japanese, and our marksmanship is so crushingly inferior to theirs, that one or more of our ships would, in their present condition, inevitably suffer humiliating defeat at the hands of an equal number of enemy's vessels of the same class and displacement."[32] Roosevelt, though not yet convinced, was encouraging and respectful, replying directly to Sims on December 12, 1901:

> I value your letter. I think you unduly pessimistic, as you certainly were at the outset of the Spanish-American War, when as you may remember, you took a very gloomy view of our vessels, even as compared with those of Spain. Nevertheless, I would a hundred-fold over that you erred upon the side of thinking us not good enough than thinking us too good; and

> many of the suggestions you have made in the past, both upon the need of improving our gun practice and of doing away with or removing faulty construction in our battleships have been genuinely fruitful. . . . I shall always be pleased to hear from you, in criticism, or suggestion.[33]

Roosevelt also ordered that all of Sims's reports be printed and distributed to every officer of the navy. The transformation of America's naval presence—from an eighteenth-century coastal defense force to a twentieth-century instrument of global power—was now fully launched. (Sims would continue to play an important role in this transformation. He was appointed inspector of target practice for the Asian Fleet and began training American gunners in Asia in the continuous-aiming technique, resulting in dramatically improved rates of practice hits. He was then recalled to Washington, where he performed similar training oversight for the Atlantic Fleet—again, greatly increasing the fleet's accuracy rates. He was eventually promoted to admiral and served with distinction in World War I.)

That development of a world-class navy would be one of the new president's principal priorities in office (thanks in part to the alarms sounded by Sims) was confirmed by his first annual message to Congress in December 1901 in which Roosevelt devoted as much or more space to the subject than any other. His theme was the same as in his Naval War College speech of 1897: peace through naval strength. "Far from being in any way a provocation to war," he wrote in his message, "an adequate and highly trained navy is the best guaranty against war, the cheapest and most effective peace insurance." This required, in Roosevelt's view, not only the building of more and better ships but also more and better-trained officers and seamen. "Good ships and good guns," he said, "are simply good weapons, and the best weapons are useless save in the hands of men who know how to fight with them. The men must be trained and drilled under a thorough and well-planned system of progressive instruction." He advocated for construction of three new battleships in the coming year, heavy armored cruisers and auxiliary and lighter craft in proportion, four thousand additional seamen, one thousand additional marines, and expansion of class size at the Naval Academy in Annapolis.[34]

Roosevelt would sound this theme again and again in subsequent annual messages, as well as in his address at the John Paul Jones commemoration in 1906. At first, there was significant congressional opposition. Gradually, though, the president prevailed. By 1909, when he left the presidency, the navy was much larger and stronger than when he took office. The number of battleships had doubled (from seventeen to thirty-three); the size, speed, and firepower of the new ships far outclassed the old; and the number of navy personnel had grown by 40 percent. Roosevelt had also reshaped naval operations in important and controversial ways.[35]

But we are getting ahead of our story. In the years 1902–5 immediately preceding the Jones commemoration, Congress approved construction of ten new battleships.[36] This was fewer than Roosevelt had cumulatively asked for in his annual messages but probably the full complement of what he hoped to get. Indeed, he was so pleased with the progress of naval development during his first term that in March 1905, shortly after his second inauguration, he wrote to General Leonard Wood, a friend, that further expansion of the fleet was unnecessary.

> When I became President three years ago, I made up my mind that I should try for a fleet with a minimum strength of forty armor-clads; and though the difficulty of getting what I wished has increased from year to year I have now reached my mark and we have built or provided for twenty-eight battleships and twelve armored cruisers. This navy puts us a good second to France and about on a par with Germany, and ahead of any other power in point of material, except, of course, England. For some years now, we can afford to rest and merely replace the ships that are worn out or become obsolete.[37]

Roosevelt officially confirmed this change of policy in his annual message to Congress in December 1905. It was no longer necessary, he wrote, to increase the fleet "beyond the present number of units." All that was needed was to replace "worn-out or inefficient units," and this could be done by building but one new battleship per year.[38]

Yet a mere four months later, in April 1906, Roosevelt would change course again and use the occasion of his John Paul Jones address to revive his earlier call for a further buildup of the navy: "We can afford as a people to differ on the ordinary party questions; but if we are both farsighted and patriotic, we can not afford to differ on the all-important question of keeping the national defenses as they should be kept; of not alone keeping up, but of going on with building up the United States Navy."[39]

What caused this quick change of heart? In a word: *Dreadnought*.

For several years, a debate had raged among politicians and naval personnel both in America and abroad about the optimal balance among battleship size, weight of armor, speed, and range, as well as size and number of guns that should be deployed on a fleet's battleships. Until recently, the tactical goal in a typical sea battle (not materially different from the time of John Paul Jones) was to close with the enemy and pound them with everything you had at close range. But times were changing. Battleship technology was evolving rapidly, steam-powered warships were able to fire accurately at ever-lengthening distances (due to developments such as continuous-aim firing), and a ship's speed and maneuverability were becoming more important.[40] The two battleships Congress authorized in 1902 (*Connecticut* and *Louisiana*, the so-called *Connecticut* class), plus the next four ships of this class authorized the following couple of years, each displaced sixteen thousand tons, making them larger than the warships constructed in the 1880s and 1890s (which ranged from sixty-five hundred to fifteen thousand tons). The *Connecticut*-class vessels were meant to be the equal of any battleship in the world at the time, but in reality they were only a little larger and faster, and only moderately more lethal, than their immediate predecessors.[41]

What was new—radically new—was the design for an all-big-gun battleship, a ship much bigger, faster, and more powerful than anything afloat. In 1904 Roosevelt had tried to persuade the Board of Construction to build an all-big-gun ship instead of the *New Hampshire* (the sixth *Connecticut*-class ship Congress authorized), but the board refused. Roosevelt had asked Sims for an opinion, and Sims was all for the bigger ship. But Mahan and the Board of Construction were both against it, and they prevailed. Moreover, since Congress typically specified, in its appropriations bills, the maximum displacement as well as cost ceiling for each ship authorized, there was no way to use the appropriation for anything larger or more powerful than a *Connecticut*-class vessel.[42]

The British, by contrast, embraced the all-big-gun ship design. Their first such vessel, *Dreadnought*, was laid down in October 1905, launched in February of the following year, deemed completed in October, and commissioned in December.[43] The launching of *Dreadnought* in February 1906, two months before the Jones commemoration, took the world by storm. The following headline from the *Chicago Daily Tribune* (not atypical) conveys a sense of the force of the storm: "Will Be a Terror on Sea. England's New Battleship Can Whip Entire German Fleet. Dreadnought

Is to Be So Big and So Powerful That It Can Stand Off 10,000 Yards and Wipe Out the Biggest Ships Now in British Navy and Not Be Touched."[44] No one questioned the revolutionary nature of the new ship. "The *Dreadnought*," wrote a reporter for a Washington newspaper, "is apparently invincible, capable at one discharge of her guns of throwing with unparalleled force twice as much metal as any foreign man-of-war now afloat, while her armor will render her immune from attacks by any enemy's guns, and, some claim, even against torpedoes, fired at the usual battle range."[45] Another observer summarized it this way: "Every other fighting ship in every navy of the world became obsolete when the British Battleship Dreadnought took the water last February."[46] Indeed, it was not only in America that *Dreadnought* gained attention. Navies around the world began scrambling for appropriations to build their own all-big-gun ships.

At the same time as news of *Dreadnought*'s launching was being broadcast around the world, the United States was suffering a sharp setback in its relations with Japan. The Russians and the Japanese had recently been at war for two years. In May 1905, in the culminating battle of that war (the battle of Tsushima), the Japanese, with little loss of men or materials, shockingly destroyed most of the Russian navy, sinking eight battleships and many smaller vessels and killing five thousand men. Russia sued for peace, Roosevelt offered to mediate a settlement, and the parties agreed. The peace treaty, signed at Portsmouth, New Hampshire, in September 1905, won Roosevelt a Nobel Peace Prize. But the peace terms Roosevelt pressed on the Japanese gave them neither territory nor financial compensation, despite their crushing victory. The Japanese public was outraged, riots ensued, and the United States was blamed. Relations between the United States and Japan deteriorated rapidly. There was even talk of war. If *Dreadnought* itself was not sufficient provocation to rethink U.S. naval policy, *Dreadnought* combined with this sudden deterioration in Japanese-American relations and the consequent possibility of war in the Far East surely was. For Roosevelt anyway, this confluence of events meant that his recently adopted replacement-only policy had already become obsolete. It was necessary to advocate once again for new construction—this time of American dreadnoughts.[47]

In his commemoration address at Annapolis on April 24, Roosevelt used the celebration of John Paul Jones to implore his colleagues in Washington to build up the navy—in effect, to resume the rebuilding program he had declared done only the previous year. He began with a history lesson: America's lack of preparedness before the War of 1812.

> As a people we are too apt to remember only that some of our ships did well in that war. We had a few ships—a very few ships—and they did so well as to show the utter folly of not having enough of them. Thanks to our folly as a nation, thanks to the folly that found expression in the views of those at the seat of government, not a ship of any importance had been built within a dozen years before the war began, and the Navy was so small that, when once the war was on, our opponents were able to establish a close blockade throughout the length of our coast, so that not a ship could go from one port to another, and all traffic had to go by land. Our parsimony in not preparing an adequate navy (which would have prevented the war) cost in the end literally thousands of dollars for every one dollar we thus foolishly saved. After two years of that war an utterly inconsiderable British force of about four thousand men was landed here in the bay, defeated with ease a larger body of raw troops put against it, and took Washington.[48]

Roosevelt then "applied" his history lesson to the contemporary scene, declaring that no one in public life who was present at the commemoration had a right to be there unless he was prepared to build up the American navy. "Spare [your] breath," he chided those who confined their criticism to the British for having burned Washington. The greater sin was "the failure of our own people . . . to make ready an adequate force to defeat the attempt." The United States had been guilty of "such shortsightedness, of such folly, of such lack of preparation" that it was "forced supinely to submit to the insult and was impotent to avenge it." Such mistakes, insisted Roosevelt, must not be repeated. It was only worthwhile to "applaud patriotic sentiments" and "honor dead heroes . . . if we are prepared to show that our energies do not exhaust themselves in words." Roosevelt's audience at the commemoration included senators and representatives who had opposed his repeated calls for naval preparedness. Now, as he neared the end of his remarks, he addressed them directly with a withering rebuke: "Those of you who are in public life have a moral right to be here at this celebration today only if you are prepared to do your part in building up the Navy of the present; for otherwise you have no right to claim lot or part in the glory and honor and renown of the Navy's past."[49]

There was no mention in the president's address of dreadnoughts or number of new ships; the policy specifics would be for another day. But the message was clear, and no one who was there missed the point. Many of the headlines of stories reporting on the commemoration ceremony sounded the theme across the country: "Nation Is Lashed by the President. Denounces the Folly That Permitted the Country to Be Ill-Prepared for the War of 1812" (*Chicago Daily Tribune*); "Honors Memory of John Paul Jones. President Speaks of Lessons of War in Which Jones Participated, and Advocates Efficient and Larger Navy to Meet Whatever Dangers May Come. Dwells upon Sin of Failure to Make Ready and Admonishes Congress" (*Washington Post*). In the coming months there would be controversy about specifics. Mahan, for example, would publish an analysis in June 1906 of the battle of Tsushima purporting to prove that all-big-gun battleships were not needed. Sims, at Roosevelt's invitation, would write a devastating rebuttal. It did not matter. Before Sims replied, Congress voted for a dreadnought. It did so on June 29, 1906, when it authorized construction of the single battleship Roosevelt had requested in his annual message the previous December (the battleship that was supposed to be the first of the replacement-only battleships going forward). But this time, Congress did not specify any maximum displacement for the ship—in effect authorizing construction of the biggest, fastest, most heavily gunned ship that could be built.[50] The *Delaware,* displacing twenty thousand tons, with a speed of twenty-one knots and carrying ten twelve-inch guns, became the first American dreadnought.

Roosevelt had won the first round of the dreadnought debate. But the *Delaware* alone could not redress the imbalance that the dreadnought revolution created. Other navies would soon be ordering dreadnoughts of their own (seventy over the next three years). Roosevelt judged that America needed at least three more. How to persuade Congress and the American people to continue investing in these expensive all-big-gun battleships? More broadly, there were important, unanswered, questions regarding the effectiveness of the expensive naval buildup undertaken during Roosevelt's first term. The prospect of war in the Far East seemed to be growing, as relations with Japan deteriorated further. Yet most of America's navy was located in the Atlantic (including the new battleships authorized during Roosevelt's first term that were coming on line in 1906 and 1907).

In the event of war with Japan, could the Atlantic Fleet be effectively redeployed to the Pacific? (The highly touted Russian fleet had arrived at Tsushima after its long voyage from the Baltic in such poor condition that it could not stand up to the Japanese navy—a fact not lost on American naval planners.)[51] More broadly still, the American economy was becoming the envy of the world, and Roosevelt had been urging a more robust, permanent American presence on the world stage—a foreign policy that required a world-class navy. Would Congress and the American people support such a permanent shift in naval strategy from coastal defense to instrument of foreign policy?

The president's way of addressing these questions was quintessential Roosevelt: send a fleet of sixteen battleships plus auxiliary vessels, manned by fourteen thousand sailors and marines, to circumnavigate the globe—a cruise of fourteen months that would cover forty-three thousand miles and call at twenty ports on six continents. Called by the press the Great White Fleet (because all of the ships were painted white except for gilded bows), the cruise would be one of the most audacious peacetime displays of naval power in the history of the world.[52]

The voyage of the Great White Fleet was intended to serve three purposes.[53] The first (the original purpose when the plan was developed in June 1907) was to determine how quickly and effectively the Atlantic Fleet could be transferred to the Pacific. Given the distance that had to be traversed and the variable sea conditions (around the southern tip of South America through the tumultuous Straits of Magellan), this was a consequential and necessary exercise if the United States hoped credibly to threaten a military response in the event of a future provocation in the Far East. The part of the Great White Fleet's world cruise from its starting point at Hampton Roads, Virginia, to Magdalena Bay, Mexico, was designed to facilitate this purpose. The second purpose, to reassure citizens on the West Coast that the much larger Atlantic Fleet could be deployed to support the smaller Pacific Fleet if needed to protect them, would be met by scheduling a series of port calls from San Diego to Seattle. The third purpose was to serve foreign policy goals, the principal goal being the projection of American power. This would be served by having the fleet visit numerous ports in Asia, the Middle East, and Europe on its journey back to Hampton Roads via the Pacific, the Indian Ocean, and the Mediterranean. Moreover, extending the cruise around the world would provide not only a platform from which to project American power but also a rigorous test of fleet and infrastructure capabilities—the ultimate test, short of war itself, of America's preparedness for distant combat.

There was substantial opposition to the cruise when it was announced during the summer of 1907. Congress threatened to deny funding (Roosevelt, not intimidated, said he had enough money to get the fleet to the Pacific; it was up to Congress to get it home). Many feared the cruise would provoke rather than prevent war with Japan. Some feared America would be defenseless for the duration of the cruise and that its cities would be destroyed, others that foreign enemies would sink the fleet far from home. Several newspapers called for Roosevelt's impeachment.[54]

It was by no means certain that the cruise would succeed; no navy on earth had ever before sent so many warships such a long distance to call at so many ports.[55] There was, therefore, reason for concern. Nevertheless, Roosevelt persisted. The public at large was intrigued, opposition waned, and a departure date was set. On December 16, 1907, amid much fanfare, the ships of the Great White Fleet steamed out of Hampton Roads at four-hundred-yard intervals and onto the open sea. Roosevelt, with William Sims at his side, watched from aboard the presidential yacht.[56]

Several days after the Great White Fleet departed Hampton Roads, *McClure's Magazine* published an article titled "The Needs of Our Navy." It was authored by Henry Reuterdahl, an associate of the Naval Institute and American editor of *Jane's Fighting Ships,* who was best known at the time as a maritime illustrator, not as a journalist. Reuterdahl's drawings of warships in the Spanish-American War, for *Harper's,* were highly regarded, so much so that Roosevelt had asked him to serve as illustrator for the Great White Fleet, and he was on board one of the fleet's battleships, steaming toward the Straits of Magellan, when "The Needs of Our Navy" hit the newsstands. The article's opening paragraphs asserted that the American navy was unprepared for war:

> Every one knows now that if we have war it must come by sea. Every one knows that it will be decided, not by months or years of campaigning, but by one day's battle—a few hours of tremendous conflict between two fleets of fighting ships. And everyone who considers it at all must understand that for those few hours our fleet must be continually prepared. We are a great

> sea power now, and we have all the deep concern of a sea power in its navy. If war should ever come and find our navy unprepared, our losses would be incalculable.
>
> The fleet of the United States by mere statistics is now the second strongest in the world. But mere statistics mean nothing by themselves. Three years ago Russia was a great sea power; in one afternoon of fighting she was obliterated by a nation statistically weaker than herself. Her fleet was unprepared.[57]

The article then detailed, with illustrations, a litany of defects indicating that the American navy was unprepared for war—among them shell-proof armor belts located below, rather than above, the waterline on all twenty-one battleships built in the past ten years as well as on five ships then under construction, thus making them vulnerable to shell holes on the waterline that could sink a ship (this was a defect as well of the Russian battleships at Tsushima, and several were in fact sunk by well-placed shells that penetrated the vessels on the waterline, above the armor); low rather than high bows on the battleships and cruisers, with the result that when a ship was moving in rough seas tons of water could slap up over the forward gun turrets, short-circuiting and burning out the electrical machinery that turns the turret, hoists the ammunition, and elevates the guns, thereby rendering useless one-half of the ship's heaviest guns; broadside guns on the twelve latest battleships and most of the navy's new armored cruisers only eleven feet above water, too close to the waterline to be fired windward (the preferred direction because it was free from funnel and gun smoke) if steaming at battle speed in moderate or rough seas; open gun turrets leading straight down into the ship's powder magazines, allowing either burning powder grains when the gun was fired or bursting shells from enemy gunfire to fall directly down into the magazine and set the charges there on fire (something analogous to which had happened to *Serapis* toward the end of the battle of Flamborough Head); inefficient ammunition hoists that delivered ammunition to the firing crews much more slowly than they were capable of firing; an insufficient number of torpedo destroyers to fend off enemy torpedo boats; and the wrong kinds of battleship guns to fight off an enemy's torpedo destroyers during an attack on enemy vessels.

In addition to cataloging equipment deficiencies such as those just mentioned, Reuterdahl lamented the advanced age of the navy's senior officers (the average admiral was said to be sixty-one, the average battleship and cruiser commander fifty-eight), arguing that fighting was work for men in their prime, not their dotage. Moreover, the age of retirement being sixty-two, no one at the top had sufficient experience of command; by the time they reached positions of command, they were near retirement. This, according to Reuterdahl, was the result of a flawed system of promotion unlike that of any other major navy in the world.

Finally, Reuterdahl excoriated the navy's bureau management system. How, he asked, could equipment defects of the sort he detailed be possible? "How can any human being, or set of human beings, place the armor of a battleship under water? How can they place their greatest guns directly above an open shaft leading to a powder-magazine? How can they, year after year, build ships so low that they cannot fire a great percentage of their guns under conditions which almost certainly must be met in naval warfare? How is it possible that blunders of these proportions can be perpetuated?"[58] His answer was the bureau system, which by its nature was impervious to demands for reform and incapable of initiating meaningful improvements on its own. What was needed was a board of expert advisers to back up the secretary of the navy, a board whose opinions the secretary should be legally authorized by Congress to accept.

> There must be in our navy some general expert board, made up of men with ample experience in sea-going service in which is centered responsibility for advising the Secretary on all matters pertaining to the efficiency of the navy. It will see that requests for improvements by sea-going officers of the service are given attention; it will present the requirements demanded for new fighting-ships to the Secretary, who will see that the bureaus fulfill them, regardless of tradition; it will enlist the genius of American inventors into the service of the department; it will advise the secretary as to the proper men to command our ships; and it will see that our fleet is properly drilled for battle. It will not bring about the millennium, but it will bring about a reasonable efficiency of equipment and preparation for war, and place us in this respect on a basis of equality with foreigners.[59]

The substance of Reuterdahl's charges was not new; it was a repetition of claims that others had made before (his friend William Sims among them). Indeed, Reuterdahl said as much, conceding that his various points had been published previously in the technical journals. But this was the first time such charges were aired in a popular magazine, and therefore the first time they were given widespread exposure. "The Needs of Our

Navy," therefore, caused an immense uproar—as well as considerable embarrassment for Roosevelt, coming as it did at the very moment the Great White Fleet had departed on a two-year world cruise intended in part to demonstrate to the American people and the world the coming of age of the U.S. Navy. Important voices came forward to defend Reuterdahl, but many opposed him.[60] The Senate Naval Affairs Committee held hearings at which Sims and other reform advocates were called to testify—and given a rough time. They argued, as they had before, that the latest battleship designs were flawed and that a general naval staff needed to be created to replace the bureau system. The committee chair, not a reformer, cut them off; a fellow senator proposed that Reuterdahl be dumped on a deserted Pacific island and left to rot.[61] Reuterdahl himself decided to abandon the Great White Fleet and return to the United States to defend his views; at the end of February, he boarded a supply ship at Magdalena Bay bound for San Diego and arrived in New York several weeks later after a cross-country rail trip. In July he met with Roosevelt at Oyster Bay, New York, to discuss naval affairs and then published a second article in *Pearson's Magazine* about his meeting with the president and predicting major changes to come in the navy and its organization.[62]

The cruise of the Great White Fleet did not address, much less test, the material and organizational deficiencies about which Sims, Reuterdahl, and the other reformers were warning. The alleged battleship-design errors (for example, placement of armor below the waterline) and the fragmented authority of the bureau system that was said to perpetuate these errors therefore went unexamined. Moreover, the battleships that made up the fleet (the majority of them new construction put in service only in the past two years) were not the mighty warships they appeared to be but rather obsolete predreadnought designs; the cruise would test their capabilities as ships, but not as battleships—and would do so under favorable conditions not likely to be duplicated in the event of war (for example, traversing the Straits of Magellan in summer, not winter, weather).[63] Nevertheless, the cruise was an operational, diplomatic, and public relations triumph. Importantly, it also pushed the debate about battleship design and naval organization into public view (the Reuterdahl article was published when it was, and became the sensation it became, precisely because it coincided with the fleet's departure and the public's intense interest in the cruise), even if it did not test the major premises of that debate. This public scrutiny would eventually reveal that the reformers were mostly correct and thereby facilitate completion of the navy's modernization.

Operationally, the Great White Fleet circumnavigated the globe without breakdowns, serious accidents, or significant repair and maintenance problems. This fact alone rendered the cruise a success, since many had feared the opposite would happen.[64] The navy itself had assumed that the fleet, once in the Pacific, would need substantial time for shipyard repairs and maintenance before it could be battle ready; now, based on the experience of the cruise, the navy was able to revise downward its estimate of the time required to mount naval operations in the Pacific from 120 to 90 days.[65] In addition, the cruise revealed a number of ship-design defects that would be corrected in future construction: for example, the size and displacement of the ships was too small comfortably to handle the heaviest weather, quarters and ventilation were inadequate, water breached the hull-casement shutters in rough seas, and the rapid-fire guns located near the waterline were often ineffective because spray and water got into the gun ports, affecting the gunners.[66]

The cruise also exposed major shortcomings in naval infrastructure. Most important, the fleet had to rely on foreign coal and foreign-flag colliers to supply its prodigious appetite for coal, as the United States had only two colliers of its own and there was no reliable U.S. merchant marine to fill the gap. This dependence on foreign logistic support might be acceptable in peacetime but could not be relied on in times of war.[67] ("Undoubtedly," wrote *Scientific American*, "the greatest need of the navy today is a fleet of large and fairly fast colliers, built expressly for naval purposes," a need the navy began to address in 1909, after the fleet returned to the United States, when Congress authorized construction of five colliers.) Also, most of the navy's docking and repair facilities were concentrated on the Atlantic Coast; there were not nearly enough on the West Coast, and the situation was worse still in Hawaii, Guam, and the Philippines. Therefore, American docking and repair facilities in the Pacific could provide, at best, only short-term support for a fleet in the Pacific. The cruise showed that America must develop Pacific bases if it was to keep a fleet in the Pacific.[68]

Besides operational feedback, the cruise provided valuable training experience for the fleet's crews. At Magdalena Bay, the gunnery practice, daily range-finding exercises, and recorded target practice improved the gunners' skills. The long periods of formation steaming and daily tactical drills during the cruise honed the skills of commanders and watch-keeping officers. Equally important, infrequent access to navy shipyards meant that the crews themselves had to take on more responsibility for repair and maintenance, thus enabling the fleet to become more efficient through self-help.[69]

But the signal achievements of the Great White Fleet were the diplomatic and public relations ones. As James Reckner has written, the cruise "commanded the world's attention. For the people of host ports it provided a unique entertainment opportunity, the significance of which they were quick to grasp. Indeed, the arrival of sixteen gleaming white and buff-colored first class battleships was the event of a lifetime. One million people lined the shores of the Golden Gate to welcome the fleet to San Francisco; half a million gathered in Sydney; hundreds of thousands turned out in other ports."[70] The behavior of the American seamen at the ports visited was exemplary—astonishingly so, given the rowdy reputation of sailors on shore leave—and contributed in no small part to the favorable impression of the American navy that the cruise aroused at each port of call. Relations were (temporarily at least) improved wherever the fleet stopped. The Australians, for example, fearing the expansionist intentions of the Japanese, became reassured that the American navy would provide protection that the British, having withdrawn its fleet from the Pacific, seemed unwilling to provide.[71] Perhaps most important, the visit to Japan greatly eased tensions with that country and led to the signing of the Root-Takahira Agreement under which the United States and Japan agreed to respect each other's possessions in the Pacific and maintain the status quo there.[72] The fleet also performed important humanitarian work, providing rescue assistance and aid at Messina, Italy, following a devastating earthquake.

The cruise was, finally—Reckner's assessment again, surely correct—"a highly successful exercise in national public awareness" that "greatly expanded popular understanding of American foreign relations and defense considerations, particularly in regard to the Pacific Basin. In every corner of the nation it promoted public knowledge of, interest in, and sympathy for the navy."[73]

The U.S. Navy was at last poised to become what John Paul Jones had presciently envisioned and his recovered memory at Annapolis would help secure: the wonder and envy of the world.

Epilogue

OUT FROM UNDER THE STAIRCASE

To whom do the dead belong?
—Michael Sledge, *Soldier Dead* (2005)

AT THE END OF CHAPTER 1, we left the remains of John Paul Jones in a flag-draped casket under the staircase of Bancroft Hall (the midshipmen's dormitory), awaiting final transfer to the not-yet-completed Naval Academy Chapel for burial. That was April 24, 1906, following the magnificent commemoration ceremony earlier in the day at the academy's armory. Six years later—long after the Great White Fleet had returned to Hampton Roads—Jones was still there, under the Bancroft staircase, not yet laid to rest.

The chapel, unfinished at the time of the commemoration, was part of a wholesale redesign and rebuilding of the academy's physical plant that began in the 1890s. The original buildings had deteriorated since the academy opened in 1845. In 1895 the Congressional Board of Visitors declared them a menace to health and safety, not fit for use. The renowned Beaux-Arts architect Ernest Flagg (whose designs included St. Luke's Hospital in New York, the Scribner and Singer Buildings in New York, and the Corcoran Gallery in Washington) was then engaged to design a new academy plant, which he did. The design included a new chapel, in the form of a Greek cross, with a dome two hundred feet high. The building was given place of honor in the overall plan, at the center of one side of the campus, and on the highest land within the enclosure. "By its height and form it will, to a certain extent," wrote Flagg, "be the dominating feature of the design."[1]

Below the chapel's main floor was a crypt, which Flagg proposed should contain catacombs and be used as the last resting place of naval heroes. The building would become, in his vision, the Pantheon of the Navy.[2] However, the $400,000 budgeted for the chapel did not include the crypt, which was to be separately funded. Flagg would later write that he had intended from the beginning (before the search for Jones's lost grave had even begun) that John Paul Jones in particular should be buried there if his remains were ever found. He even tried to take credit for inspiring the search for Jones's lost grave:

> I have always been a great admirer of John Paul Jones, and when I made the first rough sketch for the rebuilding of the Academy in 1896, I had in mind that the Chapel should be his burial place, if his remains could be found. In 1900, when I met Mr. Long, then Secretary of the Navy, on the spot, I suggested to him the advisability of using the crypt under the Chapel, which I had provided in the plans for that purpose, and that a search be made in Paris for the body. He seemed to like the idea. At various times afterwards I wrote to the Department, urging that the search be made. To one of these letters I received a reply that General Porter was to institute such a search. When the body was finally found, it occurred to me that perhaps my importunities might have had something to do with the initiation of the work; and I wrote to the Secretary, asking if it was so, but he dashed my hopes of a share in the honor by saying that I was in no way responsible for the movement; be that as it may, it is of interest to note that the crypt of the Chapel was designed from the start with the idea that it might serve as the final resting place for the remains of the father of the American Navy.[3]

The chapel was completed in 1908, but the unfunded crypt was left "in the rough, with exposed concrete and brick work," hence Jones's continuing presence under the staircase. The lack of funding was not for want of asking. Two days after the commemoration ceremony, Secretary of the Navy Charles Bonaparte appealed to Congress for an appropriation of $135,000 to finish the work. He reminded Congress that the contracts for the chapel did not cover the crypt; that Flagg had, however, provided a preliminary design for it; and that Ambassador Horace Porter had declined to be reimbursed the $35,000 of private funds he had expended in the search for Jones's lost grave, preferring that such sum be allocated to finishing the crypt. "This sum,"

Bonaparte concluded ($135,000), would be sufficient—though just barely—"to complete the work in a simple, but suitable and substantial manner."[4]

The requested appropriation was not approved. Although the Senate did, eventually (two years after the commemoration, in 1908), pass a bill appropriating such sum, the companion bill died in the House.[5] Various subsequent efforts to persuade or shame Congress to act were also unavailing. The Board of Visitors to the Naval Academy issued a report lamenting that Jones had remained "without permanent sepulcher for three years, owing to lack of money." It urged Congress to appropriate the sum.[6] *Collier's* complained that Jones's "earthly remains are not properly cared for by the nation," resting instead "on two ordinary wooden saw-horses behind the stairs in one of the Academy buildings. . . . It remains for some patriot in the House of Representatives to make its members understand that it is a national shame that the founder of the American navy has not what is accorded to every decent citizen—the right to a final resting place." The Vermont Legislature passed a joint resolution asking its senators and representatives in Congress to urge their fellow congressmen to make the appropriation. Take Jones "out from underneath the stairs," pleaded the *Syracuse (NY) Post-Standard,* even if only to give him "the headstone which the government allows all war veterans." Alternatively, a Kansas state senator proposed, let them bury him in Kansas—Kansas being preferable, he said, to the "rubbish at Annapolis" where his body now reposed.[7]

It is not entirely clear why funding for the crypt was not forthcoming. Parsimony was probably the principal reason, the House of Representatives in particular being reluctant to spend the people's money (as one speaker put it) on "building a gilded mausoleum for people who are not yet dead [the crypt having been designed for more than just Jones]. . . . You do not know how much it will cost, how many are going to be buried there; you just know you are taking people's money to start a kind of military graveyard." There may have been lingering doubts as well about whether the remains in the casket beneath the Bancroft stairway were really Jones's. Representative Augustus Stanley said as much in a speech on the House floor: "Nobody knows if it is John Paul Jones or John Paul Jones's coachman; but that does not keep the Committee on Naval Affairs from throwing away money like a drunken sailor." Some even saw the crypt as a hiding place, not a memorial or tomb—a popish plot to bury the memory, not just the bones, of the Protestant sailor so that the Roman

Catholic John Barry could be promoted as the real father of the American navy. "Hide him away in the dark underground cellar beneath the chapel, that's enough for John Paul. He was a Presbyterian—no toe-kissing subject of the Pope. The monument, the orations, the brilliant military display must all go to Commander Barry, a man whose achievements were so negligible that they had no influence whatever on the results of the Revolutionary War. But Barry was a most devout Roman Catholic, and the energies and the money of this Federal Government are now being subtly directed to the glorification of all things Romish and popish."[8]

Cumulatively, the drumbeat of those advocating completion of the crypt gradually grew louder. Ambassador Porter wrote an important letter to the chair of the House Naval Committee, in essence threatening to raise private funds to bury Jones elsewhere than at Annapolis if Congress did not act. "A number of patriotic gentlemen are willing to provide the means for taking the body for burial . . . to a lot in a city cemetery, if this session of Congress refuses it a sepulcher so that the remains may rest at least in consecrated ground."[9] Arthur Dadum, secretary of the Navy League, published (in 1911) an open letter to Congress, summarizing the many efforts theretofore made to induce Congress to act and appealing for resolution. The letter was a verbatim reprint of Porter's earlier letter, but under Dadum's name:

> This appropriation . . . has been urged by Presidents Roosevelt and Taft, by Secretaries Bonaparte. Metcalf, Newberry and Meyer, by the Navy League, by Paul Jones Clubs, patriotic societies of men and women, the press and hosts of public-spirited citizens. . . . For 130 [*sic*] years the body of this great figure in our naval history was allowed to be neglected in a sort of dumping ground in a distant land. Since being brought back to this country it has lain for five years equally neglected, stowed away like old lumber in a building at Annapolis, while every effort to have it placed at least in consecrated ground has been defeated. . . .
>
> The question is not the erection of a monument to a hero's memory or the conferring of any title, gift or distinction, but a decent burial in consecrated ground in the country he so eminently served. . . . The grateful people are appealing to the patriotic instincts of the present Congress to put an end to this unparalleled and inexplicable neglect of the remains of one who contributed so conspicuously to securing the establishment of our Republic.[10]

Finally, in 1911, five years after the commemoration ceremony, Congress appropriated seventy-five thousand dollars for the crypt—but only as a final resting place for Jones, not (as originally contemplated) for other naval heroes. The secretary of the navy and the superintendent of the Naval Academy were jointly tasked with approving final plans. The preliminary Flagg design was abandoned, and Beaux-Arts architect Whitney Warren (whose many other works include Grand Central Station in New York City) was commissioned to redo it. (Flagg was not solicited; at the time, he was engaged in a fee dispute with the navy regarding his prior work.) In the end, President Taft himself approved the design, the P. F. Gormley Company was awarded the construction contract, and the crypt, at the center of which was a huge marble sarcophagus, was finished.[11]

The final burial ceremony—Jones's fourth—was held on Sunday, January 26, 1913. Sunday was evidently chosen because the authorities wished to avoid display and the gathering of large crowds. According to the Navy Department, sufficient honor had been paid to Jones at the 1906 commemoration; now it was time for a simpler ceremony committing Jones to his final resting place.[12] There were, nevertheless, many distinguished attendees, including the secretary of the navy, the French ambassador, and the governor of Maryland. At one o'clock, the casket was taken from Bancroft Hall and placed on a wagon drawn by a squad of bluejackets. The navy band played dirges. Seven hundred midshipmen escorted the coffin to the chapel. The coffin was carried into the crypt, placed in the sarcophagus, and the marble lid was closed. The ceremony concluded with a memorial service in the chapel.[13]

The crypt is circular, ninety-six feet in diameter. It consists of Jones's twenty-one-ton marble sarcophagus at the center, surrounded by eight marble columns, all black-and-white Royal Pyrenees marble, the work of French sculptor Sylvain Salieres. The seven-and-a-half-foot-high sarcophagus, somewhat ostentatious by today's standards but in a style that surely would have pleased Jones, rests on bronze dolphins and is covered with cast garlands of bronze sea plants.[14] The names of the Continental navy ships that Jones commanded during the Revolutionary War are set in brass around the base of the tomb. Various relics of Jones's life and career are exhibited around the circular periphery of the crypt, including the Houdon bust, Jones's congressional gold medal, and the gold-hilted sword that Louis XVI gave Jones to commemorate his victory over the *Serapis*.[15]

On the marble floor, at the head of the sarcophagus, the following inscription is set in brass. The words are those of Secretary of the Navy Charles Bonaparte, in his introduction of President Roosevelt at the 1906 commemoration ceremony:

JOHN PAUL JONES, 1747–1792
U.S. NAVY, 1775–1883
HE GAVE OUR NAVY ITS EARLIEST
TRADITIONS OF HEROISM AND VICTORY

The twentieth century killed on a scale unimaginable to the eighteenth. Viewed from today's perspective, the casualties suffered on that becalmed, moonlit September night more than two centuries ago at Flamborough Head may seem unremarkable, hardly worthy of remembrance. Yet Flamborough Head was one of the bloodiest single-ship battles in the history of naval warfare to that time. Combined casualties exceeded three hundred dead and wounded—fully half of the combined *Serapis* and *Bonhomme Richard* crews. Harm's way is not pretty. Nathaniel Fanning, Jones's captain of the maintop, was appalled: "I now took a full view of the mangled carcasses of the slain on board our ship; especially between decks, where the bloody scene was enough to appall the stoutest heart. To see the dead lying in heaps—to hear the groans of the wounded and dying—the entrails of the dead scattered promiscuously around, the blood (American too) over one's shoes, was enough to move pity from the most hardened and callous breast."[16] The surgeons on both ships were overwhelmed.[17] The outcome was victory for America and glory for Jones, the price in lost life and limb a heavy one, the appalling carnage a consequence of Jones's celebrated refusal to surrender when surrender was called for by convention and common sense.

Those who advocated that Jones's remains should stay in Paris ("This business of removing bones and ashes of distinguished men is unworthy the thought of government"), those who lamented the many graves disturbed in the search for his, were well intentioned.[18] They failed, however, to grasp that ownership of his remains had passed, by virtue of the carnage for which he was responsible, into the victor's public domain. The imbalance created by his burial in a forgotten foreign cemetery far from American shores could be righted only by repatriation to the adopted land he helped free. The French understood this. So did his fellow warriors who searched those many decades for his memory and lost grave.

The commemoration of John Paul Jones did not end with his crypt. As if to make amends for its tardy appropriation, Congress also authorized funds for a monument in Washington DC, to honor Jones. The monument is located in Potomac Park, on the northwest shore of the tidal basin. It consists of a rectangular marble pylon approximately fifteen feet high and a ten-foot bronze statue of Jones, designed by American sculptor Charles Niehaus, standing on a marble base in front of the pylon, Jones's right hand clenched and his left hand clutching a sword. The following words are inscribed under the statue: "First to compel foreign-men-of-war to strike colors to the Stars and Stripes." The pylon and statue are in the middle of a circular fountain into which water spews from two dolphin heads, one dolphin on each side of the pylon. There are two inscriptions on the back of the pylon: "Surrender? I have not yet begun to fight" and "In life he honored the flag. In death the flag shall honor him." The former inscription is at the top of the pylon, the latter near the bottom, below a bas-relief depicting Jones raising the American flag for the first time on an American warship. The monument was unveiled and dedicated on April 17, 1912, nine months before the transfer of Jones's remains to the Naval Academy Chapel crypt. President Taft and Ambassador Porter each gave speeches. Admiral Dewey pulled the cords that released the flags covering the monument.[19]

Other monuments have been established in Jones's honor over the years, including the Ranger Memorial at Kittery, Maine, a small granite marker originally erected in 1905 on Badger's Island by the Paul Jones Club and the Sons of the American Revolution to mark the site where *Ranger* was launched (the marker was moved to its current location in John Paul Jones Park, near Memorial Bridge, in 1963); the John Paul Jones House plaque, erected in 1910 by the Daughters of the American Revolution, marking the house in Fredericksburg, Virginia, where Jones lived for a time with his brother; the John Paul Jones statue in William M. Reilly Memorial Park, Philadelphia, sculpted by Walker Hancock in 1957; and John Paul Jones Park in Brooklyn, New York, dedicated in 1980. There is also a John Paul Jones Award presented annually by the Navy League since

1957 to a naval officer "who has made an outstanding contribution to the high standards of leadership traditional in the naval service."

Five American naval vessels have been named for Jones since 1862, including, most recently, USS *John Paul Jones* (DDG 53), a 505-foot *Arleigh Burke*–class destroyer commissioned in 1993. Based at Pearl Harbor and recently modernized to include the latest version of the Aegis ballistic-missile system, it is said to be the most sophisticated and capable warship in the world today. Its motto is "In Harm's Way."[20]

NOTES

1. Commemoration Ceremony, April 24, 1906

1. H. Marion, *John Paul Jones' Last Cruise and Final Resting Place: The United States Naval Academy* (Washington, DC: George E. Howard, 1906), 58. For ceremony details, see "Honors Memory of Paul Jones," *Washington Post,* April 25, 1906; Josephine Tighe, "With Holiday Spirit," *Washington Post,* April 25, 1906; "Two Nations at Bier of Paul Jones," *New York Times,* April 25, 1906; and "Nation Honors Paul Jones," *New York Sun,* April 25, 1906. There are discrepancies among the reports. For example, estimates of the number of attendees ranged from four thousand to ten thousand—a large difference. H. Marion, a professor at the academy, said the hall could "easily hold several thousand people." Six thousand invitations were sent out, limited to government officials and members of patriotic organizations because of space restrictions. There were also academy midshipmen and marines from American and French ships present in the hall, as well as a large chorus and some unspecified number of others. Although most of the newspaper accounts report the higher number (ten thousand), that number seems too large, given the size of the hall. The actual number inside was probably closer to five thousand. Many who could not get inside thronged the academy grounds, those outside likely making up the difference. See "Brilliant Ceremony," *Coffeyville (KS) Daily Journal,* April 24, 1906.
2. "Paul Jones' Squadron," *Washington Post,* June 23, 1905.
3. "May Break Havre Windows," *Washington Post,* June 10, 1905.
4. Marion, *Jones' Last Cruise,* 15.
5. Ibid., 17.
6. "Cherbourg: Crowd Views Coffin of John Paul Jones," *Washington Post,* July 8, 1905.
7. "Jones' Body on Ocean," *Washington Post,* July 9, 1905; Marion, *Jones' Last Cruise,* 51.
8. Marion, *Jones' Last Cruise,* 51.
9. Ibid., 54.
10. Ibid.; "Ships Meet Sigsbee: Salute Fired in Honor of John Paul Jones," *Washington Post,* July 23, 1905.
11. Marion, *Jones' Last Cruise,* 55–58; "Jones' Body Received with Admiral's Honor," *New York Times,* July 23, 1905; "Jones' Body Entombed at the Naval Academy," *New York Times,* July 25, 1905; "Jones' Body in Vault," *Washington Post,* July 25, 1905.

12. "Is It the Body of Paul Jones?," *Literary Digest,* July 29, 1905, 133. For an example of a doubting Thomas, see "Paul Jones' Body or Another's," *Cleveland Plain Dealer,* July 7, 1905 ("The identification [of the body exhumed in Paris] was complete in the minds of those who had set their hearts on establishing the identity, but it is to be feared the evidence appealed to their hearts rather than to their heads. It seems fairly certain that though Ambassador Porter and his equally enthusiastic associates are convinced that they have found the great sea fighter's body, the evidence they have adduced would not carry conviction to the mind of an American judge or jury in, say, a murder trial. At all events the body will answer all practical purposes, at least until another shall be found in Paris bearing somewhat more convincing evidence of genuineness").
13. "Body of John Paul Jones," *Washington Post,* July 12, 1905; Tighe, "With Holiday Spirit."
14. "Find Paul Jones' Body," *Washington Post,* April 15, 1905.
15. "Ships That Will Bring Paul Jones' Body Home," *Washington Post,* June 25, 1905.
16. "Remains Those of Jones," *Washington Post,* April 16, 1905; "Burial of Paul Jones," *Washington Post,* April 17, 1905; "John Paul Jones' Sepulcher," *Washington Post,* May 15, 1905.
17. "Philadelphia Claims Paul Jones' Body," *Philadelphia Inquirer,* April 18, 1905; "Want Paul Jones Body, Governor Says Philadelphia Should Have It by All Means," *Philadelphia Inquirer,* April 20, 1905; "City Asks Body of John Paul Jones," *Philadelphia Inquirer,* April 21, 1905; "Letter to Editor," *New York Evening World,* April 27, 1905; *Montgomery Advertiser,* April 29, 1905.
18. "Congressmen Say Paul Jones's Body Should Rest Here," *New York Evening World,* April 24, 1905.
19. "Aldermen Adopt *Evening World's* Paul Jones Plan," *New York Evening World,* April 25, 1905; "Women Urge Burial of John Paul Jones Here," *New York Evening World,* April 27, 1905; "'Bury Paul Jones Here,' Asks New York Legislature," *New York Evening World,* May 2, 1905.
20. "Address of President Roosevelt," in *John Paul Jones: Commemoration at Annapolis, April 24, 1906,* edited by Charles W. Stewart (Washington, DC: Government Printing Office, 1907), 16.
21. Tighe, "With Holiday Spirit."
22. "Honors Memory of Paul Jones"; "Two Nations at Bier of Paul Jones."
23. "Address of President Roosevelt," 16–17.
24. Ibid., 17.
25. "Address of Ambassador Jusserand," in *Commemoration at Annapolis,* edited by Stewart, 21–24.
26. "Address of General Porter," ibid., 25–26.
27. Tighe, "With Holiday Spirit"; "Address of General Porter," 34.
28. Tighe, "With Holiday Spirit."
29. "Everybody Works but John Paul Jones," quoted in *The Long Road to Annapolis,* by William P. Leeman (Chapel Hill: University of North Carolina Press, 2010), 233.

2. The Deeds of John Paul Jones

1. The fabricated biography was Augustus Buell's *Paul Jones, Founder of the American Navy: A History* (New York: Charles Scribner's Sons, 1902). It was convincingly debunked by, among others, Anna De Koven, "A Fictitious Paul Jones Masquerading as the Real," *New York Times,* June 10, 1906. For several egregious examples of Buell's fabrications, see Samuel Eliot Morison, *John Paul Jones: A Sailor's Biography,* Time Reading Program Special Edition (New York: Time-Life Books, 1964), 427–31.

2. Commencement Address of President Roosevelt to the Naval Academy, May 2, 1902, http://www.theodore-roosevelt.com.
3. Charles W. Stewart, ed., *John Paul Jones: Commemoration at Annapolis, April 24, 1906* (Washington, DC: Government Printing Office, 1907), 19.
4. The following narrative, including details of John Paul's deeds of preparation and courage, has been compiled, for the most part, from three modern Jones biographies: Joseph Callo, *John Paul Jones: America's First Sea Warrior* (Annapolis, MD: Naval Institute Press, 2006); Morison, *John Paul Jones;* and Evan Thomas, *John Paul Jones: Sailor, Hero, Father of the American Navy* (New York: Simon & Schuster, 2003). Except for direct quotes, I do not identify which of the three is the source of any particular detail, although I do identify the particular source when the three disagree on details. Sources other than these three are separately cited as relevant.
5. "The favorite pastime of his earliest years was to launch his 'fairy frigate' on the waters, and issue commands to his supposed officers and crew." Robert Charles Sands, ed., *Life and Correspondence of John Paul Jones, Including His Narrative of the Campaign of the Liman* (New York: D. Fanshaw, 1830), 14–15.
6. John Paul Jones to Benjamin Franklin, March 6, 1779, in *The Life and Letters of John Paul Jones,* by Anna De Koven, 2 vols. (New York: Charles Scribner's Sons, 1913), 2:440.
7. Morison, *John Paul Jones,* 14–15; Certified Statement of Currie, Beck & Co., January 30, 1773, in *Life of Jones,* edited by Sands, 20.
8. Morison (*John Paul Jones,* 22) and Thomas (*John Paul Jones,* 30–31) disagree, respectively, as to whether the crewman had been with Jones on the voyage out or was a new recruit, taken on in Tobago while the ship was undergoing repairs.
9. Morison, *John Paul Jones,* 20.
10. Different authorities give slightly different figures for the size of the British navy. Callo (*John Paul Jones,* 20) says the British had 108 ships of the line. The website All Empires (http://www.allempires.com) says there were 117 ships of the line and 82 cruisers, citing N. A. M. Rodgers, *The Command of the Ocean: A Naval History of Britain, 1649–1815* (New York: W. W. Norton, 2004), 608. Thomas (*John Paul Jones,* 43n) says there were 270 ships, including 131 ships of the line, citing Peter Kemp, *The British Sailor: A Social History of the Lower Deck* (London: J. M. Dent, 1970), 136–37.
11. Jones to Robert Morris, October 17, 1776, in *Life and Character of the Chevalier John Paul Jones, a Captain in the Navy of the United States, during Their Revolutionary War,* by John Henry Sherburne (Washington, DC: Vanderpool & Cole, 1825), 20, 21–22.
12. Morison, *John Paul Jones,* 79.
13. *Journals of the American Congress: From 1774–1778,* 4 vols. (Washington, DC: Way and Gideon, 1823), 2:165.
14. Benjamin Franklin and Silas Deane to Jones, January 16, 1778, in *Life of Jones,* by De Koven, 1:247.
15. Jones to Morris, October 17, 1776, in *Life of Jones,* by Sherburne, 22; Morris to Jones, February 1777, in *Life of Jones,* by De Koven, 2:140.
16. Jones to American Commissioners at Paris, May 27, 1778, in *Life of Jones,* by Sherburne, 43, 46.
17. The last time, in 1338, French troops briefly landed at Southampton and set the town on fire. In 1688 the Dutch landed fourteen thousand troops at Devon, but this later incursion was at the express invitation of William of Orange, who then seized the throne from James II with the aid of the invited Dutch invaders.

18. "Morning Post, London," *Morning Post and Daily Advertiser* (London), April 28, 1778. John the Painter was a pseudonym for James Aitkin, a Scottish highwayman who terrorized the Scottish countryside and threatened to burn British naval dockyards before he was apprehended and hanged in 1777.
19. Quoted by an anonymous correspondent in "A Letter from Edinburgh, April 24," *Morning Chronicle and London Advertiser,* April 29, 1778.
20. Thomas (*John Paul Jones,* 133) says there were three Americans killed, not four.
21. *Cromwell,* a privateer, had captured *Lynx* in May 1776; *Hancock* and *Boston* had captured the twenty-four-gun *Fox* in June 1777. Morison, *John Paul Jones,* 161.
22. Extract of letter dated April 29, 1779, *Gazetteer and New Daily Advertiser,* May 7, 1778, in *Paul Jones, His Exploits in English Seas during 1778–1780: Contemporary Accounts Collected from English Newspapers,* by Don C. Seitz (New York: E. P. Dutton, 1917), 18.
23. "Morning Chronicle, London, May 9, 1778," *Morning Chronicle and London Advertiser,* May 9, 1778.
24. In America there was some appreciation for what Jones had done, including in the press. For politicians' plaudits, see Thomas, *John Paul Jones,* 156. For newspapers, see, for example, "Boston, July 6," *Independent Ledger and American Advertiser* (Boston), July 6, 1778 ("All Europe rings with the exploits of the gallant Capt. Jones, in the Ranger [including] his taking of the Drake sloop of war. . . . At what an height of glory would an equal spirit in all our commanders, have placed the American navy at this day?").
25. Jones to Thomas Bell, November 15, 1778, quoted in *John Paul Jones,* by Callo, 62.
26. Morison, *John Paul Jones,* 188.
27. Thomas, *John Paul Jones,* 157.
28. Gerald W. Gawalt, trans., *John Paul Jones' Memoir of the American Revolution Presented to King Louis XVI of France* (1979; reprint, Honolulu: University Press of the Pacific, 2001), 29.
29. Quoted in Thomas, *John Paul Jones,* 166, citing Testimony of Captain Wybert, November 28, 1781, Charges and Proofs Respecting the Conduct of Peter Landais.
30. Jones to Franklin, June 1, 1778, in *Life of Jones,* by Sherburne, 68, 69.
31. Le Ray du Chaumont to Jones, June 14, 1779, ibid., 96, 97.
32. Sir Walter Scott, *Waverley; or, 'Tis Sixty Years Since* (London: Adam and Charles Black, 1897), xxix–xx.
33. Sherburne originally attributed the prayer, erroneously, to the cruise of *Ranger* (*Life of Jones,* 64); the incident occurred during the *Bonhomme Richard* cruise. For a different version of what happened from that of Sherburne, see "Commodore Paul Jones," *Philadelphia Recorder,* December 24, 1825.
34. *The Life of Paul Jones* (London: John Murray, 1825), v. Disraeli is not identified in the publication as its editor, nor as author of the preface from which this quote is taken. However, Seitz, in his Jones bibliography, says Disraeli was the author (*Exploits in English Seas,* 167, 214). Similarly, James R. Thursfield, in an essay on Jones, says he was assured by a descendant of the publisher John Murray that the book is "substantially the work of Disraeli." Thursfield, *Nelson and Other Naval Studies* (New York: E. P. Dutton, 1909), 195n1.
35. Morison, *John Paul Jones,* 226–27.
36. Thomas, *John Paul Jones,* 151.
37. These estimates are from Morison, *John Paul Jones,* 322. No one has been able to pin down the casualties with precision. An article written in 1816 claimed that *Richard* suffered 165 killed, 137 wounded and missing; *Serapis* 137 killed and 76 wounded. "Life

of John Paul Jones," *Analectic Magazine and Naval Chronicle* 8 (July–December 1816): 1, 21. The size of *Richard*'s crew at the time of the battle was 322 men (the balance of the original crew having deserted or gone to man prizes captured during the cruise). The *Analectic* numbers would mean that more than 90 percent of *Richard*'s crew was killed, wounded, or missing in action—a percentage that is surely too high. Thomas's conclusion—that "the casualty rate on both ships was close to 50 percent"—seems about right (*John Paul Jones,* 197). Even 50 percent was a very high casualty rate for a single-ship action in the Age of Sail.

38. Quoted in Morison, *John Paul Jones,* 379. Ivak served under Jones in 1788 during the battles of the Liman, where Jones commanded a Russian fleet against the Turks.
39. "This famous battle, probably, made more noise in the world than any engagement between single ships in ancient or modern times. The whole European world was astonished at seeing an English ship of war strike to an American under such circumstances. The superiority of the enemy—the conduct of Landais—and the desperate resistance of both parties, combined with the novelty of the catastrophe, excited both admiration and wonder. Jones became hero of the day, and his name rung both in the old and the new world. The circumstance of the striking of the British flag, was not then so common as it has since become [1830]; nor was the idea of its invincibility so completely dissipated as it is now, in consequence of the gallant and glorious efforts of our little navy." "Art. VI. Memoirs of Rear Admiral Paul Jones," *American Quarterly Review* 7 (June 1, 1830): 409, 423.
40. Quoted in Morison, *John Paul Jones,* 250, citing Adams's comment in *Autobiography* (reel no. 180 of Adams Mss. microfilm).
41. "Paris, April 24, 1780," *Pennsylvania Packet* (Philadelphia), September 12, 1780. France's celebration of Jones was partly genuine admiration for his singular achievement: procuring the surrender of a British warship against great odds. But it was also a national catharsis. France had recently fought—and lost—a long, bloody war with Great Britain (1754–63), resulting in British confiscation of most of France's territories in North America. More recently (as discussed earlier in this chapter), while Jones was circumnavigating the British Isles on his way to Flamborough Head, an immense French-Spanish armada that had been assembled to cross the Channel and invade England was forced to abort its mission mid-Channel when disease overcame the fleet. Jones's capture of *Serapis* was a small but sweet taste of revenge.
42. James Fenimore Cooper, *Lives of Distinguished American Naval Officers,* 2 vols. (Philadelphia: Carry and Hart, 1846), 2:110, 112.

3. The Mantle of Forgetfulness

1. Jones, commanding *Ariel,* arrived in Philadelphia on February 18, 1781. There, in early March, he participated in the festivities celebrating ratification of the Articles of Confederation. "The evening was closed by an elegant exhibition of fire-works. The Ariel frigate, commanded by the gallant John Paul Jones, fired a feu de joye, and was beautifully decorated with a variety of streamers in the day, and ornamented with a brilliant appearance of lights in the night." "Philadelphia, March 7," *Maryland Gazette* (Annapolis), March 22, 1781.
2. There were two congressional commendation resolutions, the first one adopted on February 27, 1781, the second on April 14, 1781. *Journals of the American Congress: From 1774 to 1788,* 4 vols. (Washington, DC: Way and Gordon, 1823), 3:581–82, 610–11. Con-

gress unanimously approved Jones's appointment to command *America* on June 26, 1781 (ibid., 639). It authorized the gold medal on October 16, 1787 (ibid., 4:799). The February 27 resolution was specific to the victory at Flamborough Head and read in relevant part: "That Congress entertain a high sense of the distinguished bravery and military conduct of John Paul Jones, esq, captain of the navy of the united states, and particularly in his victory over the British ship of war Serapis, on the coast of England." The April 14 resolution was broader in scope but specifically cited Jones's efforts on behalf of American prisoners abroad: "That the thanks of the united states in congress assembled, be given to capt. John Paul Jones, for the zeal, prudence and intrepidity, with which he hath supported the honor of the American flag; for his bold and successful enterprises to redeem from captivity the citizens of these states who had fallen under the power of the enemy; and in general, for the good conduct and eminent services by which he added lustre to his character, and to the American arms."

3. The French decommissioned the ship three years later (it was riddled with dry rot and could not be repaired) and replaced it with a larger vessel of the same name.
4. Colonel Samuel Blackden to Janet Taylor, August 8, 1792, in *The Life and Letters of John Paul Jones,* by Anna De Koven, 2 vols. (New York: Charles Scribner's Sons, 1913), 2:410–11.
5. Gouverneur Morris, *A Diary of the French Revolution,* 2 vols. (Boston: Houghton Mifflin, 1939), 1:441–42, 2:64, 59; Thomas Carlyle, *The French Revolution: A History* (London: Thomas Nelson & Sons, 1903), 285–86.
6. "Letter from Col. Blackden to the National Assembly, July 19, 1792," *Diary; or, Woodfall's Register* (London), August 11, 1792; "Funeral of Paul Jones," *Federal Gazette and Philadelphia Daily Advertiser,* September 25, 1792. Morris, in a letter to Jones's executor, says his instruction was to bury Jones "in a private and economical manner "—slightly softer wording, but in substance the same. Anne Cary Morris, ed., *The Diary and Letters of Gouverneur Morris,* 2 vols. (New York: Charles Scribner's Sons, 1888), 2:46.
7. Gouverneur Morris to Robert Morris, May 1793, in *Diary and Letters,* edited by A. C. Morris, 2:46.
8. "Letter from Col. Blackden." An English translation of relevant parts of the assembly's proceedings, responding to Blackden's letter, is at "Burial of Paul Jones," *Russell's Magazine* 5 (June 1859): 268. See also Horace Porter, "The Recovery of the Body of John Paul Jones," *Century Magazine* 70 (May–October 1905): 932; and De Koven, *Life of Jones,* 2:416–17. The lead coffin and its purpose are from Blackden to Taylor, August 8, 1792, in *Life of Jones,* by De Koven, 2:410–11. The figure 462 francs was a considerable sum, the cost of an ordinary funeral being only 128 francs. Porter, "Recovery of the Body," 936.
9. See Burial Registry (translation) in "Burial of Paul Jones," 268–69. A translation of the registry can also be found in "The Contributor's Club: Paul Jones's Funeral," *Atlantic Monthly* 65 (May 1890): 712–13.
10. "Letter from Col. Blackden"; "From a Virginia Paper of May 5," *Pittsburgh Gazette,* June 8, 1793.
11. "France, Paris, July 21," *Times* (London), July 25, 1792.
12. "Letter from Col. Blackden." A huissier was a minor French functionary, sometimes translated as "bailiff" (the word *usher* is derived from it). His responsibility was to confirm that the funeral was done as ordered.
13. Excerpts from Griffith's unpublished journal are compiled under the title "Reminiscences of an American Gentleman Resident in Paris from 1791 to 1799," in *My Scrap-Book of the French Revolution,* edited by Elizabeth Wormeley Latimer (Chicago: A. C.

McClurg, 1898), 9–69. The excerpt from which the quoted language was taken reads in full as follows: "Commodore Paul Jones died in Paris soon after my arrival there; and I, with the American gentlemen I have named [apparently referring to Colonel James C. Mountflorence of North Carolina; Griffith had met Mountflorence and the American poet Joel Barlow at Morris's when he met Jones], and a small deputation from the National Assembly, attended his funeral. His internment took place in one of the common cemeteries of the town. There was no priest, nor any funeral service, but a few soldiers fired a volley of muskets in honor of the naval hero over his grave" (ibid., 21). Griffith and Mountflorence, but not Barlow, signed the Burial Registry cited at note 10. (Barlow was not in Paris when Jones died, having gone to England earlier in July.)

14. "Letter from Col. Blackden."
15. "Death of Paul Jones," *Evening Mail* (London), July 27, 1792.
16. "Monthly Obituary for August 1792," *European Magazine and London Review* 22 (August 1792): 167.
17. *Boston Gazette,* September 17, 1792; "The French Army," *Maryland Gazette* (Annapolis), September 20,1792; "July 30," *State Gazette of North Carolina* (New Bern), October 5, 1792.
18. Some say Jones was forgotten long before he died. The fact that readers of his obituaries were presumed to know who "Paul Jones" was without further elaboration than the name itself suggests he had not been entirely forgotten at the time of his death.
19. James Fenimore Cooper, *Lives of Distinguished American Naval Officers,* 2 vols. (Philadelphia: Carry and Hart, 1846), 2:110; Alexander Slidell Mackenzie, *The Life of Paul Jones,* 2 vols. (New York: Harper & Brothers, 1845), 2:291–92.
20. Mackenzie, *Life of Paul Jones,* 2:287, 289, 296, 302. See also "Art. VI. Memoirs of Rear Admiral Paul Jones," *American Quarterly Review* 7 (June 1, 1830): 409, 417, 428–29.
21. In February 1780, after the cruise of the *Bonhomme Richard* and Jones's return to France, Franklin informed Jones that Congress had ordered his return to America in *Alliance.* His assigned mission was to transport arms and cloth for army uniforms to America as well as several distinguished passengers. Jones prevaricated, in part for good reasons (*Alliance* needed some repairs; his crew had not received their pay or prize money, and Jones wanted that settled), in part not (romantic entanglements; the adulation of Paris). In June Franklin again ordered Jones to leave and ordered Jones's nemesis Peter Landais back to America to face a court-martial arising out of charges brought against him by Jones relating to his conduct during the *Bonhomme Richard* cruise. Landais, with the connivance of one of the American ministers in Paris (Arthur Lee, who detested Jones), took control of *Alliance.* Jones, instead of confronting Landais, returned to Paris. Landais then sailed *Alliance* to America himself. Franklin rebuked Jones for coming to Paris instead of staying with *Alliance.*
22. Quoted in Samuel Eliot Morison, *John Paul Jones: A Sailor's Biography,* Time Reading Program Special Edition (New York: Time-Life Books,1964), 91.
23. The third letter, from which the quote is excerpted, is in De Koven, *Life of Jones,* 1:142. De Koven sees this incident very much as Jones did: Hopkins deliberately slighting his former subordinate and refusing to implement orders from Congress. But Jones's later biographers have generally sided with Hopkins (for example, Morison, upon whose account my take on the incident is based). See Morison, *John Paul Jones,* 92–96; and Evan Thomas, *John Paul Jones: Sailor, Hero, Father of the American Navy* (New York: Simon & Schuster, 2003), 79–81.

24. Delia to Jones, July 1780, in *Life of Jones*, by De Koven, 2:163–64.
25. Thomas Jefferson Randolf, ed., *Memoirs, Correspondence, and Private Papers of Thomas Jefferson, Late President of the United States*, 4 vols. (London: Henry Colburn and Richard Bentley, 1829), 3:174.
26. Morison, *John Paul Jones*, 190, 191.
27. George Washington to John Paul Jones, May 19, 1781, in *Life and Character of the Chevalier John Paul Jones, a Captain in the Navy of the United States, during Their Revolutionary War*, by John Henry Sherburne (Washington, DC: Vanderpool & Cole, 1825), 235.
28. Joseph Wheelan, *Jefferson's War: America's First War on Terror (1801–1805)* (New York: Carroll & Graf, 2003), 47; Thomas Jefferson to William Carmichael, August 12, 1788, in *The Writings of Thomas Jefferson*, edited by Andrew A. Lipscomb and Albert E. Bergh, 20 vols. (Washington DC: Thomas Jefferson Memorial Association, 1903), 7:125–26.
29. Diary, May 13, 1779, in *The Works of John Adams, Second President of the United States: With a Life of the Author, Notes, and Illustrations*, edited by Charles Francis Adams, 10 vols. (Boston: Charles C. Little and James Brown, 1850–56), 3:202.
30. Quoted in Joseph Callo, *John Paul Jones: America's First Sea Warrior* (Annapolis, MD: Naval Institute Press, 2006), 130–31, citing James C. Bradford, ed., *The Papers of John Paul Jones*, 9 microfilm reels (Alexandria, VA: Chadwyck-Healey, 1986), 7:1419.
31. John Adams to Benjamin Rush, 1809, in *Life of Jones*, by De Koven, 1:84n1.
32. Morison, *John Paul Jones*, 89; Adams to John Langdon, January 24, 1813, in *Works of John Adams*, edited by C. F. Adams, 10:28; Adams to Elbridge Gerry, January 28, 1813, in *Works of John Adams*, edited by C. F. Adams, 10:30.
33. "Character of Commodore John Paul Jones," *Fayetteville (NC) Observer*, August 28, 1851; Adams to Langdon, January 24, 1813, in *Works of John Adams*, edited by C. F. Adams, 10:28. See also Adams to Gerry, January 28, 1813, ibid., 10:30.
34. Cooper, *Naval Officers*, 111; Sherburne, *Life of Jones*, vii.
35. "The Heirs of Paul Jones," *Charleston (SC) Mercury*, March 13, 1846.
36. For savage and dark assassin, see "Anecdote of Paul Jones's Cruelty," *Morning Post and Daily Advertiser* (London), September 30, 1779. For convicted murderer, see *Morning Chronicle and London Advertiser*, May 8, 1778.
37. "Anecdote of Paul Jones's Cruelty."
38. *General Advertiser and Morning Intelligencer*, September 28, 1779, in *Paul Jones, His Exploits in English Seas during 1778–1780: Contemporary Accounts Collected from English Newspapers*, by Don C. Seitz (New York: E. P. Dutton, 1917), 52.
39. "Morning Post, London," *Morning Post and Daily Advertiser* (London), October 15, 1779.
40. For an overview of how Jones was portrayed in the chapbooks, see "John Paul Jones," http://www.electricscotland.com.
41. Seitz is the source for the statement that this work was copied from the English chapbooks (*Exploits in English Seas*, 199).
42. *The Life, Travels, Voyages, and Daring Engagements of John Paul Jones, Containing Numerous Anecdotes of Undaunted Courage* (Hartford, CT: John Russell Jr., 1813), 5, 14, 15.
43. Ibid., 49.
44. Nathaniel Fanning, *Fanning's Narrative: The Memoirs of Nathaniel Fanning, an Officer of the American Navy, 1778–1783* (1808; reprint, New York: William Abbott, 1913), 104. For a photograph of the Grub print, see "John Paul Jones—Photographs," Miriam and Ira D. Wallach Division of Art, Prints, and Photographs: Print Collection, New York Pub-

lic Library Digital Collections, New York Public Library, http://digitalcollections.nypl.org. For the "Paul Jones the Pirate" print, see Copy of Engraving, circa 1779, National Archives and Records Division, National Archives Identifier 535749, https://catalog.archives.gov. The earliest date of the Grub print is unknown, but it was no later than the beginning of the nineteenth century. A reviewer in 1816 wrote of seeing it "many years ago" as a boy when it was displayed in the window of a small bookshop as part of a "little book called An Account of the Life of Paul Jones, with a frontispiece placed against the inside of the glass, wherein he is represented on the deck of a ship, in the very act of shooting lieutenant Grubb through the head." "Life of John Paul Jones," *Analectic Magazine and Naval Chronicle* 8 (July 1816): 3–4.

45. Published by Schoolmaster Hackston, reprinted in Arthur Guiterman, "Songs of Paul Jones," *New York Times,* August 18, 1901.
46. Samuel Chase of Maryland and Edward Rutledge of South Carolina, respectively, quoted in Charles Brodine, "A Look at the Birth of the Continental Navy," http://www.navy.mil. See also Tim McGrath, *Give Me a Fast Ship: The Continental Navy and America's Revolution at Sea* (New York: Caliber, 2014), 19.
47. Callo, *John Paul Jones,* 20. See also chapter 2, section titled "The Enemy; Cruise of *Providence.*"
48. On the supporting role of the navy, see Callo, *John Paul Jones,* 21; and Michael Palmer, "The Navy: The Continental Period, 1775–1890," http://www.history.navy.mil. On General Washington's small navy and the capture of *Nancy,* see Morison, *John Paul Jones,* 33.
49. Callo, *John Paul Jones,* 21.
50. "June 27," *New York Herald,* July 2, 1796.

4. The Search for John Paul Jones, Part 1

1. Will of John Paul Jones made July 18, 1792, in *The Life and Letters of John Paul Jones,* by Anna De Koven, 2 vols. (New York: Charles Scribner's Sons, 1913), 2:413–16. Gouverneur Morris sent a copy of the will to Janet Taylor and Mary Ann Louden on October 22, 1792, responding to their written request for a copy. He advised them he had sold certain of Jones's personal effects to satisfy claims against the estate (they apparently sold at a "good price," an acquaintance of Morris having bid up the prices "considerably"). He retained certain items for the sisters, including the sword given by the king of France. Morris, *A Diary of the French Revolution,* 2 vols. (Boston: Houghton Mifflin, 1939), 2:470.
2. Samuel Eliot Morison, *John Paul Jones: A Sailor's Biography,* Time Reading Program Special Edition (New York: Time-Life Books, 1964), 319.
3. De Koven, *Life of Jones,* 1:ix; [Janette Taylor, ed.], *Memoirs of Rear-Admiral Paul Jones, Chevalier of the Military Order of Merit, and of the Russian Order of St Anne, &c. &c.,* 2 vols. (Edinburgh: Oliver and Boyd; London: Simpkin and Marshall, 1830), 1:vi. The *North American Review* says the deposit was made "when Paul Jones left America for the last time," which would make it 1787, not 1783, and that the deposit comprised "several packages of manuscript papers, consisting of letters, journals, and vouchers of his landed and other property in America." "Materials for American History," *North American Review* 23 (October 1826): 292. But this seems to be an interpolation from the 1797 Hyslop receipt—and perhaps inferences based on Sherburne's 1825 description of sources. While Jones may well have left items with Ross twice, that is, both in 1783 and

in 1787, there is no way to be sure. What is clear is that sometime between 1783 and 1787, Jones left some of his personal papers in America with Ross.

4. The Hyslop power of attorney is in De Koven, *Life of Jones,* 2:478–81. The Hyslop receipt is in John Henry Sherburne, *Life and Character of the Chevalier John Paul Jones, a Captain in the Navy of the United States, during Their Revolutionary War* (Washington, DC: Vanderpool & Cole, 1825), 351–52. For examples of Hyslop applying to settle claims, see "To Be Sold," *New York Daily Gazette,* January 15, 1797; "Congress, Tuesday, Nov. 21," *New York Gazette,* November 24, 1797; and "New York, November 24," *New York Time Piece,* November 24, 1797.
5. "Died," *New York Daily Advertiser,* September 24, 1798; Taylor, *Memoirs of Jones,* vi.
6. "John Paul Jones," *New York Evening Post,* July 30, 1824.
7. *Columbian Centinel* (Boston), August 14, 1824.
8. See note 4. The October 1824 notice is in "John Paul Jones," *Washington Daily National Intelligencer,* October 28, 1824. The 1825 prospectus is in "Life of the Chevalier John Paul Jones: By John Henry Sherburne, Register of the Navy of the United States," *Washington Daily National Intelligencer,* February 2, 1825. Sherburne's version of how he got the documents is in Sherburne, *Life of Jones,* viii. The alternative, more sinister, explanation is in "Art. 37. Life and Character of Chevalier John Paul Jones," *New York Review and Atheneum Magazine* 1 (November 1825): 455.
9. Plutarch [pseud.], "Paul Jones," *New Hampshire Republican* (Dover), August 30, 1825.
10. Disraeli is not identified in the work as its author. The attribution is in Don C. Seitz, *Paul Jones, His Exploits in English Seas during 1778–1780: Contemporary Accounts Collected from English Newspapers* (New York: E. P. Dutton, 1917), xiv, 214.
11. "Materials for American History," 293. Jared Sparks, editor of the *North American Review* at the time, or Gulian Verplanck, a frequent contributor, probably wrote the article. It is likely that the author obtained information for it from Janet Taylor's daughter, Janette—an impeccable source for the Louden story, if true.
12. "France," *Star* (London), March 22, 1793. The article states, erroneously, that Jones's "widow and heirs" addressed the convention rather than sister and heirs. The error was repeated in other newspapers but eventually corrected. See "France," *E. Johnson's British Gazette and Sunday Monitor* (London), March 24, 1793.
13. Robert Charles Sands, ed., *Life and Correspondence of John Paul Jones, Including His Narrative of the Campaign of the Liman* (New York: D. Fanshaw, 1830), 549–50.
14. "To the Editor," *New York Commercial Advertiser,* July 11, 1825. It is evident, from a letter Jones sent his sister Janet Taylor in 1790, the sisters did not get along. Jones to Janet Taylor, December 27, 1790, in *Life of Rear-Admiral John Paul Jones, Chevalier of the Military Order of Merit, and of the Russian Order of St. Anne, &c, &c.,* edited by B. Walker (Philadelphia: Walker & Gillis, 1845), 380 ("I shall not conceal from you that your family discord aggravates infinitely all my pains. My grief is inexpressible, that two sisters, whose happiness is so interesting to me, do not live together in that mutual tenderness and affection which would do so much honour to themselves and to the memory of their worthy relations").
15. "Items," *Philadelphia Inquirer,* November 14, 1833.
16. Quoted in "From the New York Commercial Advertiser, Paul Jones," *Franklin Gazette* (Philadelphia), June 27, 1820.
17. "To Booksellers," *New York Commercial Advertiser,* September 30, 1823.
18. "Paul Jones," *New York Commercial Advertiser,* July 1, 1825.

19. The question was put publicly to Sherburne in "Paul Jones," *New York Commercial Advertiser,* July 1, 1825. Sherburne's response is in "Letter to Editor," *New York Commercial Advertiser,* July 11, 1825.
20. See note 3. Taylor is not identified in the work as the author or editor. Seitz believed the work was edited by Sir John Malcolm (*Exploits in English Seas,* xiv). I have not found any corroboration for this. Based on Janette Taylor's correspondence and the style and content of the work, Taylor seems to me the likely editor. Moreover, the 1823 solicitation made "To Booksellers" on Taylor's behalf, quoted above, identifies Jones's "niece in Scotland" (that is, Taylor) as the writer of the manuscript there being offered for sale. In a letter to the editor written by her in 1830, in which she tries to downplay the recently published Edinburgh work and solicit subscriptions for the forthcoming Sands work, Taylor writes that the Edinburgh work was edited by "a gentleman in Edinburgh." "Memoir of Paul Jones," *New York Commercial Advertiser,* April 6, 1830. Given the purpose of the letter, it seems to me unlikely Taylor would have admitted to authorship herself. Therefore, I do not regard this as a repudiation of her authorship. An American edition of the work, apparently edited by Benjamin Walker, was published in Philadelphia in 1845, with some additional material and reworking. See note 14.
21. Janette Taylor to James Fenimore Cooper, October 28, 1843, published under the title "New Light upon the Career of John Paul Jones," *U.S. Naval Institute Proceedings* 33 (Part 1, 1907): 695. The following discussion of the Converse negotiations and publication of the Sands compilation is based on this letter.
22. Ibid.
23. Ibid.
24. Ibid.
25. Francis, along with W. L. Stone and J. Pintard, made up the committee of the New-York Historical Society to which Taylor's 1820 letter was referred.
26. The Bread and Cheese Club is discussed in "The Sketch Club," *New York Times,* January 5, 1901.
27. See note 13.
28. See, for example, "Literary Notices," *New York Mirror: A Repository of Polite Literature and the Arts,* October 30, 1830.
29. Alexander Slidell Mackenzie, *The Life of Paul Jones,* 2 vols. (New York: Harper & Brothers, 1841); James Fenimore Cooper, *John Paul Jones* (Philadelphia: G. R. Graham, 1843). Taylor's critique of the Mackenzie book is in Taylor to Cooper, October 28, 1843, in *U.S. Naval Institute Proceedings* 33 (Part 1, 1907): 685, 689–90, 699, 701–2, 706–8. Her critique of Cooper is the principal subject of her October 28 letter and is based on the version of Cooper's work published in *Graham's Magazine* 23 (July 1843): 13–25; (August 1843): 73–88. She begins her letter thus: "I have recently perused your sketch of the Life of Commodore John Paul Jones, my uncle, published in Graham's Magazine, and find it substantially though not precisely correct—its errors are of minor importance, it is true, but still they are errors and as I am informed the sketch will be introduced in another work, I think it right to correct them, to the end that you may avail yourself of the same, if you think fit."
30. The parenthetical quote is from "Literary Notices." Another American example of the reset: "Paul Jones was an irregular character, but his good qualities predominated over his bad ones; and as the man who first hoisted the American flag at sea, and received the first salute offered it by a foreign nation, and the first who carried it victoriously through

the fight on the waves, he deserves our highest praise and most grateful remembrance. With such a man to lead the American navy, and stand before it as the model of a brave man, no wonder it has covered itself with glory." "Paul Jones," *American Review* 4 (September 1846): 238. The English, too, began to see Jones differently than "a demon of the deep." This more balanced biographical sketch, published in a London journal, was based on Sherburne's *Life of Jones:* "Biographical Sketches: Paul Jones," *London Saturday Journal* (September 1839): 202–5.

31. Peter Force was a publisher and politician whose *American Archives* (as it came to be known) was the largest private collection of American history printed and manuscript sources in the country to that time. The Jones portion of the collection is catalogued in Charles Henry Lincoln, *A Calendar of John Paul Jones Manuscripts in the Library of Congress* (Washington, DC: Government Printing Office, 1903). There have been several attempts to trace the history of the John Paul Jones papers. See "Special Editorial Notes: I. Paul Jones," in *Narrative and Critical History of America,* edited by Justin Winsor, 6 vols. (Boston: Houghton Mifflin, 1887), 6:589–91; and Seitz, *Exploits in English Seas,* xii–xix.
32. For biographical details of Lieutenant Pinkham's life, see generally Renny A. Stackpole, *Sea Letters: Letters and Journals of the Andrew Pinkham Family of Nantucket and Ohio, 1813–1870* (Rockland, ME: Maine Authors, 2013).
33. "Journal of Alexander B. Pinkham," ibid., 85–86.
34. Reciting from memory: John McDiamid, "Paul Jones—Arbigland—Lieutenant Pinkham," *Dumfries and Galloway Courier,* July 30, 1834, reprinted in *Military and Naval Magazine of the United States* 6 (October 1835): 128; reading to shipmates: Stackpole, *Sea Letters,* 87.
35. "Pinkham's Journal," 83–85.
36. Ibid., 102, 100–101.
37. McDiamid, "Paul Jones," 128.
38. Ibid.
39. Ibid.
40. Stackpole, *Sea Letters,* 105.
41. McDiamid, "Paul Jones," 128. The restored cottage survives to this day and is now part of the John Paul Jones Cottage Museum, which includes the cottage, a nearby exhibition gallery with museum shop, and a picnic area with views of the Solway and the Lake District. The museum's website is http://www.jpj.demon.co.uk.
42. Stackpole, *Sea Letters,* 106–7. See also Mackenzie, *Life of Jones,* 2:25.
43. "Paul Jones," *North American and United States Gazette* (Philadelphia), April 12, 1851. For the Atlantic crossing with Jones and Crèvecouer, see H. E. Scudder, ed., *Recollections of Samuel Breck with Passages from His Note-Books (1771–1862)* (Philadelphia: Porter & Contes, 1877), 85. See also J. Francis Fisher, *Memoir of Samuel Breck, Late President of the Pennsylvania Institution for the Instruction of the Blind* (Philadelphia: C. Sherman, Son, 1863), 12. Breck's brief description of Jones during their Atlantic crossing is also of interest: "He was admiral in the Russian service, and wore several crosses at his button-holes. His manners were genteel and gentle, and his demeanor polished, although reserved—I might almost say taciturn." Scudder, *Recollections of Breck,* 85.
44. *Washington Daily National Intelligencer,* September 7, 1839; "John Paul Jones: Curious History of His Prize Money after the Victory over the Serapis," *New York Times,* June 4, 1898.

45. John Henry Sherburne, *The Tourist's Guide; or, Pencilings in England and on the Continent* (Philadelphia: G. B. Zieber, 1847), 155–56.
46. William A. Graham to Sherburne, January 30, February 21, 1851, in *Life of Jones* (1851), by Sherburne, 369–70.
47. Sherburne, *Life of Jones* (1851), 370; "Paul Jones," *Boston Daily Atlas,* April 1, 1851.
48. The only one of Jones's early biographers who got the cemetery right was Cooper, in his revised sketch of Jones published in 1846: "He was interred in a cemetery that no longer exists, but which then was used, near la Barriere du Combat, for the interment of Protestants." Cooper added it was "probable" that no trace of the grave could now be found. "John Paul Jones," in *Lives of Distinguished American Naval Officers,* by James Fenimore Cooper, 2 vols. (Philadelphia: Carry and Hart, 1846), 2:108. Cooper's source for the cemetery was, apparently, Janette Taylor. She had read the first version of Cooper's sketch, published in 1843, in which he stated that Jones was buried at Père Lachaise. "John Paul Jones," pts. 1–2, *Graham's Magazine* 23 (July 1843); (August 1843): 87. Taylor then wrote to Cooper as follows: "Pere la Chaise, if I mistake not, was not opened as a public cimetiere 'till 1812, at any rate, that and other public burial grounds, in Paris, were not open when Paul Jones died.—He was interred in the old Protestant burial ground, purchased by Lord Viscount Stormont (afterwards Earl of Mansfield) when British Ambassador at the Court of France—it was situated near the Barriere du Combat, and is now, I believe, totally covered with buildings." Taylor to Cooper, October 28, 1843, 692.
49. "Arrival of the Pacific Four Days Later from Europe," *Boston Daily Atlas,* June 9, 1851. Sherburne encountered an additional problem in Paris. A grandniece of Jones's, then living in that city, hired an attorney who threatened to block any exhumation and repatriation of Jones's remains. The matter was resolved quickly, the threat was withdrawn, and the attorney ended up trying to help Sherburne in his unsuccessful search for the grave. Scott Martelle, *The Admiral and the Ambassador: One Man's Obsessive Search for the Body of John Paul Jones* (Chicago: Chicago Review Press, 2014): 141–43.
50. "Washington, June 5th," *Boston Daily Evening Transcript,* June 7, 1851.
51. "Paul Jones," *Times* (London), May 27, 1851. Cronstadt (Kronshtadt) is a city on Kotlin Island in the Gulf of Finland. There is a fort at Cronstadt that was built in 1703 to guard the approaches to St. Petersburg.
52. For example, "Burial Place of John Paul Jones, to the Editor," *New York Daily Tribune,* June 12, 1851; "Mr. Sherburne; United States; John Paul Jones; Paris," *New London Daily Chronicle,* July 1, 1851; "Paul Jones, to the Editor," *Times* (London), July 3, 1851.
53. "The French Republic," *Times* (London), July 10, 1851.
54. "Chronology," in *John Paul Jones: Commemoration at Annapolis, April 24, 1906,* edited by Charles W. Stewart (Washington, DC: Government Printing Office, 1907), 183.
55. "Monument to John Paul Jones," *Newark (NJ) Daily Advertiser,* August 8, 1851.
56. Sherburne, *Life of Jones* (1851), 373–74. Seventeen years earlier, on June 30, 1834, Congress had unanimously passed, and the president approved, an act appropriating fifty thousand dollars for construction of a frigate to be called "Paul Jones," but the Navy Board never followed through. Ibid.

5. The Search for John Paul Jones, Part 2

1. The letter was first published by the *Washington National Intelligencer* and reprinted under the title "American Sepultures Abroad," *Wilmington (NC) Journal,* December 26, 1851.

2. There are two Porter biographies: Elsie Porter Mende (in collaboration with Henry Greenleaf Pearson), *An American Soldier and Diplomat, Horace Porter* (New York: Frederick A. Stokes, 1927); and Richard Owens, *A Biography of General and Ambassador Horace Porter, 1837–1921: Vigilance and Virtue* (Lewiston, NY: Edwin Mellen Press, 2002). See also Scott Martelle, *The Admiral and the Ambassador: One Man's Obsessive Search for the Body of John Paul Jones* (Chicago: Chicago Review Press, 2014). The latter, though not strictly a biographical work, nevertheless contains a good amount of biographical detail.
3. Horace Porter, "Lee's Surrender at Appomattox," *Outlook* 84 (December 22, 1906): 973; "The Century Exhibit," *New York Times*, May 12, 1893.
4. "General Horace Porter, Ex-Ambassador, Dies," *Brooklyn Daily Eagle*, May 30, 1921; "Gen. Horace Porter, Long in Coma, Dies," *New York Times*, May 30, 1921; "The Man of the Week: General Horace Porter," *New York Herald*, July 30, 1905, magazine section.
5. See, for example, Michael A. Palmer, "The Navy: The Oceanic Period, 1890–1945," http://www.history.navy.mil.
6. Biographies: Cyrus Townsend Brady, *Commodore Paul Jones* (New York: D. Appleton, 1900); Charles Walter Brown, *John Paul Jones of Naval Fame: A Character of the Revolution* (Chicago: M. A. Donohue, 1902); and A. Van Doren Honeyman, *Admiral Paul Jones* (Plainfield, NJ: Honeyman, 1905). Articles: Josiah C. Pumpelly, "A Short Sketch of the Life and Character of John Paul Jones," *New York Genealogical and Biographical Record* 23 (April 1892): 51–61; and Molly Elliot Seawell, "Paul Jones," *Century Illustrated Magazine* 49 (April 1895): 873–93. Fiction: Winston Churchill, *Richard Carvel* (New York: Macmillan, 1899); and W.L., "John Paul Jones," *New York Times*, July 30, 1899. Drama: Edward Ross and Alfred M. de Lesser, *Captain Paul*, performed at the Columbus Theater in New York; and "The Choice of Plays," *New York Tribune*, September 15, 1895. Operetta: H. B. Farney (author) and Robert Planquette (composer), *Paul Jones* (1890). An earlier version had been performed in Paris in 1887. See Dennis Robinson, "Miss Huntington Plays Paul Jones," http://www.seacoastnh.com.
7. Horace Porter, "The Recovery of the Body of John Paul Jones," *Century Magazine* 70 (October 1905): 927. This article was a reprint of Porter's official report of July 1905: Horace Porter, "Report of General Porter," in *John Paul Jones: Commemoration at Annapolis, April 24, 1906*, edited by Charles W. Stewart (Washington, DC: Government Printing Office, 1907), 49–79.
8. See note 2.
9. Horace Porter, *Campaigning with Grant* (New York: Century, 1897), 252–55.
10. The *Trent* Affair refers to an incident early in the Civil War when a U.S. Navy vessel captured two Confederate envoys while they were traveling to England on board the British mail ship *Trent*. Great Britain accused the United States of violating British neutrality. The resulting diplomatic crisis was one of Lincoln's first foreign affairs tests. See "The *Trent* Affair," https://history.state.gov.
11. Porter, *Campaigning with Grant*, 254–55.
12. One Union general did make a Jones comparison in 1862, but his was a comparison of the elusive Jones who had evaded capture by the English with the elusive captain of the Confederate *Kearsarge* who (to that point in time) had evaded capture by the Union. "Speech of General Butler," *Janesville (WI) Weekly Gazette*, April 17, 1863.
13. Owens, *Horace Porter*, 67, 68n23; Mende, *Soldier and Diplomat*, 110. An international arbitral tribunal, established by the Treaty of Washington (1871), awarded the United

States a substantial sum of compensation in connection with U.S. claims arising out of the *Alabama*'s raids on U.S. shipping during the Civil War. Great Britain paid the award promptly, but the United States sat on the money. The Court of Alabama Claims was then established as a forum for injured private claimants to assert their claims to a share of the award.

14. "At Gen. Grant's Tomb," *New York Times,* April 18, 1897.
15. Delmonico's dinner: "Voice of a Republican: Theodore Roosevelt to the Federal Club," *New York Times,* May 12, 1887; Admiral Hopkins dinner: "Farewell to the Englishmen," *New York Times,* May 10, 1893; National Defense Association: "Gen. Porter's New Post," *New York Times,* January 23, 1897.
16. "The Sons of the American Revolution," *New York Times,* April 3, 1898.
17. "Honors to Prof. John Fiske," *New York Times,* December 17, 1893.
18. "Sons of Patriots Dine," *New York Times,* January 19, 1895.
19. "First United States Flag: Story of Its Making and of the Flag Used by Paul Jones," *New York Tribune,* April 28, 1893; "Marking a Historic Spot: Sons of Revolution Lay a Cornerstone at Dobbs Ferry," *New York Times,* June 15, 1894.
20. Owens, *Horace Porter,* 91.
21. "Honors for Dead Heroes: Eighteen Monument Bills Pending in Congress," *New York Tribune,* June 7, 1896.
22. J. K. Gowdy to Kenesaw Landis, January 2, 1899, in *Commemoration at Annapolis,* edited by Stewart, 195–96. See also Sterling Heilig, "John Paul Jones Lies in an Unknown Grave," *Cleveland Plain Dealer,* December 31, 1899.
23. The veteran's letter to McKinley is excerpted at Martelle, *Admiral and Ambassador,* 147. For Vignaud's reply to Hay, see "Grave of John Paul Jones," *New York Times,* July 13, 1899. After learning about Vignaud's reply, the veteran (his name was James Johnson) wrote a follow-up letter, informing the government that Jones was buried in the cemetery for foreign Protestants, citing and quoting from an obscure copy of Jones's funeral register previously published by Charles Read, a French antiquary, in 1859. Clearly, Mr. Johnson had been doing some research of his own! "John Paul Jones' Grave," *Washington Morning Times,* August 4, 1899; "Special Telegram to the Times," *Philadelphia Times,* August 5, 1899. The Read copy of the funeral register is at Charles Read, "Le hero d'un roman de Fenimore Cooper," *La Correspondance Littéraire* 3 (March 20, 1859): 172, 173.
24. Porter, "Report of General Porter," 49.
25. C.I.B., "John Paul Jones's Grave Located by a French Antiquarian in an Abandoned Paris Cemetery," *New York Tribune,* November 12, 1899.
26. The report is reprinted in Stewart, *Commemoration at Annapolis,* 49–79. It was also published as both an article in *Century Magazine* (see note 7) and part of a collection of Jones's letters: Horace Porter and Franklin B. Sanborn, *Letters of John Paul Jones* (Boston: Bibliophile Society, 1905), 59–123.
27. Porter, "Report of General Porter," 55. See also "John Paul's Remains: Buried in Scotland, Not in Paris, as Has Been Assumed," *Washington Post,* April 6, 1905 (quoting the editor of a California newspaper: "It is true [Jones] died in Paris, and it is natural to suppose he is buried there. But this very reasonable assumption turns out to be incorrect, as Gen. Porter will be surprised to learn as soon as he receives a letter addressed to him by an old lady. . . . Mrs. Preston is a native of Dumfries . . . and when she saw this story of the Ambassador's quest she immediately wrote to tell him that the grave of this hero was there. . . . She well remembers it, for it is marked with a stone which bears the sinister

inscription, 'John Paul Jones, the Black Pirate'"); "Tomb of Paul Jones's Father: Pastor of Dumfries Denies Report That Admiral Was Buried There," *New York Times*, April 26, 1905.

28. For example, "Grave of John Paul Jones" ("In another quarter it is intimated that owing to a custom prevailing in Paris, the remains of John Paul Jones were deposited in a rented grave for a term of years, and that upon expiration of the lease, a great many years ago, the bones of this distinguished American patriot were thrown into the Potter's Field").
29. In 1846 James Fenimore Cooper, apparently relying on corrections by Jones's niece Janette Taylor of an earlier sketch of Jones he had published, wrote that Jones was "interred in a cemetery that no longer exists, but which then was used, near la Barriere du Combat, for the interment of Protestants." Cooper, "John Paul Jones," in *Lives of Distinguished American Naval Officers*, by Cooper, 2 vols. (Philadelphia: Carry and Hart, 1846), 2:108. The various published copies of Marron's funeral oration identified Marron as a Protestant clergyman who presided at Jones's funeral.
30. C.I.B., "Jones's Grave Located."
31. Porter, "Report of General Porter," 49.
32. Read, "Hero d'un roman de Fenimore Cooper," 173. Read republished the text of Jones's funeral registry in 1887, including additional information about the cemetery. Charles Read, "Registre No. 89 (Suite), 1779–1792," *Bulletin Historique et Littéraire* (Paris: Societé de l'Histoire du Protestentism Français) 36 (1887): 135–41. For the English translations of the registry, see "Burial of Paul Jones," *Russell's Magazine* 5 (June 1859): 268–69; and "The Contributor's Club: Paul Jones's Funeral," *Atlantic Monthly* 65 (May 1890): 712–13.
33. Read, "Hero d'un roman de Fenimore Cooper," 173; Read, "Registre No. 89," 135–41; Porter, "Report of General Porter," 49, 51–52.
34. Porter, "Report of General Porter," 51, 54.
35. Ibid., 55.
36. "People Met in Hotel Lobbies," *Washington Post*, October 18, 1905.
37. J. K. Gowdy to Kenesaw Landis, May 26, 1907, in *Commemoration at Annapolis*, edited by Stewart, 195.
38. P. Weiss, "Report of Engineer Weiss," May 9, ibid., 95.
39. Porter, "Report of General Porter," 56.
40. Ibid., 56–57, 60–61; Weiss, "Report of Engineer Weiss," 96. For Swiss guards, see also Samuel Eliot Morison, *John Paul Jones: A Sailor's Biography*, Time Reading Program Special Edition (New York: Time-Life Books,1964), 409.
41. Theodore Roosevelt, "Message of the President," February 13, 1905, in House Committee on the Library, *Searching for Remains of Admiral John Paul Jones: Etc.*, 58th Cong., 3rd sess., 1905, H. Doc. 340, 1. Porter's report to Secretary Hay dated January 24, 1905, on which Roosevelt relied for the information in his message, is annexed to the message. The message, but not the annexed report, is reproduced in Stewart, *Commemoration at Annapolis*, 43–44.
42. Porter, "Report of General Porter," 57.
43. Martelle, *Admiral and Ambassador*, 156–57, citing Porter to Hay, November 9, 1899, Record Group 59, Dispatches from U.S. Ministers to France, 1789–1906, roll 27, National Archives. The naval attaché in Paris, William S. Sims, also sent the Navy Department a copy of Ricaudy's October 29, 1899, preliminary report to Ambassador Porter. House Committee on the Library, *John Paul Jones*, 58th Cong., 3rd sess., 1905, H. Rep. 4887, 6.

44. A. de Ricaudy, "Célébrités dont les restes sont perdus ou égarés," *L'Echo du Public* (October 28, 1899): 762–63, http://gallica.bnf.fr; C.I.B., "Jones's Grave Located," 2; Porter, "Report of General Porter," 59.
45. Martelle, *Admiral and Ambassador,* 157.
46. Porter, "Report of General Porter," 59.
47. Martelle, *Admiral and Ambassador,* 158.
48. See, for example, "Plans to Honor Jones' Memory," *Boston Herald,* October 7, 1903; George E. Light [attaché at Paris Consulate], "Where Is the Grave of John Paul Jones?," *Munsey's Magazine* 31 (July 1904): 576–78.
49. "Reward for Bones of John Paul Jones," *Richmond (VA) Times Dispatch,* October 18, 1903.
50. "Paul Jones' Remains, Consul General Gowdy Offers Reward for Their Location," *New Orleans Times-Picayune,* October 19, 1903.
51. Letter to editor, "Another Hero's Grave Unmarked," *New York Herald,* September 16, 1903. Porter report: Porter to Roosevelt, October 20, 1903, Theodore Roosevelt Center at Dickinson State University, Digital Library, http://www.theodorerooseveltcenter.org. Secretary Moody, press speculation: "Will Ask Congress to Bring Back Body of John Paul Jones," *Washington Times,* October 6, 1903; and "John Paul Jones," *Washington Times,* October 8, 1903.
52. House Committee on the Library, *John Paul Jones,* H. Rep. 4887. The House Report includes Porter's letter to Secretary Hay dated January 24, 1905, and the president's message dated February 13, 1905, requesting the appropriation. Notwithstanding the terms of the options that Porter negotiated, damage to the property of the owners and tenants resulting from the subsequent excavation led to claims and litigation. In 1909 the French courts awarded one of the tenants fifteen hundred dollars in damages. "Award in John Paul Jones Search," *New York Tribune,* July 7, 1909.
53. Porter, "Report of General Porter," 60.
54. Ibid.
55. Ibid., 60–61.
56. Ibid., 61.
57. Ibid., 62.
58. Ibid., 64.
59. Third floor: "Testament of Paul Jones, July 18, 1792," in *Life and Character of the Chevalier John Paul Jones, a Captain in the Navy of the United States, during Their Revolutionary War,* by John Henry Sherburne (Washington, DC: Vanderpool & Cole, 1825), 349; only building with mezzanine: Porter, "Report of General Porter," 72.
60. Porter, "Report of General Porter," 72.

6. Was It Really Jones?

1. "Paul Jones' Body or Another's," *Cleveland Plain Dealer,* July 7, 1905 ("What will detract from the significance of the transfer from France to America of the body exhumed in Paris is the lingering doubt in many minds as to whether the remains are, after all those of Paul Jones").
2. Adam Goodheart, "Home Is the Sailor," *Smithsonian,* April 2006, 3.
3. "Bonaparte Cabinet Wit," *Washington Post,* July 9, 1905.
4. Park Benjamin, "Is It Paul Jones's Body?," *Independent* 59 (July 20, 1905): 125.

5. The forensic evidence is set out in four reports, published in *John Paul Jones: Commemoration at Annapolis, April 24, 1906*, edited by Charles W. Stewart (Washington, DC: Government Printing Office, 1907): Louis Capitan, "Report of Dr. Capitan," 81–85; George Papillault, "Report of Dr. Papillault," 87–92; V. Cornil, "Report of Professor Cornil," 93–94; and P. Weiss, "Report of Engineer Weiss," 95–99. The key forensic findings are highlighted in the same work in Horace Porter, "Report of General Porter," 49–79. See also Georges Hervé, Georges Papillault, and Louis Capitan, "The Identification of John Paul Jones's Body: By the Professors of the Anthropological School," *Independent* 59 (July 13, 1905): 65–72. For commentary on the forensic evidence cited in this chapter, see Benjamin, "Is It Paul Jones's Body?," 121–25; Philip Marshall Dale, *Medical Biographies: The Ailments of Thirty-Three Famous Persons* (Norman: University of Oklahoma Press, 1952), 127–35; Goodheart, "Home Is the Sailor," 1–5; Charles Henry Hart and Edward Biddle, *Memoirs of the Life and Works of Jean Antoine Houdon* (Philadelphia: printed for the authors, 1911), 125–54; and Nikki L. Rogers et al., "The Belated Autopsy and Identification of an Eighteenth Century Naval Hero: The Saga of John Paul Jones," *Journal of Forensic Sciences* 49 (September 2004): 1036–49. See also "John Paul Jones: A Twentieth Century Post-Mortem," *U.S. Navy Medicine* 70 (April 1979): 12–14; P. P. Hollingsworth, "Review of the Autopsy Reports on the Body of Admiral John Paul Jones," *Medical World* 53 (1935): 305; Irving I. Lasky, "Autopsy of Admiral John Paul Jones, 113 Years Postmortem: Historic and Forensic Aspects," *New York State Journal of Medicine* 82 (June 1982): 1110–15; Philip A. Mackowiak, *Diagnosing Giants: Solving the Medical Mysteries of Thirteen Patients Who Changed the World* (New York: Oxford University Press, 2013), 65–81; E. H. Vincent, "Death Comes for the Admiral," *Surgery, Gynecology and Obstetrics* 89 (1949): 778–83; and Matthew R. Weir, Lori L. Bogle, and Phillip A. Mackowiak, "The Death of John Paul Jones and Resurrection as 'Father of the US Navy,'" *American Journal of Nephrology* 31 (January 2010): 90.
6. Weiss, "Report of Engineer Weiss," 99.
7. "Plan of the Shafts Sunk and Galleries Excavated," in *Commemoration at Annapolis*, edited by Stewart, 56.
8. The position of Jones's grave near the southwest wall of the cemetery, just to the southeast of the walkway running northeast to southwest from the courtyard entrance, is well illustrated in the map of the cemetery in Porter's report. "Plan of the Cemetery of Saint Louis in 1792," ibid.
9. Weiss, "Report of Engineer Weiss," 97–98.
10. Papillault, "Report of Dr. Papillault," 87.
11. Horace Porter, "Report of General Porter," 64.
12. Weiss, "Report of Engineer Weiss," 98.
13. Colonel Blackden to Janet Taylor, August 8, 1792, in *The Life and Letters of John Paul Jones*, by Anna De Koven, 2 vols. (New York: Charles Scribner's Sons, 1913), 2:410–11.
14. This was Porter's surmise. See Porter, "Report of General Porter," 64.
15. "De Paris, le 25 juillet 1780," in *Correspondance Secrète, Politique & Littéraire* (London: John Adamson, 1787), 10:84. See also Hart and Biddle, *Life and Works of Houdon*, 132.
16. James Madison to John H. Sherburne, April 28, 1825, in *Life and Character of the Chevalier John Paul Jones, a Captain in the Navy of the United States, during Their Revolutionary War*, by John Henry Sherburne (Washington, DC: Vanderpool & Cole, 1825), iv; Thomas Jefferson to Sherburne, July 2, 1825, MS, Correspondence, Library of Congress, http://memory.loc.gov. Jefferson originally wrote "perfect likeness," but then crossed out "perfect" and substituted above it "excellent."

17. Resolution of October 16, 1787, in *Journals of the American Congress: From 1774 to 1788*, 4 vols. (Washington: Way and Gideon, 1823), 3:799–800.
18. Porter, "Report of General Porter," 66n. The bust is referred to in Papillault's "Report of Dr. Papillault"—erroneously—as the "Philadelphia bust," because it was mistakenly thought to be a copy of a replica in Philadelphia.
19. Papillault, "Report of Dr. Papillault," 91–92.
20. Hart and Biddle, *Life and Works of Houdon*, 125–54.
21. Ibid., 144.
22. Goodheart, "Home Is the Sailor," 5, quoting Nicholas Penny, senior curator of sculpture at the National Gallery of Art.
23. Guilhem Scherf, "Houdon, 'Above All Modern Artists,'" in *Jean-Antoine Houdon: Sculptor of the Enlightenment*, edited by Anne L. Poulet, Guilhem Scherf, and Ulrike Mathies (Chicago: University of Chicago Press, 2005), 20.
24. Rogers et al., "Belated Autopsy," 1045.
25. Goodheart, "Home Is the Sailor," 5, quoting Penny.
26. Benjamin, "Is It Paul Jones's Body?," 122.
27. Rogers et al., "Belated Autopsy," 1046.
28. Stewart, *Commemoration at Annapolis*, 48. See also Rogers et al., "Belated Autopsy," 1043, fig. 9.
29. Rogers et al., "Belated Autopsy," 1042–43.
30. De Koven, *Life of Jones*, 2:473; "Paul Jones's Body, Says Mrs. De Koven," *New York Times*, December 25, 1911.
31. Papillault, "Report of Dr. Papillault," 91.
32. Porter, "Report of General Porter," 67.
33. Papillault, "Report of Dr. Papillault," 90–91.
34. Hart and Biddle, *Life and Works of Houdon*, 151.
35. Ibid., 152, quoting Porter.
36. Ibid., 153–54.
37. Rogers et al., "Belated Autopsy," 1046.
38. "Finding of the Body of Admiral Paul Jones in Paris," *Scientific American* 92 (May 1905): 367.
39. Papillault, "Report of Dr. Papillault," 87.
40. Hervé, Papillault, and Capitan, "Identification of Jones's Body," 66–67.
41. Augustus C. Buell, *Paul Jones, Founder of the American Navy: A History*, 2 vols. (New York: Charles Scribner's Sons, 1902). For stature, see 1:138n, 1:322, and 2:209; for hair color, see 1:71, 1:103, and 1:322. For Sands's "middling stature," see Robert Charles Sands, ed., *Life and Correspondence of John Paul Jones, Including His Narrative of the Campaign of the Liman* (New York: D. Fanshaw, 1830), 87, quoting from "London papers of 22d February, 1778," whose "date may be erroneous as to year."
42. Anna De Koven, "A Fictitious Paul Jones Masquerading as the Real," *New York Times*, June 10, 1906; Samuel Eliot Morison, *John Paul Jones: A Sailor's Biography*, Time Reading Program Special Edition (New York: Time-Life Books,1964), 427–31. Until De Koven published her exposé, the Buell biography was widely celebrated. See, for example, H. Watterson, "The Paul Jones Revival," *Louisville (KY) Courier Journal*, July 3, 1905 ("an epoch-making book. No such contribution to American history was made between 1800 and 1900. Buell found Paul Jones a myth, he left him an immortal. He found him a hero of melodrama, he left him a personage in the drama of the ages").
43. Hart and Biddle, *Life and Works of Houdon*, 149.

44. Morison, *John Paul Jones,* 313.
45. Alexander Slidell Mackenzie, *The Life of Paul Jones,* 2 vols. (New York: Harper & Brothers, 1841), 1:39.
46. Morison, *John Paul Jones,* 155; Evan Thomas, *John Paul Jones: Sailor, Hero, Father of the American Navy* (New York: Simon & Schuster, 2003), 301. The letter from Lord Daer to his father, cited by these biographers, is dated April 20, 1791. It is reprinted in De Koven, *Life of Jones,* 1:325.
47. Fanning's "about five feet six inches": Nathaniel Fanning, *Fanning's Narrative: The Memoirs of Nathaniel Fanning, an Officer of the American Navy, 1778–1783* (1808; reprint, New York: William Abbott, 1913), 105; Abigail Adams's "small of stature": extract from letter to unknown addressee, written in 1874 while resident in Paris, printed in De Koven, *Life of Jones,* 2:284; Hancock's "little Jones": John Hancock to Robert Morris, January 17, 1777, quoted in Thomas, *John Paul Jones,* 78; Taylor's "middling stature": Janette Taylor, ed., *Memoirs of Rear-Admiral Paul Jones, Chevalier of the Military Order of Merit, and of the Russian Order of St Anne, &c. &c.,* 2 vols. (Edinburgh: Oliver and Boyd; London: Simpkin and Marshall, 1830), 1:174n; Sands's "middling stature": Sands, *Life of Jones,* 87, quoting from "London papers of 22d February, 1778"; Mackenzie's "middling stature" from a "contemporary letter": Mackenzie, *Life of Jones,* 1:214; Disraeli's "short in stature": Benjamin Disraeli, *The Life of Paul Jones, from Original Documents in the Possession of John Henry Sherburne, Esq., Register of the Navy of the United States* (London: John Murray, 1825), 318. The "London papers" referred to by Sands and the "contemporary letter" referred to by Mackenzie may relate to the following: An article in a London paper in 1779 describes Jones as "of middling stature," *London Chronicle,* October 19, 1779, excerpted in *Paul Jones, His Exploits in English Seas during 1778–1780: Contemporary Accounts Collected from English Newspapers,* by Don C. Seitz (New York: E. P. Dutton, 1917), 106. Another, quoting a letter from Amsterdam dated October 14, 1779, says Jones was "of the middle height": *Gazetteer and New Daily Advertiser,* October 22, 1779, extracted ibid., 113.
48. John Komlos and Francesco Cinnirella, "European Heights in the Early 18th Century," *Vierteljahrschrift für Sozial-und Wirtschaftsgeschichte* 94 (July 2007): 271–84; John Komlos, "On the Biological Standard of Living of Eighteenth Century Americans: Taller, Richer, Healthier," http://econhist.userweb.mwn.de, figs. 2 and 4.
49. Papillault, "Report of Dr. Papillault," 88–89. The earlier study is G. Papillault, "L'homme moyen a Paris," *Bulletins de la Société d'Anthropologie de Paris* 3 (May 1902): 393–526.
50. Papillault, "Report of Dr. Papillault," 87.
51. Porter, "Report of General Porter," 70.
52. Sands, *Life of Jones,* 198–99.
53. Ibid., 199.
54. Ibid., 257, quoting from a letter fragment written by Jones in 1792. See also Gerald W. Gawalt, trans., *John Paul Jones' Memoir of the American Revolution Presented to King Louis XVI of France* (1979; reprint, Honolulu: University Press of the Pacific, 2001), 47 ("Dr. Franklin accompanied me to Versaille and the minister of marine [Sartine], upon our request, issued orders for the sale of prizes. Although it was evident that I had suffered from the extraordinary fatigue I had undergone, having slept less than 3 hours out of every 24 during the entire campaign from Lorient to the Texel, the minister, nevertheless, received me coldly and did not even ask me if I felt any ill effects from the wounds I had received").
55. "A Fellow Lodger's Letter," in *Life of Jones,* by De Koven, 2:437–39, 438.

56. Sherburne, *Life of Jones,* 362.
57. Jones's malaria or yellow fever: Rogers et al., "Belated Autopsy," 1043. On seamen and malaria: Dale, *Medical Biographies,* 129. Jones's fever at Cork in 1773: Morison, *John Paul Jones,* 21. Later fevers in 1779 and 1783: Dale, *Medical Biographies,* 130; Morison, *John Paul Jones,* 196, 334; Joseph Callo, *John Paul Jones: America's First Sea Warrior* (Annapolis, MD: Naval Institute Press, 2006), 137–38; and Thomas, *John Paul Jones,* 165, 256. "Almost blind with sore eyes" in 1780: Jones to M. Le Duc De Vauguyon, February 18, 1780, in *Life of Jones,* by Sherburne, 195–96. Pneumonia in Russia in 1788: John Paul Jones, "Narrative of the Campaign of the Liman," in *Life of Jones,* edited by Sands, 459–60; Morison, *John Paul Jones,* 386; and Thomas, *John Paul Jones,* 296. Other illnesses, such as lung infection in April 1788: Jones to Jefferson, April 8, 1788, in *Life of Jones,* edited by Sands, 389; and Thomas, *John Paul Jones,* 269.
58. Blackden to Taylor, August 8, 1792, in *Life of Jones,* by De Koven, 2:410–12.
59. The French phrase in the burial record is "de suite d'hydropisie de poitrine." The burial record is translated in "Burial of Paul Jones," *Russell's Magazine* 5 (June 1859): 268–69; and "The Contributor's Club: Paul Jones's Funeral," *Atlantic Monthly* 65 (May 1890): 712–13.
60. Dale, *Medical Biographies,* 134.
61. Ibid.
62. Rogers et al., "Belated Autopsy," 1041–42.
63. Hacking cough: Thomas, *John Paul Jones,* 302; inaudibility: Thomas Carlyle, *The French Revolution: A History* (London: Thomas Nelson & Sons, 1903), 285–86.
64. "Official Certification of the American Embassy and Consulate of the Identification of the Body of Admiral John Paul Jones," in *Commemoration at Annapolis,* edited by Stewart, 76–78, 77 ("a shirt of fine linen, handsomely made, with plaites and ruffles").
65. Benjamin, "Is It Paul Jones's Body?," 121. Cyrus Townsend Brady asserts that Jones *was* buried in his American uniform (together with sword and other articles), but does not provide any authority for this. Brady, *Commodore Paul Jones* (New York: D. Appleton, 1900), 422–23. There is no other account of which I am aware, contemporary or otherwise, that makes a similar claim.
66. Porter, "Report of General Porter," 62–63.
67. Porter, in his telegram to the secretary of state announcing he had found Jones's remains, speculated that, although no nameplate was found, "one may have been put on outer wooden coffin, few vestiges of which are left." Ambassador Porter to the Secretary of State, telegram, April 14, 1905, in *Commemoration at Annapolis,* edited by Stewart, 44.
68. Hervé, Papillault, and Capitan, "Identification of Jones's Body," 66.
69. Papillault, "Report of Dr. Papillault," 87, 92.
70. Benjamin, "Is It Paul Jones's Body?," 122.
71. Hervé, Papillault, and Capitan, "Identification of Jones's Body," 70.
72. Stewart, *Commemoration at Annapolis,* 78–79.
73. Ibid., 79.
74. Morison, *John Paul Jones,* 15n.
75. One contemporary newspaper suggested that Porter's eagerness to find Jones's grave and identify his remains before his term of office ended "may have made him more ready than he otherwise would have been to accept negative evidence—evidence which goes to show that the body exhumed may be that of Jones, but which does not prove that it is." "The Unidentified Corpse," *Chicago Daily Tribune,* May 2, 1905.
76. Goodheart, "Home Is the Sailor," 5.

7. The Great White Fleet

1. "Message of the President to the Senate and House of Representatives," February 13, 1905, in *John Paul Jones: Commemoration at Annapolis, April 24, 1906,* edited by Charles W. Stewart (Washington, DC: Government Printing Office, 1907), 44.
2. "Paul Jones' Remains, Squadron under Admiral Sigsby Will Convey Them to United States," *Washington Post,* May 13, 1905. Porter, among others, had urged that a U.S. naval fleet be sent for this purpose. Scott Martelle, *The Admiral and the Ambassador: One Man's Obsessive Search for the Body of John Paul Jones* (Chicago: Chicago Review Press, 2014), 233, citing Porter to Loomis, April 21, 1905.
3. "Paul Jones for Annapolis," *Atlanta Constitution,* May 13, 1905; "Paul Jones' Remains."
4. "Anniversary of Great Fight, Morton Wishes John Paul Jones Ceremonies to Be Held September 23," *Washington Post,* June 7, 1905; "Porter Visits Roosevelt, Discusses the Plan for Paul Jones's Internment at Annapolis," *New York Times,* July 20, 1905; "In Honor of Paul Jones: Celebration Fixed for April 24, 1906, Anniversary of Capture of Drake," *Washington Post,* August 24, 1905; "Keeping His Body Moving," *Washington Post,* August 26, 1905. For further detail on the choice of dates, see Martelle, *Admiral and Ambassador,* 252–54; and Stewart, *Commemoration at Annapolis,* 11.
5. Louis Auchincloss, *Theodore Roosevelt* (New York: Times Books, 2001), 12 (quote), 10.
6. Quoted in Henry J. Hendrix II, "Roosevelt's Naval Thinking before Mahan," in *Theodore Roosevelt, the U.S. Navy, and the Spanish-American War,* edited by Edward J. Marolda (New York: Palgrave, 2001), 51, citing F. C. Iglehart, *Theodore Roosevelt: The Man as I Knew Him* (New York: Charles Scribner's Sons, 1919), 121–22.
7. Reveling in Marryat's novel: Theodore Roosevelt, *An Autobiography* (New York: Charles Scribner's Sons, 1920), 16; reading Cooper's nautical tales: Donald Wilhelm, *Theodore Roosevelt as an Undergraduate* (Boston: John W. Luce, 1910), 37.
8. Roosevelt, *An Autobiography,* 2; Roosevelt to Putnam, November 1, 1897, in *The Letters of Theodore Roosevelt,* edited by Elting E. Morison, 8 vols. (Cambridge, MA: Harvard University Press, 1951–54), 1:705.
9. Theodore Roosevelt, *The Naval War of 1812* (New York: G. P. Putnam's Sons, 1882). For contents, War College textbook, and copies on ships, see Hendrix, "Roosevelt's Naval Thinking," 52; and John A. Gable, "Theodore Roosevelt and the Heritage of the U.S. Navy," in *Theodore Roosevelt,* edited by Marolda, 42.
10. J. L. Harrison, "Review of 'The Naval War of 1812,'" http://userpages.umbc.edu.
11. [Theodore Roosevelt,] "The Influence of Sea Power upon History," *Atlantic Monthly* 66 (October 1890): 563; Kenneth Wimmel, *Theodore Roosevelt and the Great White Fleet: American Sea Power Comes of Age* (Washington, DC: Brassey's, 1998), 58.
12. The discussion of the navy in 1880 is based on Elting Morison, *Admiral Sims and the Modern American Navy* (New York: Houghton Mifflin, 1942), 19–21.
13. "Report of the Secretary of the Navy," 4th Cong., 1st sess., November 28, 1881, House Ex. Doc. 1, pt. 3.
14. David Colamaria, "The Story of the New Steel Navy," http://www.steelnavy.org.
15. Peri Arnold, "Policy Leadership in the Progressive Presidency: The Case of Theodore Roosevelt's Naval Policy and His Search for Strategic Resources," *Studies in American Political Development* 10 (Fall 1996): 338–39.
16. Wimmel, *Great White Fleet,* 65.
17. Theodore Roosevelt, "Naval War College Address," June 2, 1897, Almanac of Theodore Roosevelt, http://www.theodore-roosevelt.com.

18. Wimmel, *Great White Fleet,* 116–25, 136–46, 148.
19. Morison, *Admiral Sims,* 63–65.
20. Ibid., 65–69.
21. Ibid., 69–76.
22. Roosevelt lobbied to be awarded the Medal of Honor for his bravery ("If I didn't earn it, then no commissioned officer can ever earn it"), but was unsuccessful in his lifetime. Auchincloss, *Theodore Roosevelt,* 34. He was eventually awarded the medal in 2001, one hundred years after San Juan Hill.
23. Wimmel, *Great White Fleet,* 157.
24. Quoted in Morison, *Admiral Sims,* 50.
25. Roosevelt to Sims, December 2, 1897, in William Sowden Sims, "Roosevelt and the Navy," *McClure's Magazine* 54 (November 1922): 32–41, 34.
26. Theodore Roosevelt, "The Strenuous Life," April 10, 1899, Almanac of Theodore Roosevelt, http://www.theodore-roosevelt.com.
27. Wimmel, *Great White Fleet,* 157–58. Sims focused on armaments. He said the machinery to deliver ammunition to the guns was too slow, the turrets were misplaced so as to attract concentrated enemy fire, the large gun apertures needlessly exposed the crews, and the ammunition hoists were open shafts through which a wayward spark could ignite the magazines.
28. Ibid., 159–60.
29. Morison, *Admiral Sims,* 83–84.
30. Ibid., 84.
31. Elting E. Morison, *Men, Machines, and Modern Times* (Cambridge, MA: MIT Press, 1966), 17–20.
32. Sims to Roosevelt, November 16, 1901, in *Admiral Sims,* by Morison, 103.
33. Roosevelt to Sims, December 12, 1901, ibid., 104–5.
34. Theodore Roosevelt, "State of the Union Message, December 3, 1901," Almanac of Theodore Roosevelt, http://www.theodore-roosevelt.com. See also Wimmel, *Great White Fleet,* 174.
35. Arnold, "Policy Leadership," 342.
36. James R. Reckner, *Teddy Roosevelt's Great White Fleet* (Annapolis, MD: Naval Institute Press, 1988), 4–5.
37. Roosevelt to General Leonard Wood, quoted in Wimmel, *Great White Fleet,* 189.
38. Theodore Roosevelt, "State of the Union Message, December 5, 1905," Almanac of Theodore Roosevelt, http://www.theodore-roosevelt.com.
39. Theodore Roosevelt, "Address of President Roosevelt," in *Commemoration at Annapolis,* edited by Stewart, 18–19.
40. Wimmel, *Great White Fleet,* 178.
41. Ibid., 176–77.
42. Ibid., 179, 181–82.
43. Kennedy Hickman, "World War I: HMS *Dreadnought,*" http://militaryhistory.about.com.
44. "Will Be a Terror on Sea. England's New Battleship Can Whip Entire German Fleet. Dreadnought Is to Be So Big and So Powerful That It Can Stand Off 10,000 Yards and Wipe Out the Biggest Ships Now in British Navy and Not Be Touched," *Chicago Tribune,* January 21, 1906. See also "Britain's Mysterious Battleship Launched, Giant Dreadnought May Revolutionize Naval Warfare, Biggest and Fastest Afloat," *New York Times,* February 11, 1906; and "Biggest of Warships. Dreadnought Launched at Portsmouth, England. Secrets Carefully Guarded," *Washington Post,* February 11, 1906.

45. "Biggest of Warships." While the details of the *Dreadnought* design were secret, its leading characteristics were known: displacement was increased by two thousand tons; the secondary battery was eliminated and armaments reduced to two types of guns, twelve-inch and three-inch; the armor protection was particularly heavy and complete; steam turbines were used; and it was estimated the ship could travel twenty-one knots per hour. "The 'Dreadnought,'" *Scientific American* 94 (February 24, 1906): 166; "The New British Battleship 'Dreadnought,'" *Scientific American* 94 (March 10, 1906): 208–9.
46. "The Revolution in Battleships as Exemplified in the Dreadnought," *Current Literature* 11 (April 1906): 436–37, 466.
47. Reckner, *Great White Fleet,* 5–6.
48. Roosevelt, "Address of President Roosevelt," in *Commemoration at Annapolis,* edited by Stewart, 18.
49. Ibid., 18–19.
50. "Nations Is Lashed by the President. Denounces the Folly That Permitted the Country to Be Ill-Prepared for the War of 1812," *Chicago Daily Tribune,* April 25, 1906; "Honors Memory of John Paul Jones. President Speaks of Lessons of War in Which Jones Participated, and Advocates Efficient and Larger Navy to Meet Whatever Dangers May Come. Dwells upon Sin of Failure to Make Ready and Admonishes Congress," *Washington Post,* April 25, 1906; Wimmel, *Great White Fleet,* 198–201.
51. Reckner, *Great White Fleet,* 14.
52. Except for gilded bows: Mike McKinley, "The Cruise of the Great White Fleet," http://www.history.navy.mil.
53. The following summary of the three purposes is based on Reckner, *Great White Fleet,* 13.
54. Leroy Dorsey, "Sailing into the 'Wondrous Now': The Myth of the American Navy's World Cruise," *Quarterly Journal of Speech* 83 (November 1997): 448, citing Reckner, *Great White Fleet,* 17; and R. A. Hart, *The Great White Fleet: Its Voyage around the World, 1907–1909* (Boston: Little, Brown, 1965), 26, 31–32.
55. McKinley, "Cruise of the Great White Fleet"; Reckner, *Great White Fleet,* xi.
56. McKinley, "Cruise of the Great White Fleet"; photo of Roosevelt and Sims aboard the presidential yacht: Wimmel, *Great White Fleet,* 170.
57. Henry Reuterdahl, "The Needs of Our Navy," *McClure's Magazine* 30 (January 1908): 251.
58. Ibid., 260.
59. Ibid., 263.
60. For supporting voices, see, for example, "[Admiral] McCalla Stands by His Navy Criticism," *New York Times,* February 4, 1908; and "Defects in Warships Noted by Officers," *New York Times,* March 1, 1908. For opposing voices, see, for example, "Scientific Bombardment of Naval Critic Reuterdahl," *Los Angeles Times,* January 29, 1908; and "What a Real Expert Says," *Washington Post,* April 22, 1908.
61. Wimmel, *Great White Fleet,* 233–34; "Reuterdahl Wrong, Say Naval Experts," *New York Times,* February 26, 1908.
62. "Reuterdahl Quits Fleet to Face Critics," *Los Angeles Times,* March 1, 1908; "President Has Twelve Guests; Talks with Reuterdahl on Naval Matters," *Los Angeles Times,* July 16, 1908; "Hunters at Sagamore Hill," *New York Times,* July 16, 1908; "Navy Needs Change," *Washington Post,* November 25, 1908.
63. Reckner, *Great White Fleet,* xi; Wimmel, *Great White Fleet,* 243.
64. McKinley, "Cruise of the Great White Fleet."
65. Reckner, *Great White Fleet,* 160–61.

66. McKinley, "Cruise of the Great White Fleet."
67. Reckner, *Great White Fleet,* 16–17.
68. "Lessons and Results of the Battleship Cruise," *Scientific American* 100 (February 20, 1909): 146; Reckner, *Great White Fleet,* 161, 15.
69. Reckner, *Great White Fleet,* 160.
70. Ibid., x.
71. Ibid., 158.
72. McKinley, "Cruise of the Great White Fleet."
73. Reckner, *Great White Fleet,* x.

Epilogue. Out from under the Staircase

1. H. W. Desmond, ed., "The Works of Ernest Flagg," *Architectural Record* 11 (April 1902): 90, fig. 86. The caption was written by Flagg.
2. Ibid.
3. Ernest Flagg, "New Buildings for the United States Naval Academy, Annapolis, Md., Part I," *American Architect and Building News* 94 (July 1, 1908): 6.
4. Secretary Bonaparte to Senator Eugene Hale and Representative George Edmund Foss, April 26, 1906, in "$135,000 More for Crypt," *Baltimore Sun,* April 27, 1906; Senate, Committee on Naval Affairs, *Permanent Resting Place for Body of John Paul Jones: Report (to Accompany S. 8868),* 61st Cong., 3rd sess., January 11, 1911, S. Rep. 955, 2; House, Committee on Naval Affairs, *John Paul Jones: Report (to Accompany S. 8868),* 61st Cong., 3rd sess., February 9, 1911, H. Rep. 2114, 1–2.
5. "Legislative Briefs," *Washington Post,* March 3, 1908; "The Paul Jones Crypt," *Baltimore Sun,* January 29, 1911.
6. "Crypt for Paul Jones' Body," *Washington Post,* June 26, 1908.
7. "John Paul Jones, Our Graveless Hero," *Collier's* 45 (April 9, 1910): 18; A.J.C., "Slow Erecting Tomb," *Washington Post,* December 19, 1910; "Why Not Bury Paul Jones?," *Syracuse (NY) Post-Standard,* December 19, 1910; "Shades of John Paul Jones!," *Baltimore Sun,* January 24, 1911.
8. Representative Augustus Stanley, speaking on the Naval Appropriation Bill, on February 11, 1911, 61st Cong., 3rd sess., Cong. Rec. 46, pt. 3:3027; "John Paul Jones, the Greatest of Sea-Captains," *Jeffersonian* (Thomson, GA), January 23, 1913.
9. Horace Porter to Representative George A. Loud, December 3, 1910, in House, Committee on Naval Affairs, *John Paul Jones: Report (to Accompany S. 8868),* 3.
10. Arthur Dadum, "The Paul Jones Crypt," *Baltimore Sun,* January 29, 1911.
11. "Memorial to Paul Jones," *New York Times,* March 5, 1911; "Bids for Paul Jones Crypt," *New York Times,* February 25, 1912; "To John Paul Jones," *Baltimore Sun,* January 26, 1913. For Flagg fee dispute, see "Flagg Sues Government," *New York Times,* May 9, 1911; and "Architect Sues Government," *Washington Post,* May 9, 1911.
12. "To John Paul Jones."
13. "Place in Great Crypt Body of Paul Jones," *New York Times,* January 27, 1913.
14. "Crypt Now His Tomb: Body of John Paul Jones Laid in Final Resting Place," *Washington Post,* January 27, 1913; Bill Kelly post, "Remember the Intrepid: John Paul Jones Autopsy and Burial," http://remembertheintrepid.blogspot.com.
15. The sword, inherited by Jones's sister Janet Taylor, had been given by her to the other celebrated Revolutionary War commodore John Barry, with a view that it should be passed from time to time to the senior ranking officer of the navy. Barry gave it to Richard Dale,

Jones's first lieutenant on *Serapis*. It remained in the Dale family until it was lent to the Naval Academy for permanent display in Jones's crypt beneath the chapel.

16. Nathaniel Fanning, *Fanning's Narrative: The Memoirs of Nathaniel Fanning, an Officer of the American Navy, 1778–1783* (1808; reprint, New York: William Abbott, 1913), 48.
17. Evan Thomas, *John Paul Jones: Sailor, Hero, Father of the American Navy* (New York: Simon & Schuster, 2003), 197.
18. "Washington, June 5th," *Boston Evening Transcript*, June 7, 1851. See also "Patriotic Relics," *Independent* 59 (July 27, 1905): 222, 223 ("The presence at Annapolis of the remains of Commodore Jones, or whoever the gentleman is, will be a great object lesson to American youth, as, indeed, others have said before. It will teach them that if they in their turn become naval heroes they, too, will not be allowed to rest in peace in their graves, but will be liable to be dug up and Bertilloned like a criminal and transported to another continent whenever larger appropriations are needed for the navy"). As noted in chapter 4, the lamenters, at least for a time, included one of Jones's descendants, a niece then living in Paris (1851), who threatened to sue Colonel Sherburne if he went ahead with his plan to dig up Jones and send his remains to the United States.
19. "Late Honor Paid John Paul Jones," *Atlanta Constitution*, April 18, 1912; "Honor Naval Hero, Taft and Dewey Unveil Statue of John Paul Jones," *Washington Post*, April 18, 1912.
20. For more on the John Paul Jones–named vessels, see http://www.history.navy.mil. USS *Zumwalt*, a larger and technologically more advanced destroyer than USS *John Paul Jones*, was commissioned in Baltimore on October 15, 2016, after the writing of this book was completed. It is the first of three *Zumwalt*-class destroyers on order.

INDEX